VOICES & VISIONS

Selected Essays

Bernard F. Rodgers, Jr.

University Press of America,® Inc.
Lanham · New York · Oxford

Copyright © 2001 by
University Press of America,® Inc.
4720 Boston Way
Lanham, Maryland 20706
UPA Acquisitions Department (301) 459-3366

12 Hid's Copse Rd.
Cumnor Hill, Oxford OX2 9JJ

All rights reserved
Printed in the United States of America
British Library Cataloging in Publication Information Available

ISBN 0-7618-2168-6 (pbk. : alk. paper)

∞™ The paper used in this publication meets the minimum
requirements of American National Standard for Information
Sciences—Permanence of Paper for Printed Library Materials,
ANSI Z39.48—1984

To Jane

Contents

Preface ... vii

Acknowledgments ... xi

I. *Posthumous Papa:* Ernest Hemingway ... 3

 The March Hare: T.S. Eliot ... 15

 Indivisible Man: Ralph Ellison ... 25

 The Ghost Writer: Philip Roth ... 35

 True Impressions: Saul Bellow ... 67

 A Novelist's Revenge: E.L. Doctorow ... 91

 Old Friends: John Updike ... 103

II. *A Father's Words:* Richard Stern ... 119

 Passionate Partiality: Susan Sontag ... 127

 The Tortoise and the Hares: Cynthia Ozick ... 147

 A First Life: William Styron ... 153

	Paradise Lost: Jamaica Kincaid	159
	Strenuous Exercise: John Ashbery	165
	As Common as Rain: John Irving	171
	The Greenhouse and the Briar Patch: Toni Morrison	175
	Stark-Naked Truth: Erica Jong	179
III.	*The Witness of Poetry:* Czeslaw Milosz	185
	Laughable Loves: Milan Kundera	195
	Life with a Star: Jiri Weil	203
	Into the Realm of Nightmare: Aharon Appelfeld	207
	Imaginary Homelands: Salman Rushdie	211
IV.	*Images and Impulses:* The Chicago Novel	225
	A Special Eloquence: Leon Forrest	245
	The Outsiders: Bette Howland	249
	Lost Illusions: Morris Philipson	253
	The Red Menace: Michael Anania	257
	A Legend of the City: Nicholas Von Hoffman	261
	The Myth of Crows: Charles Dickinson	265
	Everyday Heroes: Harry Mark Petrakis	269
About the Author		273

Preface

Every book is rooted in autobiography, and this one is no exception. I can't remember a time when I didn't love to read, but I vividly recall the summer I fell in love with literature. The place was Cape Cod, I was thirteen, and literature was Ernest Hemingway.

My parents had rented a housekeeping cottage in West Yarmouth, and within a few hours of our checking in I discovered a little bookstore a half-mile away on Route 28. In that Cape bookstore they had a shelf of Hemingway's novels in the old uniform Scribner's paperback edition— a line of gray volumes with blue, yellow, green, and red accents. That first day I bought *The Sun Also Rises* and then stayed up late into the night, long after the rest of the family had gone to sleep, reading it by the light of a sixty-watt bulb in an old chair that smelled a bit mildewed.

The next morning I was waiting at the door when the bookstore opened to get another Hemingway. And in the two weeks that we spent on that vacation I walked back and forth to that little bookstore again and again, each time returning with another Hemingway paperback clutched in my hands—*A Farewell to Arms*, *For Whom the Bell Tolls*, *The Old Man and the Sea*, *The Short Stories of Ernest Hemingway*. Each of which I then devoured in a day or two, reading on the beach, in the car, at meals, at night, wherever and whenever I could. By the time we returned home from the Cape, I was in a Hemingway daze, and the books went on my bedroom bookshelf as precious objects. Hooked, I quickly moved on to other authors, other books—my little library soon included *This Side of*

Paradise and *The Great Gatsby*, *Look Homeward, Angel* and *The Catcher in the Rye*—with the same sense of discovery and excitement.

At first, my focus was on the solitary act of reading. But within a few months I realized that there was a way to keep reading like this for the rest of my life, to share my excitement about the things that I was reading, and make a living besides. Before I turned fourteen I knew that I wanted to become a college English teacher.

Eventually I did, and along the way I found another way of sharing my experience of books by writing about them. This collection is drawn from the literary essays and reviews that I've written over the past twenty-five years. The earliest (on E.L. Doctorow's *Ragtime*) was written and published in 1975, the most recent (on John Updike's *Licks of Love*) in 2000. While these pieces range widely over modern and contemporary American and Eastern European writing, they have several things in common. From the beginning, I have been fortunate enough to be able to select my own subjects, to write about books and writers that have genuinely interested me and to find editors who were willing to publish what I wrote. As a result, most of my writing has been a combination of review and appreciation—has been intended, that is, to place a new book in the larger context of the career of a writer I admire or to introduce a new writer whose work has excited me. In almost everything that I've written, the impulse has been to speak to the interested general reader—rather than to the academic specialist—about books, writers, and ideas that have engaged and fascinated me with the hope that what I write will encourage others to read these books and writers themselves.

The first half of this collection reflects some of my abiding interests: among the American moderns, in Hemingway and Eliot; among post-World War II American writers, in Ralph Ellison, Philip Roth, Saul Bellow, E.L. Doctorow, and John Updike. I began to read most of these writers when I was a teenager, and have continued to read them with deepening appreciation ever since. The second half treats a variety of other writers. From 1972 to 1985 I studied, taught, and lived in Chicago, where I began to write reviews on modern and contemporary literature for the *Chicago Tribune Book World* and the City Colleges of Chicago's *Arts in Review* radio program. Through my involvement with several series and programs sponsored by the Chicago Public Library and the Illinois Humanities Council, I was able to express my growing affection for the city through more than a decade of lecturing and writing about both the history of literature in Chicago and the fiction of contemporary Chicagoans. Prompted by my own Eastern European heritage and the Writers from the Other Europe series that Roth edited for Penguin in the

1970s, I began to read the work of writers like Milan Kundera and Jiri Weil, Czeslaw Milosz and Aharon Appelfeld, and spent 1979-1980 as a Fulbright lecturer in American literature at Marie Curie Sklodowska University in Poland. During my stay there, Susan Sontag and John Ashbery visited on a State Department-sponsored tour. I was so impressed by them that when I returned to the United States I made it a point to read all of their work and begin to write about what I'd discovered.

Looking back, I find that I have been attracted, again and again, to exploring writers who have what I think of as distinctive voices and visions. By "voice" I mean a unique style, language, tone—what E.I. Lonoff described to young Nathan Zuckerman in *The Ghost Writer* as "something that begins at around the back of the knees and reaches well above the head." By "vision" I mean a distinctive way of looking at the world, a writer's attitude toward his or her encounter with experience, or history, or politics, or culture—or all of this and more—that, over time, creates a recognizable territory that his or her readers identify as uniquely this writer's own.

Just as I was beginning to write essays and reviews for publication, John Updike published his collection *Picked-Up Pieces*. In his foreword he outlined a set of six rules for reviewing that I have always tried to follow:

1. Try to understand what the author wished to do, and do not blame him for not achieving what he did not attempt.
2. Give enough direct quotation—at least one extended passage—of the book's prose so the review's reader can form his own impression, can get his own taste.
3. Confirm your description of the book with quotation from the book, if only phrase-long, rather than proceeding by fuzzy *precis*.
4. Go easy on plot summary, and do not give away the ending. . . .
5. If the book is judged deficient, cite a successful example along the same lines, from the author's *oeuvre* or elsewhere. Try to understand the failure. Sure it's his and not yours?

To these concrete five might be adder a vaguer sixth, having to do with maintaining a chemical purity in the reaction between product and appraiser. Do not accept a book for review that you are predisposed to dislike, or committed by friendship to like. Do not imagine yourself the caretaker of any tradition, an enforcer of any party standards, a warrior in any ideological battle, a corrections officer of any kind. Never, never . . . try to put the author "in his place," making of him a pawn in a contest with other reviewers. Review the book, not the reputation. Submit to whatever spell, weak or strong, is being cast. Better to praise and share than blame and ban. The communion between reviewer and his public is based upon the presumption of certain possible joys of reading, and all our discriminations should curve toward that end.

Most of the pieces in this collection were written as reviews, and while I've edited and refined them I haven't attempted to disguise their origins. Instead, I've left them in a form that I hope will convey the immediacy and excitement of my initial encounters with these books, as well as my attempts over time to gain a perspective on them that makes their character, and their authors', clearer both to me and to other readers.

This book is dedicated to my wife Jane, whose voice and vision have taught me most—and meant more to me than I can ever express.

South Yarmouth, Massachusetts
July 1, 2001

Acknowledgments

Grateful acknowledgment is made to the following publications and publishers who first printed all or part of essays in this book, usually under different titles and in slightly different form:

The Berkshire Eagle: for a section of *"The Ghost Writer*: Philip Roth."

Chicago Review: for a section of *"A Novelist's Revenge*: E.L. Doctorow."

Chicago Tribune Book World: for *"Into the Realm of Nightmare*: Aharon Appelfeld," *"A Special Eloquence*: Leon Forrest," *"The Outsiders*: Bette Howland," *"Lost Illusions*: Morris Philipson," *"A Legend of the City*: Nicholas von Hoffman," *"The Myth of Crows*: Charles Dickinson," *"Everyday Heroes*: Harry Mark Petrakis," and sections of *"Posthumous Papa*: Ernest Hemingway," *"The Ghost Writer*: Philip Roth," *"A Father's Words*: Richard Stern," and *"Images and Impulses*: The Chicago Novel."

Illinois Issues: for permission to reprint *"Images and Impulses*: The Chicago Novel,"* copyright © 1983, *Illinois Issues*, published by the University of Illinois at Springfield, Springfield, IL 62794-9243.

Kwartalnik Neofilologiczny (Warsaw): for a section of *"True Impressions*: Saul Bellow."

The Salem Press: for permission to reprint *"The March Hare*: T.S. Eliot," *"Indivisible Man*: Ralph Ellison," *"The Tortoise and the Hares*: Cynthia Ozick," *"Paradise Lost*: Jamaica Kincaid," *"A First Life*: William Styron," *"Life with a Star*: Jiri Weil," and sections of *"Imaginary Homelands*: Salman Rushdie," *"Posthumous Papa*: Ernest Hemingway," *"The Ghost Writer*: Philip Roth," *"A Novelist's Revenge*: E.L. Doctorow," *"Old Friends*: John Updike," and *"Passionate Partiality*: Susan Sontag," which were originally published in *Magill's Literary Annual,* copyright © 1986, 1990, 1991,

1992, 1993, 1996, 1997, 1998, 1999, 2000, 2001, Salem Press, Inc. "*The Witness of Poetry*: Czeslaw Milosz" and "*Laughable Loves*: Milan Kundera," which were originally published in *Magill's Survey of World Literature,* copyright © 1992, Salem Press, Inc. And a section of "*The Ghost Writer*: Philip Roth" which was published in *Masterplots II: American Fiction Series,* copyright © 1986, Salem Press, Inc.

The University of Chicago Press: for permission to reprint the first section of "*A Father's Words*: Richard Stern," originally published as a Foreword to their Phoenix Fiction edition of Stern's *Golk,* copyright © 1987, The University of Chicago. All rights reserved.

The World & I: for sections of: "*The Ghost Writer*: Philip Roth," "*Old Friends*: John Updike," and "*True Impressions*: Saul Bellow" which originally appeared in its April 1987, October 1997, February 1999, and August 2000 issues and are reprinted with permission from *The World & I,* a publication of The Washington Times Corporation, copyright © 1987, 1997, 1999, 2000.

Most of the pieces in this collection that have not been previously published were originally written as radio reviews for programs produced by the City Colleges of Chicago and broadcast on WBBM-AM and WNIB-FM in Chicago.

John Blades, former editor of the *Chicago Tribune Book World,* was the first to invite me to write reviews, and during my time in Chicago he regularly gave me the opportunity to share my reactions to new books with the *Tribune*'s readers. I am very grateful to him for his early encouragement and support. More recently, Clark Munsell, book editor of *The World & I,* and several editors of the Salem Press's *Magill's Literary Annual, Magill's Survey of World Literature,* and *Masterplots II: American Fiction* have invited me to contribute longer essay-reviews to their publications and I want to thank them as well.

Peter Filkins offered thoughtful suggestions on an early version of my work on Susan Sontag. My assistant Bonita Lovison helped to prepare many of these essays for both their initial and book publication with her usual efficiency and good humor. President Leon Botstein, Executive Vice President Dimitri Papadimitriou, Chairman Emily Fisher and the other members of the Board of Overseers of Simon's Rock College of Bard generously approved my taking the semester's sabbatical that provided the time for me to complete this book. U Ba Win, Patricia Sharpe, Jon MacClaren, Mary-King Austin, Leslie Davidson, John Verones, David Reed and my other colleagues in the administration and faculty at Simon's Rock made it possible for me to focus on this project throughout that sabbatical. I am very grateful to each of them for that gift.

I

Posthumous Papa

Ernest Hemingway

"Man was not made for safe havens," Aeschylus wrote; "the fullness of life is in the hazards of life." Although we have no record of Ernest Hemingway's ever having read these lines, there is ample evidence of his having lived by them. Hemingway the writer shunned the safe havens of established prose style for the hazards of trying to write "one true, simple declarative sentence." Hemingway the man fled the safe haven of Victorian Oak Park for the hazards of World War I Italy, Civil War Spain, World War II France and Germany, Africa, and points beyond and between them. Because he was such an American original, larger than life in his genius and in his faults, we still remember him; because he continues to fascinate so many of us, nearly every publishing season offers at least one more book to swell the already massive academic and popular bibliography on the writer, the man, the legend.

In the late 1970's, most of the Hemingway fare was eminently forgettable. Except for Mary Hemingway's highly selective memoir *How It Was*, Scott Donaldson's perceptive critical study *By Force of Will*, Matthew Bruccoli's meticulous reconstruction of the Hemingway/Fitzgerald relationship in *Scott and Ernest*, and the incisive chapter on Hemingway's reputation in Malcolm Cowley's—*And I Worked at the Writer's Trade*, the commercial houses published only mediocre memoirs by assorted relatives and hangers-on that capitalized on the audience for books on Hemingway but added little to our understanding of him. Just in time for Christmas 1978 things suddenly took a turn for the better, however, with the appearance of Peter Buckley's *Ernest* and Robert E. Gadjusek's *Hemingway's Paris*—two books that remain among the most memorable on the Hemingway shelf.

Peter Buckley divides his beautiful photographic study into three sections. The first consists of ninety full-page portraits of Hemingway taken between the first months of his life and the final ones. The third section is another series of photographs that show Hemingway surrounded by the people and places that touched and shaped his childhood, youth, maturity, and age. The second section—Buckley's essay on Hemingway's art and character—is the book's only weakness. Because Buckley is neither an original critic nor a distinguished writer, his text is repetitive, imitative of Hemingway's style, padded, and partisan. A text half as long would have been twice as effective.

But the pictures! Though we have seen some of them before, their cumulative effect here is absolutely hypnotic. In the portraits, especially, we encounter all of the Hemingway personae—the fisherman, the wounded young veteran, the bullfight aficionado, the big-game hunter, the boxer, and the working writer. We watch him age and, as he ages, we see him gain and lose wounds and bruises, beards and bulk. In portrait after portrait, though, the eyes are what rivet us. By turns bright and dark, open and wary, twinkling and challenging, bibulous and cold sober, at the end haunted by paranoid specters and very real death, they tell an unforgettable story that needs no commentary.

In 1960, when those eyes were a year away from closing forever, they focused on what they had seen in Paris forty years earlier. The memoir that double vision produced began with a paean: "If you are lucky enough to have lived in Paris as a young man, then wherever you go for the rest of your life, it stays with you, for Paris is a moveable feast." It concluded with the observation that "there is never any end to Paris and the memory of each person who has lived in it differs from that of any other." Between that opening and that close is some of the most perfect prose that Hemingway ever wrote—and some of the cruelest. With Hemingway's conclusion as his starting point, Robert E. Gadjusek has produced a book that will enthrall devotees of Hemingway as well as those of one of his favorite cities.

Juxtaposing present-day photographs of places in Paris that played a role in Hemingway's life with writing about them from his work and that of his contemporaries and biographers, *Hemingway's Paris* creates a vivid picture of a special man and the most special of cities. Hemingway and the whole crew from Paris in the 1920's provide the words; Gadjusek provides the photographs. What strikes the reader most is just how many "true sentences" Hemingway wrote about the place where he became an artist. Though some of the landmarks are now gone, you can still find your way around the Left Bank with *A Moveable Feast* (1964) as your guide. The Select, the Rotonde, the Dome, and Brasserie Lipp are still there, pretty much as he described them; so is Place St. Michel and the corner café where the young artist struggled to write the stories that revolutionized American prose. Shakespeare & Company has moved from the Rue de l'Odeon to a spot near the bookstalls by the quai that Hemingway frequented, but Gertrude Stein's studio—now marked with a brass plaque—is still visible at 27 Rue de Fleurus. Gadjusek shows all this and more. And as we walk with Gadjusek through the streets that Hemingway walked and see them as the young Hemingway did, we come away with a better understanding of what he meant when he once described Paris as an old mistress who is "always the same age and always has new lovers."

II

No other modern American writer captured the imagination of the general public as thoroughly, or for as long, as Hemingway. Even forty years after his death, no other modern American writer's face is as widely recognized. Though he made no lecture tours, gave very few interviews, and never appeared on a radio or television talk show, both his face and his personal history long ago became a part of American popular lore. Newspapers chronicled his deep-sea fishing, his big game hunting, his war reporting, his love of bullfighting and his many brushes with death. Highly successful films—with the biggest stars of the era, such as Tyrone Power, Ava Gardner, Gary Cooper, Ingrid Bergman, Humphrey Bogart, and Lauren Bacall—were made of his major works.

Yet in spite of all the publicity, which he occasionally courted but more often shunned, Hemingway was fundamentally an intensely private man. He wanted no biography written about him. He raged over the way analysis of his work—the work that was the longest and most enduring passion of his life—was, all too often, analysis of his personality and image. And he specifically directed that his executors *not* allow publication of any of his letters, since he felt that they were "often libelous, always indiscreet, [and] often obscene." When he committed suicide in the summer of 1961 he left the all-but-complete memoir, trunks of manuscripts of several unfinished projects, and a few short stories. But he never even began an autobiography.

Nothing that is published posthumously will (or should) alter the stature of his literary achievement, for judgment of that achievement must be based on the books that he actually had time to complete. But *The Selected Letters of Ernest Hemingway* (1981), published with the permission of Mary Hemingway and sensitively edited and annotated by

Hemingway biographer Carlos Baker, is probably the nearest that we will ever get to once again hearing his voice as he meant it to be heard. The collection includes six hundred of the more than six thousand letters that we know Hemingway wrote during his lifetime. Although many of the most important of these letters have been paraphrased over the years by scholars who have had access to them in the Hemingway Collection at the John F. Kennedy Library in Boston, this is the first time that they have been available to most readers. And while Papa is, most assuredly, growling in his grave at this invasion of his privacy, the rest of us cannot help but be grateful for the guilty pleasure that we've been handed.

For publication of *The Selected Letters* is a literary event of the first magnitude and an invaluable contribution to the history of modern American writing. It is also the closest that we will ever come to a Hemingway autobiography. And precisely because they were not *intended* for publication these letters give us a more honest and unvarnished picture of their author than most autobiographies. They do not tell us everything we might want to know, and they do not show us all of the facets of Hemingway's personality and character. But while the picture is not complete it is certainly enthralling.

Hemingway wrote letters, he told F. Scott Fitzgerald, "because it's such a swell way to keep from working and yet feel that you've done something." The letters are not as polished or literary as those of many writers, but they are vivid expressions of what was on Hemingway's mind at the time he wrote each of them. Hemingway is not always pleasant in them. Sometimes he's angry—about publishing arrangements, bad reviews, broken friendships, real and imagined betrayals, his own failures and those of his friends. Sometimes he's cruel—as in the now-famous letter to Fitzgerald about *Tender Is the Night*, where he seems to be kicking his friend when he's down. Sometimes he's coarse and obscene. But just as often he is tender, thoughtful, generous, forgiving, and understanding; and—with few exceptions—he is unfailingly honest.

There is so much to relish in these letters. Students of literature will be fascinated by the letters to Fitzgerald, his editor Max Perkins, William Faulkner, James Joyce, Ezra Pound, Archibald MacLeish, Gertrude Stein, Sherwood Anderson, Bernard Berenson, Edmund Wilson, Malcolm Cowley, critics Philip Young and Charles Fenton; and by Hemingway's comments (sometimes perceptive, sometimes foolish or rivalrous) about Nelson Algren, Saul Bellow, James Jones, Norman Mailer, Carson McCullers, Thomas Wolf, John O'Hara, Lionel Trilling, and a host of other predecessors, contemporaries, and successors. Others will be intrigued by his letters to Gary Cooper and Marlene Dietrich. And others will revel in his lovingly detailed descriptions of the hunting, fishing, and bullfighting that meant so much to him.

Certainly no one will be able to read the letters he wrote during and just after the breakups of his first three marriages without being moved to sympathy, even pity. Nor will anyone read the letters that he wrote throughout his life to his parents, his sons, and his wives and ex-wives without feeling, perhaps for the first time, the immense vulnerability that he so consciously hid behind the façade of bravado and the persona of Papa.

As you would expect, there is much here about Hemingway's views on literary craftsmanship. "Writing is something that you can never do as well as it can be done," he wrote the Soviet critic who was responsible for translating most of his works into Russian. "It is a perpetual challenge and it is more difficult than anything else that I have ever done—so I do it. And it makes me happy when I do it well." *So*—"it is more difficult than anything else that I have ever done—*so* I do it." That one word says more about Hemingway's art and character, and the relationship between them, than most of the books that have been written about him. And the letters are full of similarly revealing statements about how and why he wrote as he did.

To anyone who cares about Hemingway, or writing, or art, or psychology, or the tragedies and triumphs of a life fully-lived, *The Selected Letters of Ernest Hemingway* may well be the posthumous Papa most worth savoring.

III

Every reader of *True at First Light* (1999), which Hemingway's heirs and publishers report is the last of his posthumous works, should be reminded of John Updike's comments on the publication of the first posthumous novel, *Islands in the Stream*, in 1970. "This book consists of material that the author during his lifetime did not see fit to publish," Updike wrote in words that apply to each of the works that have been issued in Hemingway's name since his death, "therefore it should not be held against him."

> That parts of it are good is entirely to his credit; that other parts are puerile and, in a pained way, aimless testifies to the odds against which Hemingway, in the last two decades of his life, brought anything to completion. It is, I think, to the discredit of his publishers that no introduction offers to describe from what stage of Hemingway's tormented later career [this work] was salvaged, or to estimate what its completed design might have been, or to confess what editorial choices were exercised in the preparation of the manuscript. Rather, a gallant wreck of a novel is paraded as the real thing,

as if the public are such fools as to imagine a great writer's ghost is handing down books from Heaven.

The odds that Updike refers to are now well known: Hemingway's last years can only be described as a tragedy. A lifetime of hard drinking, courting physical danger, ricocheting between periods of mania and depression, and coping with the frenzy of renown had begun to affect him by the mid-1940's. The wounds, concussions, and broken bones had all taken their toll. And then, returning in January 1954 from the six-month stay in Africa that *True at First Light* recounts, two plane crashes and a brush fire within a single week left him with two spinal disks cracked and impacted, his liver and one kidney ruptured, paralysis of the sphincter, a dislocated right arm and shoulder, a concussion and a cracked skull that leaked cerebral fluid for several days, and first-degree burns on his face, arms, legs, chest and back.

He survived, physically and mentally debilitated, to return to his home in Cuba, but he would never be the same. The prescriptions and self-medications that he took to treat the after-effects of all this, together with his increasing consumption of alcohol, eventually led in 1960 to a mental breakdown and paranoid delusions. As a result, he was hospitalized at the Mayo Clinic—where he was given electroshock treatments that affected him like a series of new concussions, leaving his memory weak but his delusions intact. On July 2, 1961, after several failed attempts, he committed suicide in his Ketchum, Idaho home.

In the weeks and months that followed, his widow Mary discovered that he had left fifty pounds of unpublished manuscripts—thousands of pages, hundreds of thousands of words. As executor of his estate, she was left with the responsibility of sorting this all out and determining what, if anything, from this cache of manuscripts deserved to be published. Ultimately, she (and, after her death, his sons) determined that every one of the works that he left behind deserved to be published—the letters that he had specifically directed them not to print, the stories he had chosen not to publish or collect, and each of the long works that he had been unable to shape into a finished form that satisfied him.

The Selected Letters included a thoughtful and thorough introduction by Carlos Baker. Philip Young wrote a similarly detailed explanation of the principles and premises upon which he based his edition of *The Nick Adams Stories* (1972)—but Scribner's ultimately chose not to include it in the book. (It was published, instead, in the scholarly quarterly *Novel*.) So Hemingway's publishers have still not provided introductions for the general reader that respond to Updike's questions for any of the posthumous books except *The Selected Letters*. But thanks to Hemingway biographers such as Baker and Michael Reynolds, and to Rose Marie

Burwell's comprehensive examination of the postwar manuscripts and the books eventually drawn from them in her indispensable *Hemingway: The Postwar Years and the Posthumous Novels* (1996), we now know much more about how the posthumously published books evolved.

Hemingway returned to the Finca Vigia after the Allied victory in Europe intent on writing an epic that would treat World War II. He failed. But between 1945 and 1961 he never stopped writing—first, on projects that he referred to in his letters as "The Big Book," "The Land, Sea, and Air Book," and "The Sea Book"; later on projects he called "The African Book," "The Paris Book," and "The Bullfighting Book."

According to Burwell, "The Big Book" was an "ever expanding" novel set in the south of France during the 1920's (parts of it were published in 1986 as *The Garden of Eden*). "The Land, Sea, and Air Book" was "a dream that never became a reality." "The Air" section was never written; "The Land" section, which dealt with the war in Europe, devolved into *Across the River and into the Trees* (1950); and "The Sea" section evolved into "The Sea Book." This "Sea Book" initially had four sections. The first section, consisting of parts called "Bimini" and "Miami," he labeled "The Sea When Young"; a section called "Cuba" was known as "The Sea When Absent"; "At Sea" he referred to as "The Sea Chase"; and the last section, which Hemingway eventually extracted and published separately as *The Old Man and the Sea* (1952), had the working title of "The Sea in Being." After *The Old Man and the Sea* was published, Hemingway continued to mention "The Sea Book" to Scribner's as "a three-part work that could be published in separate volumes." When Mary Hemingway and Charles Scribner II eventually edited the book, however, they cut "Miami"—it was later published in the Finca Vigia edition of *The Complete Short Stories of Ernest Hemingway* (1987) as "The Strange Country"—and the remaining sections of "The Sea Book" were published as *Islands in the Stream*.

The last two books that Hemingway published during his lifetime were both drawn from these larger projects, then. They turned out to be one of his worst and one of his most highly praised. *Across the River and into the Trees* was variously described by reviewers as "a parody," "a travesty," "an embarrassment," "trash," and worse. Hemingway was clearly finished, many of them said. *The Old Man and the Sea*, which appeared two years later, surprised even the naysayers and was generally hailed as a small masterpiece. Shortly after it appeared, Hemingway was awarded the Nobel Prize in Literature.

In the remaining nine years of his life he published no more new books but he worked compulsively on these projects as well as three others: "The African Book" (*True at First Light*); "The Paris Book," a "fictional memoir" about Paris in the 1920's which was published as *A*

Moveable Feast; and "The Bullfighting Book" (published in 1985 as *The Dangerous Summer*)

A Moveable Feast was by far the most successful of all of these projects. Certainly, it had the most spectacular beginning. As Mary Hemingway tells the story in her memoir *How It Was* (1976), while they were stopping at the Ritz Hotel in 1956 the Hemingways were approached by a bellman who asked if Monsieur Hemingway wished to retrieve the suitcases that the hotel's baggage room had been holding for him. Hemingway had totally forgotten about the luggage, which had apparently been there at the Ritz gathering dust for thirty years. When two bags were delivered to his room he opened them to find a powerful reminder of the time when all that lay before him was promise and possibility. Inside there were a dozen of the blue and yellow notebooks that he had used during his early years in Paris as well as hundreds of pages of typed manuscript from that era. Mary describes Ernest sitting on the hotel room floor, surrounded by this treasure trove, reading and remembering. When they returned to the Finca he set aside the African Book and began the Paris memoir. Several months before his death Hemingway delivered an all but complete manuscript of this memoir to his publishers, indicating that he was still working on a final chapter and a title.

Each of the other projects was left unfinished. In each of these later works the narrator or main character is an artist or writer; in three—*True at First Light*, *A Moveable Feast*, and *The Dangerous Summer*—the artist is Hemingway himself. In *The Garden of Eden* and the Paris memoir he is looking back, mining his past to make sense of his present; in the African and bullfighting books he is returning to places that had been almost sacred to him earlier, only to find them diminished or inaccessible. Each of the unfinished manuscripts seems to have involved an effort to return to earlier sources of inspiration in the hope of recapturing a mastery that Hemingway knew had disappeared. *A Moveable Feast* and *The Garden of Eden* draw on the same period and the same autobiographical sources as some of the early stories and *The Sun Also Rises* (1926). *Islands in the Stream* recalls elements of *To Have and Have Not* (1937) and *For Whom the Bell Tolls* (1940). *The Dangerous Summer* returned to the bullfighting of *The Sun Also Rises* and *Death in the Afternoon* (1932). *True at First Light* was an attempt to recapture the spirit of *Green Hills of Africa* (1935) and the inspiration behind "The Snows of Kilamanjaro" and "The Short Happy Life of Francis Macomber."

As he worked on each of these projects at various points during the last fifteen years of his life, moving from one to the other, unable to finish or totally abandon any of them—writing, always writing—he lost his way. Each project began to grow exponentially, and as the books grew longer Hemingway tried to convince himself that their length was a virtue. He began to keep obsessive daily counts of the number of words he was writing and began to brag about the counts in his letters to his publisher, editors, and friends. As the years passed and he continued to take loans from Scribner's against future royalties without delivering a completed manuscript, he began to sound like a student whose assignment is overdue: the later the assignment, the greater the claims for what the final work will be. So, although he must have known better, he claimed that "The Sea Book" was ready to publish if he died. And as the piles of manuscript pages for the various projects began to grow and be placed in boxes and vaults in Cuba, New York, Key West, and Ketchum, he started referring to these unpublished works as "insurance," "savings," a legacy left "in the bank," to be drawn on in the future by Mary, his sons, and his publisher. (About this, unfortunately, he could not have been more right.)

Reading the letters from this period is truly painful, as the self-deceptions and boasts replace his characteristic honesty, grow and feed on one another. As if quantity were the same as quality, or loquacity were a virtue in a writer whose reputation was based on his radically paring language down to its absolute essentials. Where Hemingway had once prided himself on his "iceberg theory" of literature—on the idea that nine-tenths of his writing was beneath the surface of the carefully chosen words that were actually on the page—in these manuscripts he repeatedly told his readers much more than they wanted to know. Where once he had used repetition for effect, he now began to repeat himself endlessly, as if convinced that every word he wrote needed to be preserved.

None of these manuscripts can fairly be described as "aimless," but all of them turned out to be endless. Each metastasized. By the time he set them aside, *The Garden of Eden* and *True at First Light* each stood at 200,000 words, *Islands in the Stream* at 182,000, and *The Dangerous Summer* (a 10,000-word assignment from *Life* magazine) at 120,000. When they were eventually published by his estate, all were drastically cut. In fact, the size of cuts has grown with each successive posthumous book as the manuscripts from which the books have been drawn have become progressively worse and more unfinished. "The Sea Book" was cut by about one-third to produce *Islands in the Stream*. "The Big Book" and "The Bullfighting Book" were each cut by two-thirds to create *The Garden of Eden* and *The Dangerous Summer*. Three-fourths of "The African Book" was cut to produce *True at First Light*. And in every case this major surgery has been performed on Hemingway's manuscripts with little or no explanation to readers of who did the cutting, how, or why.

Hemingway's son Patrick is credited with editing *True at First Light*, but neither his almost incoherent introduction nor the egregious "Cast of Characters" that he appends to the book convince us of his competence to make aesthetic choices about his father's manuscript. He does not mention that a 50,000 word excerpt from the manuscript was serialized in several issues of *Sports Illustrated* in 1971-1972, does not explain how this book relates to that excerpt, and does not tell us what was eliminated. So that what we are left with here—as was the case with *Islands in the Stream*, *The Garden of Eden*, and *The Dangerous Summer*—cannot honestly be described as a book "by Ernest Hemingway." Hemingway didn't complete it, didn't decide it was ready for publication, didn't edit it, didn't order its parts and, therefore, didn't create its emphases. It would be more accurate, instead, to describe *True at First Light* and these other books as "drawn from the writing of Ernest Hemingway."

In the case of *True at First Light*, what has been drawn from Hemingway's sprawling manuscript is a first-person account of several parts of a trip to Africa that he took with his last wife, Miss Mary, in the fall of 1953-54. The subjects of the fragments that are collected here are the threat to the Hemingway camp posed by a handful of Mau Mau warriors who have escaped from jail, Miss Mary's quest to shoot a lion, her plans for a Christmas celebration, Hemingway's bantering friendships with the hunter Philip Percival, a game warden known as G.C., and his gun-bearer Ngui, and Hemingway's relationship with a native Wakamba girl named Debba, whom he describes as his *"fiancée."*

The dialogue ranges from stilted and embarrassing to very funny and sharp; the descriptions of Africa range from powerful to hackneyed. Hemingway "goes native"—shaving his head, dying his clothes the burnt orange of the Wakamba tribe, carrying a spear, acting as an elder of the tribe and the *fiancé* of Debba—and the conversations that he and Miss Mary have about this are often hilarious. At times he presents himself with a self-deprecation and a consciousness of his own pretensions that is appealing and unusual in Hemingway's work; at others—especially in all of the conversations about the "new religion" that he and his friends have invented—he loses all sense of those pretensions and appears at his self-indulgent worst as pontificating Papa. He talks too much, tries to think deeply and mostly fails, but ultimately recognizes that his fantasy of escape among the Wakamba is doomed.

We will never know what Hemingway might have made of this or his other unfinished books if he had been granted the time or the health to work on them further. That he could follow *Across the River and Into the Trees* with *The Old Man and the Sea*, could write a work as sure in its effects as *A Moveable Feast* at the same time that he was stumbling around in the gargantuan manuscript of his African book, at least suggests that he might have turned these projects into works that he would have truly wanted to publish. As it stands, *True at First Light* is not worthless—none of the posthumous books are—but it is also not a book that anyone could seriously recommend to a reader who is interested in discovering the work of Ernest Hemingway.

The March Hare

T.S. Eliot

In 1968, T.S. Eliot's *The Waste Land*, then forty-six years old, seemed about to undergo a mid-life crisis. Word leaked out that the keepers of the Berg Collection of the New York Public Library had discovered the manuscript of the poem among the papers of John Quinn, a New York lawyer and patron of modern art, and that they were planning to publish it. The rumor turned out to be true and in 1971, six years after Eliot's death, *The Waste Land: A Facsimile and Transcript of the Original Drafts*, edited with an introduction and notes by Eliot's second wife Valerie, was published.

Its appearance caused a stir in the literary world that was unprecedented and prompted a reconsideration of Eliot's life and work that continues today. The most significant aspect of that consideration—first apparent in Robert Sencourt's *T.S. Eliot: A Memoir* (1971), T.S. Matthews's *Great Tom* (1974), Lyndall Gordon's *Eliot's Early Years* (1977), and James E. Miller's *T.S. Eliot's Personal Waste Land* (1977)— is that since the appearance of *The Waste Land* facsimile the relationship between Eliot's life and his work has become an acceptable subject of discussion. Before the facsimile this was most certainly not the case, and the reasons for this are an extraordinary episode in literary history and criticism.

For nearly forty years, from the 1920's through the 1960's, T.S. Eliot reigned as both *the* modern poet and *the* modern critic. In both his art and his criticism he seemed to embody "modern" poetry and, in the process, he defined the terms by which his own work would be judged. In contemporary America, we have become accustomed to writers explaining their intentions and their work in essays and interviews. But I wonder if anyone has ever been as successful at this as Eliot was. Although he seldom gave interviews about his work, what he did say and what he wrote in his own critical essays did not just tell readers how to approach his own poems. It also established the perspective and terms of what became known as the New Criticism—terms which were then used for more than a generation to judge not only the work of his contemporaries, but of all those who came before and after him as well.

It now seems clear that Eliot's followers turned his early critical statements into the rudiments of an orthodoxy that was more rigid than any he himself ever brought to his own criticism; and many of the things that he said later in his life contradicted the critical principles and practice of his early career. At the beginning, the most famous of those principles certainly appeared to be clear. "The progress of the artist is a continual self-sacrifice, a continual extinction of personality," he wrote in "Tradition and the Individual Talent" (1917). "It is not in the personal emotions provoked by personal events in his life that the poet is in any way remarkable or interesting . . . Poetry is not a turning loose of emotion, but an escape from emotion."

On the basis of this and similar statements, the New Critics created their theory of the "impersonality" of poetry: the poem is an object, to be considered separate and apart from its creator. To focus on the author's biography, to see the poem as an expression of a unique personality and sensibility and turn to the biography to better understand the poet and the poem, is to commit the "biographical fallacy." That this approach dominated literary criticism for so long during the middle of the twentieth century now seems a tribute to the power of Eliot's own genius and needs. For it should be obvious to any reader who approaches his poems with a mind uncluttered by New Critical theory that the "Preludes," "The Love Song of J. Alfred Prufrock," "Gerontion," "The Hollow Men," *The Waste Land*, *Four Quartets*—and most of Eliot's other poems for that matter—absolutely express a personality. One very much like what Peter Ackroyd's *T.S. Eliot: A Life* (1984) presents to us in fascinating detail.

To Bertrand Russell, Eliot in his twenties was "altogether impeccable in his tastes but [had] no vigour or life or enthusiasm." His first wife Vivien once complained that "he has lost all spontaneity and can only break through his conventionality by stimulants or violent emotions." Friends nicknamed him "the undertaker," while Ezra Pound dubbed him "Old Possum" because he was always hiding behind a personality that he had painstakingly constructed. Edmund Wilson summed up the impressions of many of the friends and acquaintances that Ackroyd quotes when he wrote, after first meeting Eliot, that "he gives you the creeps a little at first because he is such a completely artificial, or rather, self-invented character . . . but he has done such a perfect job with himself that you end up by admiring him."

"There will be time . . . to prepare a face to meet the faces that you meet," Eliot wrote in his first great poem. "The longer we pretend/ The harder it becomes to drop the pretence,/ Walk off the stage, change into our own clothes/ And speak for ourselves," he wrote in his last play, *The Elder Statesman*. And in the fifty years that separate those two works he lived his personal and professional lives, shifting shapes, protecting himself from the world through a carefully controlled performance. At Lloyd's Bank, and later as Faber and Faber's most famous editor, he was an English businessman—complete with bowler hat, dark gray suits, and umbrella on his arm. But at the same time that he was beginning at Lloyd's he would sometimes visit Virginia Woolf and other artistic friends in the guise of a bohemian and poet, wearing pale green face powder and a touch of lipstick.

Just as his personality was constructed from the models around him, he wrote poetry that grew out of other poetry. "He needed a model," Ackroyd writes, "before he could explicate his own experience." In a life spent seeking order and a tradition upon which he could rely, he struggled with the disorders of constant illness, too many deadlines, a mutually destructive first marriage, repeated writer's block, and profound self-doubt. Yet through a will stronger than his weakness, through a confidence somehow stronger than his lack of self-confidence, through a need to write somehow stronger than his inability to write, through a faith somehow stronger than his doubt, through a personality finally stronger than his need for masks, he managed to write the poetry that has defined the modern condition for several generations.

Peter Ackroyd's biography cannot explain all of this. Prohibited from quoting Eliot's letters by the estate, he is forced to paraphrase much that we have been able to read as Eliot wrote it since *The Letters of T.S. Eliot: Volume I 1898-1922* appeared in 1988. Some of the generalizations that Ackroyd, an Englishman, makes about America and Americans seem foolish. He spends more time and lavishes more critical respect on Eliot's later plays than they deserve. And he seems to have almost no information about the last eight years of Eliot's life, the period from his marriage to Valerie Eliot in 1957 until his death, except that they were happy. But Ackroyd's biography succeeds, in spite of these limitations, because of his understanding of the qualities of the greatest of Eliot's poetry—and because of his discovery and judicious use of Eliot's first wife's diary. His biography does what a good literary biography should do: it sends us back to Eliot's work more sensitive to its own terms.

Ackroyd concludes, with the kind of understanding that makes his book valuable, by observing that we are confronted with a number of paradoxes.

> Eliot proclaimed the impersonality of great poetry, and yet his own personality and experience are branded in letters of fire upon his work. He was a poet who insisted upon the nature and value of a tradition, and yet he had no real predecessors or successors. He was a writer who attempted to create order and coherence, and yet his central vision was of "the Void." His poetic voice is unmistakable, and yet it was composed from a number of other poets' voices which he adapted and borrowed. He was a strange, private and often bewildered man who was raised into a cultural guru, a representative of authority and stability.

Eliot told his second wife Valerie that "he had paid too high a price to be a poet, that he had suffered too much." Readers of Peter Ackroyd's *T.S. Eliot: A Life* will probably reach a rather different conclusion, just as readers of Eliot's poetry have done for most of the past century. Finally, however—as the gaps in Eliot's biography have been filled in by the biographers who have come after Ackroyd—the poet Randall Jarrell turns out to have the last word. Writing before *The Waste Land* facsimile, before any of the biographies, before the change in attitude toward Eliot's theories, he recognized what New Critical theory had blinded most of his contemporaries to seeing. "Won't the future say of us in helpless astonishment," he wrote, "but did you actually believe that all those things about objective correlatives, classicism, the tradition, applied to *his* poetry?"

> Surely you must have seen that he was one of the most subjective and daemonic poets who ever lived, the victim and helpless beneficiary of his own inexorable compulsions, obsessions? From a psychoanalytical point of view he was far and away the most interesting poet of our century. But for you, of course, after the first few years, his poetry existed undersea, thousands of feet below the deluge of exegesis, explication, source listing, scholarship and criticism that overwhelmed it. And yet how bravely and personally it survived, its eyes neither coral or mother-of-pearl but plainly human, full of anguish!

II

Tom Eliot published his first poem in his prep school's literary magazine in 1905. Four years later, he became a poet. And eight years after that, with the publication of *Prufrock and Other Observations* (1917), he became T.S. Eliot. Christopher Ricks's edition of *Inventions of the*

March Hare (1996) is a major literary event because it allows its readers to watch this development, to accompany the callow young man from St. Louis as he discovers the voice and vision that would make him the most influential poet in English of the first half of this century.

The handful of poems that Eliot published in the *Smith Academy Record* and the *Harvard Advocate* between 1905 and 1909 were no more than talented imitations and exercises. There is nothing particularly distinguished about them, nothing that suggests what would soon follow. Collected in *Poems from Early Youth* (1950), they demonstrate that, like every beginning poet, Eliot struggled to find his voice. At sixteen he discovered the English poets of the 1890s—especially John Davidson, Ernest Dowson and Arthur Symons—and, struck by their attempt to use colloquial speech and by the dark urban images in poems such as Davidson's "Thirty Bob a Week," he began to sense other possibilities.

The decisive moment in the development of his poetic sensibility can be dated precisely. In December 1908, during his junior year at Harvard, he discovered a copy of the newly published second edition of Arthur Symons's critical anthology *The Symbolist Movement in Poetry* in the Harvard Union. He later described the anthology as more important to his development than any other book because it introduced him to the poetry of Baudelaire, Verlaine, Rimbaud, Corbiere and, most importantly, Jules Laforgue. Baudelaire, he wrote, showed him the poetic possibilities of "the more sordid aspects of the modern metropolis." And from all of these poets he learned that his own experience and emotions could be the subjects of poetry.

In his copy of the anthology, Eliot marked Symons's comment that in Laforgue "the old cadences, the old eloquence . . . are all banished." Soon after, he ordered the three volumes of Laforgue's *Oeuvres completes* from Paris. The book arrived some time in the spring of 1909 and during that summer at his family's vacation home in Gloucester, Massachusetts, he read all of Laforgue in French. "I puzzled it out as best I could," he wrote to a friend years later, "not finding half the words in the dictionary."

Apparently he understood enough for his purposes. Laforgue, he said, "was the first . . . to teach me the possibilities of my own idiom of speech." Throughout his career Eliot wrote extensively about poetic influence— about influence in general and his own influences in particular—and it is now clear that, here as elsewhere, his Olympian critical generalizations usually masked autobiographical revelations. Two of the comments he made about influence, included in an appendix to *Inventions of the March Hare*, define what Laforgue's influence meant to Eliot's own development in the critical year of 1908-1909.

A poet's most important early influences, Eliot wrote in 1950, are those that "introduce one to oneself . . . due to an impression which is in one aspect, the recognition of a temperament akin to one's own, and in another aspect the discovery of a form of expression which gives a clue to the discovery of one's own form." Such a "feeling of profound kinship, or rather of a peculiar intimacy, with another, probably dead, author," he wrote in 1917, "is certainly a crisis; and when a young writer is seized with his first passion of this sort he may be changed, metamorphosed almost, within a few weeks even, from a bundle of second-hand sentiments into a person. The imperative intimacy arouses for the first time a real, an unshakeable confidence. . . It is something more than encouragement to you. It is a cause of development . . . "

Through his own first passion for Laforgue, Eliot underwent precisely this transformation in the summer and fall of 1909. From this French dandy whom he soon began to imitate in both his life and his poetry, Lyndall Gordon writes in her *Eliot's Early Years*, Eliot learned "to broadcast secrets, to confess through the defeatist persona his own despair and, at the same time, to shield himself by playing voices against one another—the wry voice of the sufferer, the scathing or flippant voice of the commentator, the banal voice of a woman." Laforgue, she says, also helped him to develop his "central persona—a performer fixed in a silly role, unable to take command of his real self which is socially unacceptable, outcast, or elusive."

These characteristics and this persona first appear in the extraordinary series of poems Eliot wrote in November 1909 and the spring and summer of 1910, during and just after his senior year at Harvard, most of which appear for the first time in *Inventions of the March Hare*. Eliot clearly knew that these poems were significantly different—and better—than his earlier efforts. Always self-conscious, he certainly understood that through a very personal experience of the way that "tradition" can effect an "individual talent" he had begun to find his own voice. In symbolic recognition of this new beginning and as an assertion of his poetic ambitions, while on vacation in Gloucester during the summer of 1910 he bought a marble-covered notebook for a quarter from Proctor Brothers Co., Old Corner Bookstore. On the front free end paper he titled the notebook "Complete Poems of T.S. Eliot." (Some time later he added, and then crossed out, the subtitle "Inventions of the March Hare.") Eliot copied into the lined pages of the notebook the poems written since November 1909 that he wanted to preserve. He did not copy the earlier poems he had published in the *Smith Academy Record* or the *Harvard Advocate* into this notebook of "Complete Poems"—presumably because he already realized that they did not belong to "T.S. Eliot."

Eliot continued to use this notebook until 1914, copying in poems written during his year abroad in Paris and Berlin (1910-1911), his graduate school years at Harvard (1911-1914), and his first year in London (1914). Among these poems are his most important early works—the "Preludes," "Portrait of a Lady," and "The Love Song of J. Alfred Prufrock"—as well as a number of the lesser-known works from his first books.

In 1922, when he wanted to express his gratitude to John Quinn, who had helped him to arrange for his first American book publication and had negotiated the serial and book publication of *The Waste Land*, he offered to give Quinn the manuscripts of both *The Waste Land* and his early poems. Quinn agreed to accept the manuscript of *The Waste Land* as a gift if he could pay Eliot for the manuscripts of the other poems. Before mailing the package containing all of these manuscripts to Quinn on October 23, 1922, Eliot altered the notebook—excising twelve pages that included bawdy verses about "King Bolo" and "Columbo," dating some of the undated poems, changing some titles, and adding the same dedication to Jean Verdenal that he had used in *Prufrock and Other Observations*. He also inserted twenty-five loose leaves of typed and hand-written manuscripts of poems written before 1918 to make the collection both more complete and more valuable.

For thirty years after John Quinn died in 1924, both manuscripts were lost among the many cases of his papers put into storage. They were eventually rediscovered by his niece in the 1950s, and she sold them to the Berg Collection of the New York Public Library in 1958. Eliot never knew what had happened to the manuscripts. His widow Valerie only learned of their whereabouts in 1968, and Eliot bibliographer Donald Gallup reported the existence of *The Waste Land* and notebook manuscripts, and described them both, shortly afterward.

The first publication from these manuscripts was *The Waste Land* facsimile. Until *Inventions of the March Hare*, the early manuscript poems—aside from the few included among the letters collected in Mrs. Eliot's edition of *The Letters of T.S. Eliot: Volume I*—were only available to scholars, and they were not permitted to quote them. *Inventions of the March Hare* makes them available to the general public for the first time and, in presenting them, editor Christopher Ricks has performed an extraordinary act of scholarship and restoration. In addition to publishing all of the unpublished poems in the notebook and loose leaves, his edition includes a detailed preface that describes the history of the notebook; a chronology, detailing when Eliot wrote, and when and where he published, each of his early poems; a description of variant readings of the individual poems; facsimiles of Eliot's handwritten manuscripts of two of the poems, "First Caprice in North Cambridge" and "Interlude in London"; two hundred pages of notes on the poems; and four appendices. One appendix includes the poems excised from the notebook; one presents the first published texts of "Humoresque (After J. Laforgue)" and the other poems from the notebook that were included in *Prufrock and Other Observations*; one prints the texts—as they first stood in the loose leaves—of the poems Eliot published in *Poems* (1919), *Ara Vos Prec* (1920), and *Poems* (1920); and one presents quotations on "Influence and Influences" from Eliot's writing and speeches.

Much of the initial response to this edition focused on Ricks's notes and the excised poems. The notes deserve the attention, the excised poems do not. A few reviewers portrayed Ricks as an almost mad Nabokovian character—as an annotator run amok whose two hundred pages of notes are excruciatingly detailed, frequently tangential, and *prima facie* evidence of academic overkill. Many more acknowledged the obvious: Ricks is probably the best-read, most incisive and most original literary sleuth to come along in decades, and his insights on the possible influences, sources, readings and contexts behind these early poems are invaluable—in spite of their occasional excesses, tangents, and false leads—because they do exactly what he intended: assist those readers who are interested to understand the poems by suggesting "where they came from and where they went to" in Eliot's later work.

The scatological King Bolo and Columbo verses have been highlighted and cited as further evidence of the racism, sexism and anti-Semitism that commentators such as Cynthia Ozick and Anthony Julius have recently emphasized in their re-evaluations of Eliot and his career. They are not nearly that important. Eliot began writing them while a graduate student at Harvard, and they read like the off-key adolescent efforts of an uptight, sexually repressed, inexperienced young man who was trying to prove he was "one of the guys." They also reflect all of the stupidities and sexual prejudices of that time, class, and place. He composed a few more of these verses in the years before 1917 as a running joke with Conrad Aiken and Ezra Pound, two friends and fellow poets who apparently enjoyed this type of humor. These poems, which take up six pages of this 428-page book, are certainly embarassingly juvenile and tasteless, and Eliot knew it. That is why he excised them from the notebook before he sent it to Quinn, why he sent them to Pound, and why he never considered publishing them.

What most readers will feel reading *Inventions of the March Hare* is what Eliot must have felt when he wrote these poems: the excitement of discovery and the sense of a rapidly growing mastery of the images, language, and form that quickly became the signatures of his maturity. T.S. Eliot was often his own best critic and, even at this early stage, he had an unerring sense of which of his poems should be published. The best example of the rigor of his editing is his decision to cut a thirty-eight line section titled "Prufrock's Pervigilium" from the manuscript version of "The Love Song of J. Alfred Prufrock" before he gave the poem to Pound for submission to Harriet Monroe's *Poetry* magazine. Like the excisions he would later make from the original manuscript of *The Waste Land*, "Prufrock's Pervigilium" contains lines that any writer would be proud of—and the final version of the poem is stronger and more effective without them.

Eliot would not have wanted this book to be published, but readers must be grateful for it. There are no hidden gems among the previously unpublished early poems, but there are flashes of brilliance. And reading the poems that did not quite meet Eliot's standards is still a pleasure that is well worth the price of admission to *Inventions of the March Hare*.

Indivisible Man
Ralph Ellison

Ralph Ellison published his first novel, *Invisible Man*, in 1952 at the age of thirty-eight. When he died in April 1994, a little more than a month after his eightieth birthday, he had not yet completed his second. In the interim, he became the best-known and most influential one-book novelist in American literary history. The fact that the only novel he published during his lifetime is generally regarded as a masterpiece may explain Ellison's place in American literature, but it does not fully account for the larger role that he played in the debates of postwar American culture, or the attention and respect that he gained and kept for the more than forty years in which he struggled to complete its successor. The essays, reviews, addresses, and interviews that he wrote and gave during his long fictional silence do that. Taken together, they are his autobiography, his *apologia pro vita sua*, his contribution to both creating and understanding the culture and character of America, and his claim to being one of his country's most important twentieth-century men of letters.

In the years between the appearance of his first book review in 1937 and his last public address in 1992, Ellison wrote more than seventy-five essays, reviews, addresses, and conference talks. In the absence of a second novel, this nonfiction became the vehicle for Ellison to express the ideas about art, race, and American culture for which he was both praised and attacked by his contemporaries. He collected less than half of this work in the two books he published in the years following *Invisible Man*, *Shadow and Act* (1964) and *Going to the Territory* (1986). The Modern

Library *Collected Essays of Ralph Ellison* (1995), edited and introduced by John F. Callahan, includes the complete texts of both these books, as well as eleven previously published but uncollected essays, nine essays and talks that have never been published before, and two of Ellison's most extensive interviews.

While this does not make this handsome one-volume compilation a complete collection of Ellison's nonfiction, it certainly makes it an indispensable one. In his introduction, Callahan mentions that Ellison wrote more than thirty essays and reviews for *New Masses* and other publications on the Left in the 1930's and 1940's. But taking his cue from Ellison, who republished only one of these early pieces ("The Way It Is") in his own essay collections, Callahan chooses to ignore most of the work Ellison wrote while enamored with Marxism and Malraux, adding only one essay from this period of Ellison's career ("A Congress Jim Crow Didn't Attend") to *The Collected Essays*. At a minimum, it would seem, the collection should have also included Ellison's first published essay—a review of Waters Edward Turpin's novel *These Low Grounds*, commissioned by Richard Wright and published in the magazine he edited, *New Challenge*—and "Stormy Weather," his 1940 *New Masses* review of Langston Hughes' memoir *The Big Sea*. While the former may only be of historical interest, the absence of the Hughes review is particularly unfortunate—both because it would have provided readers with a fuller sense of Ellison's political and intellectual journey and because it is an important early example of Ellison's willingness to challenge demands for racial solidarity by measuring other African-American writers against the same high artistic standards he sought to meet himself.

The Collected Essays adds two of the best Ellison interviews—James Alan McPherson's "Indivisible Man" and John Hersey's "A Completion of Personality"—to the three interviews Ellison collected in *Shadow and Act*. But since Ellison's practice was to work with most interviewers to review and revise his initial comments until they met his exacting standards as prose, there are a number of other, equally interesting, interviews that might have been included. The reader who wishes to have a fuller sense of Ellison's public statements will want to go on from the five interviews included in *The Collected Essays* to the nineteen others that Maryemma Graham and Amritjit Singh have gathered in their four-hundred page *Conversations with Ralph Ellison* (1995).

Even though the previously unpublished and uncollected essays and speeches it includes do not alter the shape or character of Ellison's achievement as a thinker or writer, *The Collected Essays* offers a welcome occasion to reconsider this achievement. At its core is his insistence, early and late, on the inextricable connection between black and white Americans as co-creators of a distinctly American culture. For Ellison, that American culture is inevitably complex, pluralistic, fluid, and challenged to fully realize the democratic ideology expressed in its founding documents.

American history, he argues repeatedly, is the story of our working out the conflict caused by the Declaration of Independence's assertion that "all men are created equal," the Constitution's refusal to acknowledge this principle, and American society's failure to keep faith with it. Yet during the more than two hundred years in which the struggle to realize the democratic promise and humanist commitment of the Declaration has persisted, Ellison believed, Americans of every race and color have shaped one another's consciousnesses, constantly creating and recreating the American character in the process.

Ellison's commitment to cultural pluralism and the American promise made him a target for vicious attacks and ugly rhetoric, especially during the 1960's when literary and political radicals in the Black Arts and Black Power movements cast him as a self-hating Uncle Tom. He weathered these attacks with dignity and lived long enough to see his ideas inspire a new generation of black artists and thinkers such as Leon Forrest, Charles Johnson, Stanley Crouch, Wynton Marsalis, and Henry Louis Gates. Since he believed that integration was a cultural given—that is, that Americans of every race are part of a culture which all of them have shaped—he rejected visions of a future for black Americans based on separation or a return to Africa and African culture as both impractical and undesirable. As fashion and politics changed, as the preferred terms for black Americans shifted from "colored" to "Negro" to "Black" to "African American," Ellison also angered many and made himself seem archaic to others by continuing to insist on speaking about "Negro Americans." Since his reason for this insistence, articulated in the interview "Some Questions and Some Answers" is the philosophical foundation upon which all of his writing about race, art, and American culture is built, it deserves to be quoted at length.

The term "Negro American," he argues "describes a people whose origin began with the introduction of African slaves to the American colonies in 1619, and which today represents the fusing with original African strains of many racial blood lines."

> The American Negro people is North American in origin and has evolved under specifically American conditions: climactic, nutritional, historical, political and social. It takes its character from the experience of American slavery and the struggle for, and the achievement of emancipation; from the dynamics of American race and caste discrimination, and from living in a highly industrialized and highly mobile society possessing a relatively high standard of living and an explicitly stated equalitarian concept of freedom. Its spiritual outlook is

basically Protestant, its system of kinship is Western, its time and historical sense are American (United States), and its secular values are those professed, ideally at least, by all of the people of the United States.

Culturally this people represents one of the many subcultures which make up the great amalgam of European and native American cultures which is the culture of the United States. This "American Negro culture" is expressed in a body of folklore, in the musical forms of the spirituals, the blues and jazz; an idiomatic version of American speech (especially in the Southern United States); a cuisine; a body of dance forms . . . . It must, however, be pointed out that due to the close links which Negro Americans have with the rest of the nation these cultural expressions are constantly influencing the larger body of American culture and are in turn influenced by them. . . . Nor should the existence of a specifically "Negro" idiom in any way be confused with the vague, racist terms "white culture" or "black culture"; rather it is a matter of diversity within unity.

Every piece in *The Collected Essays* is, finally, an exploration, elaboration, defense, or clarification of these assertions. In essays on James Armistead Lafayette, William L. Dawson, Alain Locke, Roscoe Dunjee, Inman Page, and Romare Bearden, Ellison calls attention to the largely unrecognized extent of the role Negro Americans have played in the country's political and cultural history. In essays on jazz, the blues, spirituals, and individual musicians such as Charlie Parker, Mahalia Jackson, Charlie Christian, Jimmy Rushing, and Duke Ellington, he recalls the Negro's creation of America's unique contribution to world music. In interviews, he explains the importance of Negro folklore to both his own work and the larger American culture. In essays such as "Twentieth-Century Fiction and the Black Mask of Humanity," "Change the Joke and Slip the Yoke," "The Shadow and the Act," and "An Extravagance of Laughter," he argues—as Toni Morrison would later argue in *Playing in the Dark* (1990)—that both the ways in which black Americans are present in the best-known works of American fiction and the ways in which they are absent speak volumes about the essential nature of American life and American literature.

Because he considered himself a Negro American, Ellison also resisted the over-simplifications that he thought were too often applied to writers based on their race by both black and white critics. As *Invisible Man* demonstrated, his comments in interviews emphasized, and his most famous essays such as "The World and the Jug" and "The Little Man at Chehaw Station" underlined, he viewed himself as an artist whose work must be measured against the greatest achievements of all other artists—not just other black artists. He would not let anyone tell him what or how to write, and he resisted having his work classified as black rather than American as vehemently and eloquently as he could.

"Complexity" was one of his favorite words. Music was his first love. So it is no surprise that his description of the education of a jazz musician in his homage to the birth of be-bop, "The Golden Age, Time Past," reads as his version of Eliot's "Tradition and the Individual Talent." The jam session, he writes, is the "jazzman's true academy." There he learns tradition, group techniques and style. "After the jazzman has learned fundamentals of his instrument and the traditional techniques of jazz . . . he must then 'find himself,' must be reborn, must find, as it were, his soul. All this through achieving that subtle identification between his instrument and his deepest drives which will allow him to express his own unique ideas in his own unique voice. He must achieve, in short, his self-determined identity."

In the intellectual autobiography that develops over the course of *The Collected Essays*, Ellison describes his own education in Oklahoma, at Tuskegee, and in New York as the acquisition of a characteristically hybrid American culture that combined Hemingway and Dostoevsky, Richard Wright and Andre Malraux, Langston Hughes and T.S. Eliot, Ellington and Wagner, the street and the library, the jazz club Minton's Playhouse and the symphony hall. He acquired it as an individual with the encouragement and example of other individuals, Ellison writes, not because he was born into a particular group; and he struggled to make something lasting of it as an individual, not as a member of a group. This, he says, is the reality that our stereotypes mask; and it is what each of us must finally do.

In *The Collected Essays of Ralph Ellison*, readers will discover an important part of what Ellison learned about himself, his country, and his art through expressing "his own unique ideas in his own unique voice." That voice—articulate, intelligent, thoughtful, personal, witty, well-read, stubborn yet gracious—is sorely missed.

II

Shortly before he died in 1994, Ralph Ellison told his literary executor John F. Callahan that he wanted to publish a collection of his short stories and hinted that he had some unpublished stories that no one had ever seen. After Ellison's death, as Callahan began to review the thousands of pages of manuscript of Ellison's long-awaited unpublished second novel to see if they could be brought together into a final text, he discovered a box that was full of old magazines, clippings, and duplicate printouts from the novel. At the bottom of the box he found a brown imitation-leather portfolio with RALPH W. ELLISON embossed in gold letters on the front; inside, there was a manila folder labeled "Early Stories" bulging with manuscripts typed on crumbling paper, brown with age. While some of these manuscripts were fragments or unfinished stories, Callahan determined that six of them were worthy of publication.

Only the discovery of these six stories made publishing a book of Ellison's stories possible: without them, there would not have been enough short fiction for a collection. In the fifty-seven years between his first story and his death, Ellison published a total of only twenty-two pieces of short fiction: eight pieces between 1937 and 1944, two of which were excerpts from an abandoned novel called *Slick*; and just fourteen stories in the fifty years after 1944, all but one of them excerpts from *Invisible Man* or his novel-in-progress.

In the four hundred pages of *Conversations with Ralph Ellison* and the eight hundred and fifty pages of *The Collected Essays*, Ellison's references to his short stories add up to less than a few pages. In describing his relationship with Richard Wright in several interviews he mentions "Hymie's Bull" as his first story, written at Wright's invitation to appear in *New Challenge* (the magazine folded while the story was in galleys and it has not been published until now). There is a sentence or two about "Flying Home" in a 1971 interview with David L. Carson, noting that its publication in the 1944 *Cross Section* anthology was his first appearance between hard covers and confirming that its title came from a jazz piece of the same name. And he refers briefly in his thirtieth anniversary introduction to *Invisible Man* to "In a Strange Country" (without naming it) as an outgrowth of the unfinished novel he abandoned to write his masterpiece.

In other words, Ralph Ellison decided early that the short story was not the form that interested him and abandoned it when he began writing *Invisible Man* in 1945. ("A Coupla Scalped Indians" was published in 1956, but it is not clear when he actually wrote it and it seems likely that he originally conceived of it as an excerpt from his novel-in-progress rather than a free-standing story.) Since he was an inveterate collector and reviser who appears to have kept copies of every draft of decades of effort on his second novel, it is hardly surprising that Ellison kept copies of his early unpublished stories at the bottom of an old box. But, in spite of his comment to Callahan, it is still hard to believe that Ellison would have really wanted these unpublished stories to be presented to his public. He chose not to publish them during the forty-two years separating *Invisible Man* and his death, although he had ample opportunity to do so. His self-critical attitude toward his own work was legendary. Long after it had become a contemporary classic, he wondered aloud if *Invisible Man* would continue to be read; and in spite of the encouragement of many writers and critics he respected, he was never satisfied enough with his novel-in-progress to allow it to be published.

Yet readers owe Professor Callahan a debt of gratitude for preparing *Flying Home and Other Stories* (1996) and for all of the painstaking work he is doing as Ellison's literary executor. Like *The Collected Essays of Ralph Ellison*, this collection is part of his effort to make long unavailable Ellison materials easily accessible to all those who care about one of the most important figures in modern American literature. Just as readers may enjoy the version of Ellison's second novel that Callahan has edited and titled *Juneteenth* (1999)—knowing that Ellison did not consider the book ready for publication and that *Juneteenth* is, at best, a sensitive editor's approximation of what its author intended—they may read *Flying Home* with interest and pleasure for what *it* is: a collection of apprentice work which reveals the development of Ellison's talent and technique, voice and vision.

In an interview with John Hersey that suggests how these early stories should be read, Ellison said that when he began writing his first stories he approached writing as he approached music: "I knew you didn't reach a capable performance in whatever craft without work... I wrote a hell of a lot of stuff that I didn't submit to anybody." He went on to say that one of the particular problems that he was working on in these stories was "how to render Afro-American speech without resorting to misspellings—to give a suggestion of the idiom." "Some of the first things were embarrassing," he confessed. "You go from something that you've read, until you find out how you really feel about it."

The six previously unpublished stories in *Flying Home*—"A Party Down at the Square," "Boy on a Train," "Hymie's Bull," "I Did Not Learn Their Names," "A Hard Time Keeping Up," and "The Black Ball"—show what he meant by these statements. So do the four published stories about two young Oklahoma boys, Buster and Riley—"Mister Toussan" (1941), "Afternoon" (1940), "That I Had Wings" (1943), and "A Coupla Scalped Indians." From the beginning, the territory seems Ellison's own. But in all of these stories he is still trying to find his own voice. Without it, the stories are obviously imitative, shaped by his reading of Twain, Faulkner, and especially Hemingway—three of the writers he frequently cited in his essays and interviews as early influences on his own work.

"A Party Down at the Square," for example, is an exercise in the kind of innocent, child's eye, first-person point of view that is so effective in stories such as Hemingway's "My Old Man" or Sherwood Anderson's "I Want to Know Why." Told by a white boy, it vividly describes a lynching and conveys a sense of the moral and social chaos surrounding it. In his introduction to *Flying Home*, Callahan quotes an undated meditation by Ellison in which he writes of the importance of Hemingway's prose style to his own early work: "when I started trying to write fiction," Ellison notes, "I selected Hemingway for a model." (So, of course, did most of his generation.) The model is apparent in the simple words, sequence of "ands," and multiple meanings of the word "party" in the story's opening paragraph: "I don't know what started it. A bunch of men came by my Uncle Ed's place and said there was going to be a party down at the Square, and my uncle hollered for me to come on and I ran with them through the dark and rain and there we were at the Square." It also appears in the plain-spoken, deadpan reaction of the boy as he becomes morally complicit when he watches the "Bacote nigger" burn: "I had enough. I didn't want to see anymore. I wanted to run somewhere and puke, but I stayed. I stayed right there in front of the crowd and looked."

Hemingway's voice echoes throughout these early stories: in "Boy on a Train" ("The train gave a long, shrill, lonely whistle, and seemed to gain speed as it rushed downgrade between two hills covered with trees. The trees were covered with deep-red, brown, and yellow leaves"); in "I Did Not Learn Their Names" ("It was chilly up on top. We were riding to St. Louis on a manifest, clinging to the top of the boxcar. It was dark, and sparks from the engine flew back to where we were riding"); or in "A Hard Time Keeping Up" ("The streetlights and the neon signs made you think of Christmas as they sparkled on the whiteness. It was pleasant to think about the snow . . .").

In the Buster and Riley stories—the stories where Ellison is trying to find a way to render Afro-American speech—the Mark Twain of *The Adventures of Huckleberry Finn* is just as clearly a model. "I hope they all gits rotten and the worms git in 'em," the first story begins. But Ellison goes beyond Twain as "Mister Toussan" progresses, using the vernacular to introduce the boys' love of language and riffing into his narrative: "Ole Toussan was too hard on them white folks, thass why!/Oh, he was a hard man!/He was mean. . ./But a good mean . . ./Toussan was clean . . ./ . . .He was a good, clean mean. . ./Aw, man, he was sooo-preme."

These early stories do not compare with the mature Ellison in complexity, originality or style, but they certainly show that his powers of characterization and description developed quickly. In *Shadow and Act*, Ellison observed that when he began to write he was forced "to stare down the deadly and hypnotic temptation to interpret the world and all its devices in terms of race." His ability to overcome this temptation seems to have come quickly, too. With the glaring exception of "Black Ball"—the only truly embarrassing piece in *Flying Home* ("Brown's much nicer than white, isn't it, Daddy?/ Some people think so. But America is better than both, son./Is it, Daddy?/Sure it is.")—while all of these stories engage questions of race in one way or another none of them reads like propaganda rather than literature.

The best stories in *Flying Home*, by far, are the final three—all published in 1944 as Ellison was about to begin *Invisible Man*, and all expressing his unique voice and vision. There is a value, certainly, in gathering the apprentice work of a great writer; but the value is as much historical and biographical as literary. Restoring "King of the Bingo Game," "In a Strange Country," and "Flying Home" to print, however, makes this collection an important literary event. Unlike the earlier work, each stands on its own as a masterful short story that would deserve to be published even if Ralph Ellison were not its author. At the same time, reading them together is particularly fascinating because they reveal Ellison beginning to work out the style, themes, and images that would emerge fully-formed in his novel.

In "King of the Bingo Game," which describes a desperate man's trying to hit the jackpot at a movie theater's bingo game, Ellison has already gained control of the blend of realism and surrealism that characterizes the Battle Royal, Golden Day, and Liberty Paint factory episodes of *Invisible Man*. Both "In a Strange Country" and "Flying Home" are stories set during World War II about the conflicts felt by black servicemen fighting for a country which spurns them. In "In A Strange Country," Parker leaves his ship for a shore leave in a small Welsh town feeling "the excited expectancy of entering a strange land... in the morning he would see the country with fresh eyes, like those with which the Pilgrims had seen the New World." As he walks into the town, he is glad to hear the other American voices of a group of soldiers bunched at a curb—until they spring out of the darkness and attack him, yelling "It's a goddam nigger." A Welshman and his friends rescue him, take him to a pub, treat him with respect and kindness, and invite him along to a concert at a private club where the beauty of their folksongs touches him deeply. "*I believe in music!*" he thinks, "*in what's happening here tonight*" (Ellison's italics). When the Welshmen try to honor him by singing "The Star-Spangled Banner," Parker suddenly hears his own voice singing along, "like the voice of another, over whom he had no control." And, "for the first time in your whole life," he thinks, "the words are not ironic." In just nine pages, Ellison captures the complexities of Parker's emotional vulnerability, his defensiveness, his hope, his love of music, and his unrequited sense of his own Americanness.

In "Flying Home" a black aviator from a nearby base crashlands his plane in a Macon County field. "Now the humiliation would come," he thinks. "When you must have them judge you, knowing that they never accept your mistakes as your own but hold it against your whole race." Ashamed to be associated with the old black fieldhand Jefferson who tries to help him, abused by the local white landowner Mister Graves who has him placed in a straightjacket, the aviator Todd also finds himself "in a strange country"—the South, America, a land where he can never feel at home. In its frank treatment of an educated black man's ambivalence toward the pull of racial solidarity, its symbolic use of Jefferson's folk tale of flying in heaven, its allusions to the spirituals, its combination of realism and surreality, its control of its central imagery, and its use of several narrative voices, "Flying Home" is Ellison's most impressive story. A prelude to *Invisible Man* and culmination of all the experiments with the short story that preceded it.

The Ghost Writer
Philip Roth

Few novelists have been as thoroughly identified with their fictional alter egos as Philip Roth has been with his. Even fewer have spent as much time and energy challenging their readers' tendency to make such identifications. For more than forty years, in essays and interviews by turns witty and testy, eloquent and blunt, Roth has tried to convince his readers and critics of the importance of acknowledging the fundamental distinction between facts and fictions, imagined and genuine autobiographies, his characters and his own character. In his novels and memoirs, he's demonstrated how difficult making those distinctions can be.

What he describes in his "Author's Note" to *Reading Myself and Others* (1975) as his "continuing preoccupation with the relationship between the written and the unwritten world" started at the very beginning, when Roth found himself attacked by segments of the Jewish community as disloyal and self-hating for the stories in *Goodbye, Columbus* (1959). But the reaction to *Portnoy's Complaint* (1969) was certainly the critical spark that ignited his passion to explore this theme ever since. Stung by that reaction, Philip Roth found himself explaining over and over that he was not Alexander Portnoy, that his mother was not Sophie—that fiction was not life, that characters were not self-portraits but imaginary selves. In the wake of that experience, in which his own fiction turned on him in a way he had not fully expected, since *The Breast* (1972) Roth has consistently focused his work on the enigma of identity—often by exploring the conflicts between life and art, the writer and his creations, reality and invention.

Since his exploration began in that novella, Roth's approach to this subject has undergone several transformations. In *The Breast*, *My Life as a Man* (1974), and *The Professor of Desire* (1977), he began to define the terms of his exploration and experimented with several alter egos. In the trilogy and epilogue collected in *Zuckerman Bound* (1985)—*The Ghost Writer* (1979), *Zuckerman Unbound* (1981), *The Anatomy Lesson* (1983), and *The Prague Orgy* (1985)—and in *The Counterlife* (1987) he used the career of Nathan Zuckerman to develop and elaborate his theme. In *The Facts: A Novelist's Autobiography* (1988), *Deception* (1990), *Patrimony* (1991), and *Operation Shylock* (1995), his focus turned from Zuckerman to a novelist named "Philip Roth." And in his latest trilogy, composed of *American Pastoral* (1997), *I Married a Communist* (1998), and *The Human Stain* (2000), "Philip Roth" has withdrawn as Nathan Zuckerman has re-emerged—now as a witness who tries to tell the truths that lie behind the fictions of others and the facts of recent American history, rather than as the main character of his own stories.

In *The Breast*, David Kepesh, a professor of literature, tries to interpret his way out of his Kafkaesque metamorphosis into a gigantic female breast. He doesn't succeed. Faced with the inexplicable, Kepesh tries to turn his situation into a narrative that makes sense: perhaps he is actually a quadruple amputee, the victim of punitive wish-fulfillment, or of postanalytic collapse. Perhaps he has succumbed to the impulse to revert to the safety and security of the womb; is trying to escape a trauma through self-delusion; has read too much Kafka, Gogol, and Swift; is trying to out-Kafka Kafka by making the metamorphic word flesh. Perhaps he's dreaming. But, in one of the novella's most inventive twists, all of his efforts to turn his condition into a useful fiction are finally dismissed by his analyst Dr. Klinger. "It happened," Klinger insists.

In "Useful Fictions," the first part of *My Life as a Man*, Roth introduced the character of Nathan Zuckerman in two short stories. In "Salad Days," Nathan is a pampered Jewish son and precocious undergraduate English major with literary ambitions. The story ends with the warning that "he would begin to pay . . . for the contradictions: the stinging tongue and the tender hide, the spiritual aspirations and the lewd desires, the softy boyish needs and the manly, *magisterial* ambitions." In "Courting Disaster (or Serious in the Fifties)," Nathan is a University of Chicago graduate student and instructor so enamored of the Great Books, so caught up in his own contradictory impulses, that he manages to trap himself into one of the most disastrous marriages in contemporary American fiction. In the second part of the novel, titled "My True Story," Roth introduces yet another alter ego, Peter Tarnopol, who is presented as the author of the two Zuckerman stories that we have just read. By relating Tarnopol's "true story," Tarnopol's "useful fictions," and publicly known facts of his own biography, Roth explicitly investigates the relationship between autobiography and fiction for the first time.

In his next novel, *The Professor of Desire*, set before the action of *The Breast*, David Kepesh reappears. Here Roth's focus is on the relationship between the lives invented by writers (Kafka, Chekhov, Robert Musil) and the life Kepesh is trying to live. In *A Philip Roth Reader* (1980), which Roth himself edited, this focus is summed up in his title to one group of selections: "Literature Got Me into This and Literature Is Gonna Have to Get Me Out." In the lives of his semi-autobiographical characters since *The Breast*, literature invariably does the former and invariably fails to do the latter. For the early and later versions of Nathan Zuckerman, for Peter Tarnopol, for David Kepesh, for "Philip Roth," the order and moral seriousness of art are as much temptation as vocation. Trying to live by fiction, each discovers that the world's disorder is beyond the artist's control, that moral seriousness is easier to carry off in fiction than in life. Paradoxically, while their own lives and choices are shaped by their reading, Roth's heroes in all of the novels before *The Counterlife* repeatedly reject the pleas of all those who tell them that the images in books *matter*, that what they write may have real consequences for real people, including themselves.

II

Roth has described the subject of *Zuckerman Bound* as both "the moral consequences of the literary career of Nathan Zuckerman" and "the unintended consequences of art." The consequences vary, but in *Zuckerman Bound* there most certainly are consequences that Nathan's early theories of "art for art's sake" fail to recognize. Over the course of the trilogy and epilogue Zuckerman learns the hard way that this is true: that the relationship between art and life is far more complex than he imagined when he began his career.

Zuckerman Bound traces the literary and personal lives of Nathan Zuckerman from 1956 to 1976. The story begins in *The Ghost Writer*, a sensitive, deeply moving, exquisitely crafted portrait of the artist as a young man that deserves a place on that ever-lengthening list of important contemporary American novels in which the writer's subject is a writer and his subjects. Like Saul Bellow's *Humboldt's Gift*, it is cast as a memoir describing the impact of an older Jewish writer's life and work on a younger writer. Like William Styron's *Sophie's Choice*, it treats the young writer's relationship with his father, with a young woman who survived the Holocaust, and with the participants in a doomed love affair. Like Bernard Malamud's *Dubin's Lives,* its underlying theme concerns the conflict between a writer's dedication to the life of his art and his dedication to living itself.

Narrated by forty-three year-old Nathan Zuckerman, it recounts events of twenty years earlier. As a beginning writer at odds with his father and pillars of his community such as Judge Leopold Wapter over the content of his first stories—which present unflattering portraits of Jewish characters—Zuckerman visits E.I. Lonoff, "the most famous literary ascetic in America," to submit himself for candidacy as a spiritual son.

During the afternoon, evening and morning he spends at Lonoff's home he gets the validation he is seeking. Lonoff offers a toast to "a wonderful new writer," declares that Zuckerman has "the most compelling voice I've encountered in years," and encourages him to leave his nice Jewish boy's manners out of his fiction and cultivate his "turbulence" instead. But Zuckerman also gets a lesson he's not expecting about just how much the religion of art to which he has dedicated himself demands of its acolytes—and those close to them.

For just as Zuckerman's determination to write the truth as he sees it has begun to alienate him from his loving Jewish family, Lonoff's single-minded dedication to his comic parables of "terminal restraint," to a life dedicated to "turning sentences around," has long ago cut him off from connection with those closest to him—especially Hope, his wife of thirty-five years. While Zuckerman is visiting, her frustration and unhappiness explode, destroying forever the illusions he has had that the writer's life will be a serene and ordered idyll. Kinsmen in their sense of alienation as well as their art, older and younger writer each briefly fantasizes the same means of escape from his isolation: the love of Amy Bellette, the proximate cause of Hope's explosion. A refugee from Europe, a survivor of the concentration camps with a shadowy past, she is a former student of Lonoff's who has taken on the task of arranging his manuscripts. To the much older Lonoff, Amy represents the possibility of starting over, of breaking out of his fastidious life of habit and regaining a vital link to something other than his work. But this is a possibility that he is finally no more able to grasp than one of his heroes, characters whose impulses are extinguished by "the ruling triumvirate of Sanity, Responsibility, and Self-Respect" who are famously plagued by the "ambiguities of prudence and the anxieties of disorder." To Zuckerman she represents a way of reconciling with his family without compromising his art.

In the most imaginative and audacious section of the novel, Zuckerman imagines that Amy, whose background is mysterious, is actually the archetypal victim of the Holocaust, miraculously saved from the death readers of her world-famous diary believe she suffered. He sees her as a way to silence his critics by allowing him to demonstrate his own Sanity, Responsibility, and Self-Respect. As Roth once imagined that Kafka survived to become his Hebrew teacher in Newark in the story "Looking at Kafka" (1973), Zuckerman pictures how different his life will become when he and Amy are married and her "real" identity is revealed to the family that has begun to accuse him of self-hatred. The conversation as he imagines it: "I met a marvelous young woman while I was up in New England. I love her and she loves me. We are going to be married." "Married? But so fast? Nathan, is she Jewish?" "Yes, she is." "But who is she?" "Anne Frank." . . . "*Anne, says my father—the Anne? Oh how I have misunderstood my son. How mistaken we have been!*"

"But, alas," Zuckerman finally admits, "I could not lift her out of her sacred book and make her a character in this life." The fantasy is "so much fiction," and "far from acquitting me of their charges and restoring me to my cherished blamelessness, a fiction that of course would seem to them a desecration even more vile than the one they had read." For both Lonoff and Zuckerman Amy is only a *fiction*, a fantasy of escape, and each is finally left to face the consequences of his vocation without her help.

The idea of the "ghost writer" is a rich and suggestive one. Anne Frank, of course, is a ghost writer in more ways than one. Lonoff is a ghost writer too, to the extent that he withdraws from real life, is not there for his wife and family, and is brought back to life through the power of Zuckerman's memories. As the fictional phantom who is his author's alter ego, Zuckerman is a kind of ghost writer. And then there is Philip Roth, who ghost writes this memoir as well as all of the other novels in which Zuckerman writes and speaks.

In *Zuckerman Bound*, set in 1969, the consequences of his vocation multiply for Nathan Zuckerman with dizzying and hilarious effects. As the novel begins, he has recently published his fourth book, *Carnovsky*, a no-holds-barred account of growing up Jewish in Newark. Wilder than anything he has written before, it quickly becomes a best-selling *success de scandale* that disrupts his entire life. His youthful ambitions for artistic fame are fulfilled, in spades, but fame in contemporary America turns out to be a bit more than he bargained for.

His picture is on the cover of *Life*. People stop him on the street to advise him about how to invest his money and ask him about his sexual exploits. His mail is almost evenly divided between propositions and letters comparing him to Joseph Goebbels. A rock singer he has never met leaves the audience of "The Tonight Show" doubled over in laughter by describing her experiences with his sexual proclivities. His name is linked in gossip columns with other women he has never met. A jet-setting film star he *has* met, Caesara O'Shea, leaves him for Fidel Castro. And when he goes home, exhausted, and turns on his television set he finds a panel of psychiatrists analyzing his castration complex.

In Florida, his mother is being inundated by calls from the press asking what "Mrs. Carnovsky" is really like. Back in New York, he is getting calls from a mysterious kidnapper who is demanding fifty thousand dollars for *not* kidnapping her. And a nonstop talker and whiner named Alvin Pepler—who may or may not be the kidnapper *manque*—keeps popping up to regale his fellow Newarker with tales of the Gentile plot that knocked him off the quiz show "Smart Money" in the 1950's, and of the Broadway musical about his life that he is trying to get produced.

Zuckerman is not amused. At least, one Zuckerman is not. His agent can tell him to relax and enjoy his brief moment of media stardom, but careful, responsible, respectable Nathan will not just disappear after all of these years so that impulsive, irresponsible, libidinous Nathan can let go. Especially since while all of this is happening as a result of his having let loose in his fiction all of the ties that have bound, but also anchored, his life are also falling away. His third marriage, to a woman as serious and sensible as part of him, is on the rocks because he finds married life, like his earlier fiction, "stultifying." His father, whose life was totally dedicated to duty and responsibility, dies in a Miami Beach nursing home, cursing him. His brother accuses Nathan of killing their father with the shame of *Carnovsky*, and the two of them become estranged. He sees that the Jewish Newark that has inspired his work is gone, too. And so, on the novel's last page he is left fatherless, brotherless, and homeless—unmoored, adrift, unbound.

The Anatomy Lesson takes place in the Watergate summer of 1973, four years after the success/debacle of *Carnovsky*. Zuckerman's mother has recently died in Florida, and her death has severed his remaining ties to his family and his brother. Following her funeral, he finds himself unable to write, flat on his back with a crippling and unexplained pain in his neck and shoulders, suddenly going bald, and enraged by a devastating attack on his work recently published by the prominent New York Intellectual critic Milton Appel. The cause of his pain is unknown—it may be physical, it may be psychosomatic—but that does not make it any less real or debilitating. Freed of the constraints of family and wives, supposedly unbound, he finds himself almost totally immobilized. Living in Manhattan, he is as isolated as E.I. Lonoff ever was in the remote Berkshire Hills. But all is not lost: though unable to move, he is visited regularly by four women who minister to his physical and sexual needs.

In frustration and desperation with his pain and the dead end he has met as a writer—he "had lost his subject. His health, his hair, and subject. Just as well he couldn't find a posture for writing"—he concocts a scheme to start over. Inspired by alcohol and the pain-killing Percodans he begins to swallow like jellybeans, he decides to give up writing altogether. Instead, he will go to medical school at the University of Chicago and begin a new life.

In the novel's final third, Zuckerman completely loses control. Using Appel's name, on the flight to Chicago he pretends to be the publisher of the notorious pornographic magazine *Lickety Split*. Spewing anger and obscenities, he lands in Chicago, harangues an old friend who is a doctor at the university's Billings Hospital, and winds up in the hospital himself with his jaw broken and wired shut. Trying to escape his blocked career as a writer, he ends up with a pad and pencil his only means of communication.

> Yet as soon as he sat down to write, out came another explanation, causing him to recoil from his words in disgust. The same with his books: however ingenious and elaborate the disguise, answering charges, countering allegations, angrily sharpening the conflict while earnestly striving to be understood. The endless public deposition—what a curse! Best reason of all not to write again.

The novel ends with him following the interns on their rounds, still believing he can unchain himself from a future as a man apart and escape the corpus that is his.

In the epilogue *The Prague Orgy*, Zuckerman once again confronts the consequences of art. But this time the confrontation occurs in another culture: Eastern Europe. It is 1976 and Nathan has abandoned the desperate quest for another life and another career that was the subject of *The Anatomy Lesson*. Through Zdenek Sisovsky, a Czech émigré writer, and his companion Eva Kalinova, a Czech émigré actress renowned for her portrayals of Anne Frank and Chekhov's heroines, Zuckerman is drawn out of his obsession with his own life long enough to begin to put that life into some perspective.

In his own country, Sisovsky explains, "I can at least be a Czech—but I cannot be a writer. While in the West, I can be a writer, but not a Czech." Like Zuckerman, in other words, he is both unbound and bereft of a subject. When Sisovsky describes the Yiddish stories that his father once wrote—"Not only a Jew, but like you, a Jew writing about Jews; like you, Semite-obsessed all his life"—and explains that his estranged wife Olga has the stories in Prague, Zuckerman soon finds himself setting off to Czechoslovakia on a secret mission of literary and cultural retrieval not very different from the ones that Philip Roth undertook himself during the 1970's when he began editing the Writers from the Other Europe series for Penguin Books.

Zuckerman's Prague guide Bolotka soon invites him to visit the regular Tuesday night orgy hosted by the film director Klenek. "You like orgies," he says knowingly, since *Carnovsky*'s reputation has clearly preceded Zuckerman to Prague, "you come with me. Since the Russians, the best orgies in Europe are in Czechoslovakia." In fact, the orgy is rather tame. But Zuckerman does meet Olga at Klenek's and, ultimately, convinces her to hand over Sisovsky's father's stories. Shortly afterward, Zuckerman is picked up by the Prague secret police, hustled to the airport, and expelled from the country. The stories are confiscated, and the guard who checks his passport as he leaves utters the last of the trilogy's words. "Zuckerman the Zionist agent," he says to the writer whose career has been a painful struggle to escape the bonds of ethnic solidarity in the name of individual freedom and art. "An honor to have entertained you here, sir. Now back to the little world around the corner."

III

Since Nathan Zuckerman is Philip Roth's autobiographical alter ego, the salient events of Roth's life and career are frequently mirrored in Zuckerman's. Both were born and raised in the Newark of the 1930's and 1940's, and both reflect on their childhood with a mixture of nostalgia and rue. Both are talented sons with older brothers, both attended the University of Chicago. Both published a first collection of short stories in the 1950's that elicited high praise from literary critics and outrage from many Jewish leaders, then wrote several serious and stylistically restrained novels focused on Jamesian moral dilemmas. Both published a fourth book in 1969 that made them both notorious and best-selling authors. Both developed an interest in Franz Kafka that led to visits to Prague and other parts of Eastern Europe and ties with writers from the region. And both, of course, have found themselves defending their novels against hostile critics in their fiction itself.

But pursuing such biographical parallels for their own sake is finally no more the point when reading Philip Roth than it is when reading Bellow's *Humboldt's Gift* or *Ravelstein*. The point, as Philip Roth explained best in his 1984 *Paris Review* interview, is that the "mock autobiographical" method of the Zuckerman books *works* for him as a writer. The point is what he *makes* out of his autobiographical sources and echoes.

"Nathan Zuckerman is an act," he said in the interview. "It's all the art of impersonation, isn't it? That's the fundamental novelistic gift."

> Making fake autobiography, false history, concocting a half-imaginary existence out of the actual drama of my life is my life. There has to be some pleasure in the job, and that's it. To go around in disguise. To act a character. To pass oneself off as what one is not. To *pretend*....
>
> [You] have to be awfully naïve not to understand that a writer is a

performer who puts on the act he does best—not least when he dons the mask of the first-person singular. That may be the best mask of all for the second self....

You don't necessarily, as a writer, have to abandon your biography completely to engage in an act of impersonation. It may be more intriguing when you don't. You distort it, you caricature it, you parody it, you torture and subvert it, you exploit it—all to give the biography that dimension that will excite your verbal life. Millions of people do this all the time, of course, and not with the justification of making literature.

What may be taken by the innocent for naked autobiography is, as I've been suggesting, more than likely mock-autobiography or autobiography grandiosely enlarged. We know about the people who walk into the police station and confess to crimes they haven't committed. Well, the false confession appeals to writers, too.

At least to some writers. Certainly to Philip Roth, for whom the fictions we create about ourselves and others have always been the most productive novelistic subject. Roth said as much when he acknowledged later in the *Paris Review* interview that

Writing for me isn't a natural thing that I just keep doing the way fish swim and birds fly. It's something that's done under a certain provocation, a particular urgency. It's the transformation, through an elaborate impersonation, of a personal emergency into a public act (in both senses of that word). It can be a very trying spiritual exercise to siphon through your being qualities that are alien to your moral makeup—as trying for the writer as for the reader. You can wind up feeling more like a sword-swallower than a ventriloquist or impersonator.

The most obvious "provocation," the most obvious "particular urgency" that has inspired Roth's efforts since *Portnoy's Complaint*, has been the critical and popular reaction to that book and the effect of that reaction upon his sense of his vocation. But the added "dimension" that has excited his verbal life has been the combination of that personal urgency with the focus that he had long before *Portnoy's Complaint*—the focus suggested by his references in the interview to the millions of people who distort their experiences, and to those who cast themselves as guilty of crimes to which they eagerly confess. The focus, that is, that views all of us as amateur novelists, inventing characters for ourselves and others, constantly revising our life stories over time and occasion, always struggling to determine where our fictions end and reality begins. And it is this focus that has inspired the extraordinary series of mock autobiographical fictions that begin with the events and conflicts of Philip Roth's own life and end by touching the events and conflicts in ours.

Where the fiction brought together in *Zuckerman Bound* treats these themes as *subjects*, in the books since Roth has also explored them through his *form* as well. For most of his career Philip Roth has been thought of as a "traditional" novelist, linked with writers like Saul Bellow or John Updike, contrasted with writers like John Barth or Robert Coover. The distinction is not without merit. Like Bellow or Updike, Roth has continued the nineteenth century tradition of the novel as a means of treating the interaction between individuals and their particular society and has grounded his major fiction in realistic character, plot, dialogue, and description. From the beginning of his career, however, he has also been highly conscious of the possibilities of formal experiment.

In his college stories and the stories collected in *Goodbye, Columbus* he worked his way through the styles of J.D. Salinger, Irwin Shaw, Isaac Bashevis Singer and others, before finding his own voice in "Defender of the Faith," "Eli, the Fanatic," and *Goodbye, Columbus* itself. In *Letting Go* (1962) he experimented with a style that combined Henry James and Bellow; in *When She Was Good* (1967), with one that blended Flaubert, Sinclair Lewis, and popular romantic melodrama. In *Portnoy's Complaint*, he cast his novel as a psychoanalytic monologue; in his nightmarish story "On the Air" (1970), he drew on the styles of the radio programs he listened to in his youth. In *Our Gang* (1971), he blended vaudeville skits, political rhetoric, and Newsspeak; in *The Breast* and "Looking at Kafka" he experimented with the fantastic realism of Franz Kafka and Nikolai Gogol; and in *The Great American Novel* (1973), he wrote in the tradition of the tall tale. In *My Life as a Man* he exploited the techniques of the metafictionists themselves, while in *The Professor of Desire* and the works in *Zuckerman Bound* he returned to the conventions of the realistic novel. Then, in *The Counterlife, The Facts, Deception,* and *Operation Shylock* he subverted those same conventions as a way of treating familiar subjects from yet another perspective.

IV

Superficially a fiction about writing fiction, a novel about a novelist, *The Counterlife* turns out to be a provocative and stylistically startling investigation into the nature of identity. "As you well know," Roth concluded in the *Paris Review* interview, "the intriguing biographical issue—and critical issue for that matter—isn't that a writer will write about some of what has happened to him, but *how* he writes about it, which, when properly understood, takes us a long way to understanding *why* he writes about it."

The *how* of *The Counterlife*—the novel's form—is nothing less than stunning in its virtuosity and its sudden reversals. In *The Counterlife*'s five sections readers are shown—*shown*, not just told—how a writer embellishes and transforms autobiography, chance encounters, the lives of those close to him, facts and fantasies, to serve the impulses of his fiction. Roth turns his readers into detectives, constantly throws them off the scent, and leaves them, finally, unsure of where the "facts" end and the "fiction" begins.

By the time *Zuckerman Bound* appeared, some of Roth's detractors had begun to suggest, even demand, that he abandon his alter ego Zuckerman, whom they saw as the product of an increasingly boring narcissism. At the beginning of *The Counterlife*, Roth seems to have responded to his critics once again, since the main character appears to be Nathan's brother Henry, rather than Nathan himself. And midway through the novel he seems to go even further: Nathan Zuckerman dies. But in this extraordinary novel, where turning a page often means encountering a new beginning, Zuckerman doesn't stay dead. In a twist as audacious as anything Roth has ever tried, he brings Nathan back to life—*twice*—before *The Counterlife* is over.

The action of the novel begins in 1978, two years after the episodes of Zuckerman's life related in *The Prague Orgy*. The reversals start on page 13. "Basel," the novel's first section, opens with Henry's point of view. Given drugs to control a heart condition, Henry finds that he has become impotent, and we are immediately drawn into the complexities and contradictions of his apparently stable and staid suburban life. A prominent and respected South Orange, New Jersey, dentist, at thirty-nine a husband for eighteen years and the father of three, Henry seems to be everything that his estranged brother Nathan is not. *Seems*. For as the section develops, we are given a version of Henry's life that is more convoluted, more multi-faceted, than Nathan or we ever could have expected.

Henry's illness forces him to confront his hidden desires—in the shape of his dental assistant, Wendy, with whom he can no longer continue his regular afternoon trysts. Should he have the quintuple bypass operation that may restore his potency but could also kill him? He turns to Nathan, the only remaining member of his family and the family's expert on the id, for advice.

Then the voice is Nathan's, and what we have read so far turns out to be his highly inappropriate draft of a eulogy for Henry, who went ahead with the operation and died. Nathan hasn't changed much since we last saw him. His trouble is still that the "words that were morally inappropriate . . . were just the words that engaged him"; that in the midst of experience he is already re-imagining it. Even at a moment of great sorrow, he realizes that he is "going to have a very hard time getting through the day without seeing everything that happened as *more*, a continuation not of life but of his work or work-to-be."

As he moves through the day, Nathan recalls the rest of Henry's story as Henry related it to him. That story began ten years earlier, when Henry had an affair with a Swiss woman, Maria—an affair whose details Nathan recorded in the notebooks that hold the real sources of his fictional characters and situations. Having discovered passion for the first time in his life, Henry dreamed of changing his character as easily as a novelist changes that of his creations, of being "remade in Europe with a European wife, to become in Basel an unfettered, robust, fully grown-up American expatriate dentist." Instead, he remained in South Orange and later began the affair with Wendy that prompted his decision to have the bypass operation.

But this story is not the one that Nathan hears at Henry's funeral. In a moving, slightly shocking, eulogy for her late husband, Henry's wife Carol explains to the mourners that Henry had decided to have the operation because he could not settle for a less than perfect marriage—could not live with the loss of *their* physical relationship. "Henry was so dedicated to the completeness of our marriage," she explains, "that he wouldn't be deterred, not by anything." ("If your brother died to sleep with his wife, then he's already up with the angels, Nathan," Aunt Essie comments when they go back to the house. "But he always was the best boy, Esther," Nathan responds. "Son to end all sons, father to end all fathers—well, from the sound of it, the husband to end all husbands, too." "From the sound of it," she replies, "the schmuck to end all schmucks . . . I like better the [stories] you write.")

"Henry's problem," Nathan thinks, "may have been that he passed so long for a paragon, he had got himself ridiculously entangled in this brilliant disguise at just the moment he was destined to burst forth as less admirable and more desperate than anyone ever imagined." Or at least that's the explanation that fires the novelist's imagination. And Nathan is not able to check that imagination at the door, even at his brother's funeral. Every conversation that he has that day is accompanied in his imagination by a counter-conversation of his own invention. But he is struck, as well, by Henry's imaginativeness: for months he had spent every Saturday in a therapist's office, speaking with great candor about his passion for Wendy, "pretending to the therapist, however, that the passion was for Carol." His end, "Basel" suggests, is the price Henry paid for trying to become more like Nathan, or for trying to be Henry at all. The price of living a life counter to Nathan's, as well as the price of trying to reinvent a life counter to the one he has lived for thirty-nine years.

And then, seven pages into "Judea," the second section of the novel, there is another reversal. We are told that Henry didn't die at all. Instead, we are presented with yet another counterlife: Henry leaving South Orange and his family eight months after his successful surgery to join a Gush Emunim settlement on the West Bank; Henry, the assimilated Jew, realizing that "of all that I am, I am nothing, I have never been *anything*, the way that I am this Jew."

Carol asks Nathan to go to Israel to bring Henry home and Nathan agrees. Not from "filial duty alone," however. The novelist in him is "deeply curious about this swift and simple conversion of a kind that isn't readily allowed to writers unless they wish to commit the professional blunder of being uninquiring. Henry's life was no longer coming true in its most pedestrian form." On the contrary, Henry has suddenly become such an artist of his own life that "the rebellious script that he had tried to follow ten years back could hardly touch this one for originality."

The brothers' roles are suddenly reversed. Henry has acted on impulse, changed his name to Hanoch, walked away from his family and his life in search of personal fulfillment. While Nathan is now married to an Englishwoman—named, like Henry's Swiss lover, Maria—and is stepfather to her daughter Phoebe. At forty-four, after three failed and childless marriages, he is living in London and about to become a father himself—about to begin *his* counterlife. No longer the notorious Zuckerman son, he, too, is beginning again, as the domestic Zuckerman, the husband and father. Maria was reluctant to marry him, he tells us, for fear of what will happen when the novelty wears off. "Why marry me and have a child and settle down like everyone else to an impostor's life," she asked. "Because I've decided to give up the artificial fiction of being myself for the genuine, satisfying falseness of being somebody else," he answered. *"Marry me."* And she finally agreed, but not without saying that she dreaded "what happens when things start going wrong in England with your fantasy of family life."

Nathan leaves her to fly to Israel and, in the pages that follow, Roth presents us with a wide assortment of contemporary Israeli voices and visions— from the liberal (Nathan's friend Shuki) who is appalled by Menachem Begin and his militance, to Henry's Meyer Kahane-like settlement leader, Mordecai Lippman, whose combative rhetoric explodes at the center of the novel, to a half-mad Pepleresque character named Jimmy Ben-Joseph, a fan of Zuckerman's who has emigrated from West Orange to a Jerusalem yeshiva. Recently married to his fourth Gentile wife, fresh from a confrontation with upper-class English anti-Semitism, faced with the arguments of Henry, Shuki, Lippman, Ben-Joseph and others, Zuckerman becomes more conscious than ever of his own complicated relationship to the Jewish people. At first, he remains detached, aloof amid the clamor of argument and debate; but when he returns to England the emotions Israel unleashes in him shock him with their vehemence.

While he is in Israel, however, speculations about Henry's motives dominate Nathan's thoughts. Brothers know one another "as a kind of deformation of themselves," he explains to Shuki. If Nathan and his characters have been self-obsessed soul-searchers, Henry will leave *his* self behind. "The hell with *me*," he rails, "forget *me*. *Me* is somebody *I* have forgotten. *Me* no longer exists out here. There isn't time for *me*, there isn't need for *me*—here Judea counts, not *me!*" Henry now sees his desire to run off to Basel with his Maria as "the original Jewish dream of escape." And as he explains all this Nathan is struck once again by *"the kind of stories that people will turn life into, the kind of lives that people turn stories into."*

In the end, Henry's flight from South Orange earns Nathan's grudging envy, since "observed solely from the novelist's point of view, this was far and away Henry's most provocative incarnation, if not exactly the most convincing—that is, it was the most eminently exploitable by me." Henry realizes this, too, and condemns Nathan for his novelistic focus on psychology and motives with his final words. "There's a world outside the Oedipal swamp, Nathan, where what matters isn't what made you do it but *what it is you do*—not what decadent Jews like you think but what committed Jews like the people here *do*! Jews who aren't in it for laughs, Jews that have something more to go on than their hilarious inner landscape!"

Not one to be left without the last word, in "Aloft" Nathan boards a plane back to London and uses the beginning of the flight to write Henry a letter. "I asked," he writes,

> if your identity was to be formed by the terrifying power of an imagination richer in reality than your own, and should have known the answer myself. *How else does it happen?* The treacherous imagination is everybody's maker—we are all the invention of each other, everybody a conjuration conjuring up everyone else. We are all each other's authors.

Zionism itself, he goes on to say, was "the construction of a counterlife ... a species of fabulous utopianism, a manifesto for human transformation as extreme—and, at the outset, as implausible—as any ever conceived. A Jew could be a new person if he wanted to." And he ends his letter with an ironic postscript: "You will see by my signature that I haven't bothered about changing my own name, but in England embark upon the search for *my* anti-self carrying my old identity papers and disguised as N.Z."

Nathan recognizes that he has undertaken the trip to Israel, in part, to see if Henry has turned out to be more original than he had always imagined him to be. But he leaves disappointed, because he thinks

> that was like expecting the woman next door, whom you suspect of cheating on her husband, to reveal herself to you as Emma Bovary, and, what's more, in Flaubert's French. People don't turn themselves over to writers as full-blown literary characters—generally, they give you very little to go on and, after the impact of an initial impression, are barely any help at all. Most people (beginning with the novelist—himself, his family, just about everyone he knows) are absolutely unoriginal, and his job is to make them appear otherwise. It's not easy. If Henry was ever going to turn out interesting, I was going to have to do it.

After finishing his letter to Henry, Nathan reads one from Shuki. Like Judge Wapter's ten questions in *The Ghost Writer*, Shuki's letter asks Nathan to think, before he writes about his experience with Lippman, about what is good for the Jews and Israel. As Nathan begins to draft a response, he suddenly realizes that he knows his seat-mate and, within a few moments, he finds himself caught in a nightmarish twist of fate.

The next two sections of *The Counterlife*, "Gloucestershire" and "Christendom," are mirror images, counterversions, of "Basel" and "Judea." In "Gloucestershire" *Nathan* is suffering from a heart condition, made impotent by medication, and led to undertake an operation that turns out to be fatal because of his love for a woman and the new life she represents. Henry survives *him*, attends *his* funeral, hears a eulogy that *he* finds to be a false picture of his brother's life. In "Christendom" Nathan survives the operation and tries to escape his old life by fleeing to England.

The tentativeness, the speculative quality of the tone and language at the beginning of "Gloucestershire," are critical to understanding what Roth is up to here:

> If for Henry there's Wendy, who is there for me? As I haven't had to endure his marriage or suffer his late sexual start, a vampire-seductress won't really do to lure me to destruction. It can't be for more of what I've tasted that I risk my life, but for what's unknown, a temptation by which I've never before been engulfed, a yearning mysteriously kindled by the wound itself. If the uxorious husband and devoted paterfamilias dies for clandestine erotic fervor, then I shall turn the moral tables: I die for family life, for fatherhood.

If . . . It can't be for . . . If . . .—the language suggests that what follows is another of Nathan's fictions, another possible life and death, rather than actual fact. And this language continues throughout the first part of the section as he imagines the situation that *might* lead to his own destruction. "I want what I've never had as a man, starting with family happiness," he thinks. "There is nothing bizarre about my goals," he explains. "This is the choice not of a desperate adulterer crazed by a drastic sexual blow, but of a rational man drawn to an eminently sane woman with whom he plans to lead a calm, conventionally placid, conventionally satisfying life." It is, in other words, the counterlife of Henry's counterlife.

If Henry no longer wanted to spend his life as a conventional South Orange dentist, Nathan no longer wants to spend his as an unconventional writer. "There was a time when everything seemed subordinate to making up stories," he tells Maria. "When I was younger I thought it was a disgrace for a writer to care about anything else. Well, since then I've come to admire conventional life much more and wouldn't mind being besmirched by a little. As it is, I've practically written myself *out* of life." But Maria knows better. "Are you writing a book?" she asks. "Yes," he answers, "it's all for a book, even the disease."

Maria accuses Nathan of fictionalizing their relationship, of reinventing her so that she can fit into his fantasy. "You ought to take a moment and ask yourself if you're not inventing a woman who doesn't exist, making me somebody else already."

> Just as you want to make *this* something else. Things don't have to reach a peak. They can just go on. You *do* want to make a narrative out of it, with progress and momentum and dramatic peaks and then a resolution. You seem to see life as having a beginning, a middle, an ending, all of them linked with something bearing your name. But it isn't necessary to give things a shape. You can yield to them too.

The second part of "Gloucestershire" begins "So long as Nathan was alive, Henry couldn't write anything unself-consciously." Henry goes on to explain that, as he read each of Nathan's books, "he would immediately begin to sketch in his head a kind of counterbook to redeem from distortion the lives that were recognizably, to him, Nathan's starting point." After Nathan's funeral, Henry goes to his brother's apartment, determined to make sure that Nathan will not be able to further distort his and his family's lives from beyond the grave. He rummages through Nathan's notebooks and discovers the notes on his affair with the Swiss Maria. He opens the manuscript left on Nathan's desk at his death and reads "Basel" and "Judea"—both wild distortions of the events of his life—and another section titled "Christendom," in which he does not appear. He also finds drafts, in Nathan's handwriting, of the eulogy he has just heard delivered by Nathan's editor at the funeral service. In a cold sweat he takes the notebook pages and the manuscripts of "Basel" and "Judea" and rushes out of the apartment, feeling "as though he'd survived a murder attempt by himself disarming the murderer."

The last part of "Gloucestershire" is a dialogue between Nathan's Maria and a voice that turns out to belong to Nathan's ghost. She, too, has come to Nathan's apartment looking for what he has left. She finds what Henry didn't take, "Christendom." Although she feels that it distorts the character and behavior of both her and her family she chooses to leave it untouched, a monument to Nathan's "longing to shed it all and have another life, his longing to be a father and a husband, things the poor man never was." She will not be like Lady Byron and Lady Burton, she explains, who destroyed their husbands' memoirs, letters, and fragments. Besides, if "Christendom" is ever published it may well be the door that lets her out of her marriage and allows *her* to begin a counterlife. Echoing Philip Roth in the *Paris Review* interview, she explains that, to Nathan

> Making you believe what he wanted you to believe was his very reason for being. Maybe his only reason. I was intrigued by the way he'd turned events, or hints I *had* given him about people, into reality—that is, *his* kind of reality. This obsessive reinvention of the real never stopped, what-could-be always having to top what-is.

After reading about the version of herself in "Christendom," she "began to wonder which was real, the woman in the book or the one I was pretending to be upstairs . . . I was not myself just as much as Maria in the book was not myself. Perhaps she was. I began not to know which was true and which was not, like a writer when he comes to believe that he's imagined what he hasn't."

Next, we get to read what Henry and Maria have already seen, "Christendom." It begins as if "Aloft" had not occurred. After a quiet flight back from his visit to Henry in Israel, Nathan finds himself back in England and increasingly angry about real and imagined acts of anti-Semitism by Maria's family and others. He and Maria have a terrible quarrel about this. He storms out of the house, walks for a while, and then returns, terrified at the thought that Maria may have left him.

> Imagine Maria gone, my life *without* all that, imagine no outer life of any meaning . . . Imagine—instead of a life inside something other than a skull, only the isolated unnaturalness of self-battling . . . When I return . . . let me find sleeping there what I've worked for and what I want, a woman with whom I'm content, pregnant with our future, her lungs quietly billowing with life's real air. For if she should be gone, should there be only a letter beside the pillow . . .

And then *The Counterlife* offers its final twist on the theme of inventing reality. "What exactly is that letter," Nathan wonders. He imagines her words: "I'm leaving. I've left. I'm leaving you. I'm leaving the book." And he thinks "That's it. Of course. The book! She conceives of herself as my fabrication, brands herself a fantasy and cleverly absconds, leaving not just me but a promising novel of cultural warfare barely written but for the happy beginning."

Leave is exactly what Maria finally does, insisting that "I will not be locked into your head in this way. I will not participate in this primitive drama, not even for the sake of your fiction." From what she says in her parting letter, it is clear that she has read all of what has come before in the novel, and that *everything*—Henry's death and Nathan's, Henry's escape and Nathan's, Henry's visit to Nathan's apartment as well as hers—has been the fiction of Nathan Zuckerman, drafts for a novel as yet incomplete.

The Counterlife—this novel presented to us as drafts for a novel—is an incredible performance. On first reading it's easy to suffer from imaginative whiplash as the narrative makes unexpected twists, hairpin turns, and abrupt starts and stops. What holds it all together is the idea of "the counterlife." It is, first of all, fiction itself: the life a writer creates out of his transformations and embellishments of actual experience. The counterlife is also the goal that each of the novel's characters seeks, the dream of escape each imagines: to be other than one is, to act differently, to start over, to remake oneself at will, as if the past did not exist and the future had no limits. *Imagine*, the novel says again and again. And then it shows us what imagination can be and do, as well as how inadequate it sometimes is in the face of the real. If *The Counterlife* is about the way fictions are created by writers, in other words, it is also about the way fictions are created by the rest of us.

In it, all of the major themes and images of Philip Roth's Zuckerman novels are tied together as never before. Zuckerman is as complex a character as Roth has ever created, and Nathan's complexity lies in both his own confusions and ambivalences and in his being able to see, even sympathize, with the views of his critics. Just as Nathan's father was presented in *The Ghost Writer* with an unfailing respect and affection that is almost totally alien to the harsher satiric spirit of much of Roth's early work, in *The Counterlife* Henry, Maria, and all of the other major characters are given their full share of Roth's attention and understanding. Even Nathan's most severe critics—Judge Wapter and Milton Appel in the earlier books, Henry, Shuki, and Lippman in *The Counterlife*—are allowed to make their cases as best they can.

In *The Counterlife*, even more than in the previous Zuckerman books, we are constantly presented with doubles, with characters strikingly similar to yet significantly different from Nathan. The ways that Henry, Carol, Maria, Shuki, Lippman, even Jimmy Ben-Joseph, speak for and against Nathan's own ideas and attitudes are as fundamental to the book's method of characterization as the characters of Lonoff, Amy, Pepler, Appel, and Sisovsky were to the earlier books. Like Alvin Pepler, Jimmy Ben-Joseph is Zuckerman's mad secret sharer—his own dark impulses rampant and incarnate. Henry's counterlife—especially in Judea—challenges Nathan's lifelong project of distancing himself from enforced solidarity with the Jewish community. Lippman's rhetoric mirrors the power and single-mindedness of Zuckerman's own. The indictments made against Nathan by Henry, Lippman, and Maria, are the indictments most to the point and most difficult for him to simply dismiss—the same indictments he earlier made against himself in *The Anatomy Lesson*.

Finally, in this novel Philip Roth demonstrates through the style and form of his narration both *how* a writer may use autobiographical materials and *why*. The result is anything but the dry dissertation on the art of the fiction, the lifeless postmodernist exercise in leg-pulling, or the plaintive cry for understanding that it might have been in less talented hands. With *The Counterlife* Roth ended his decade-long examination of the fictions of Nathan Zuckerman, but he did not abandon the questions and issues that the Zuckerman books had explored. In the next phase of his work a writer named "Philip Roth" would replace Zuckerman as the central figure, but the relationship between fiction and "the facts" would continue to be his focus.

V

In spite of the autobiographical character of his fiction, throughout his career Philip Roth has actually been rather reluctant to become a public figure or to engage in exposing the self behind his fictions. "On the pendulum of self-exposure that oscillates between aggressively exhibitionistic Mailerism and sequestered Salingerism," he accurately notes at the beginning of *The Facts*, "I'd say that I occupy a midway position, trying in the public arena to resist gratuitous prying or preening without making a holy fetish of secrecy and seclusion."

In practice, this has meant that Philip Roth has regularly met students as a college professor at the University of Pennsylvania and Hunter College, that he has given occasional readings at colleges and libraries, that he has regularly agreed to print interviews to publicize each new book, and that he has been willing to engage in serious conversations about his work with Terry Gross of National Public Radio's "Fresh Air" or Melvyn Bragg of the BBC. But he does not make the rounds of television's morning or late-night talk shows and has not sought to become a public figure or a media star. Considering his concern for his privacy, it was more than a little surprising when Roth followed *The Counterlife* with an autobiography. Considering *The Counterlife*, however, it wasn't surprising that his "novelist's autobiography" raised as many questions as it answered.

Roth's readers must be forgiven if they approached *The Facts* with skepticism. After all, in 1974 his publishers announced another book that sounded very much like an autobiography. But those who bought *My Life as a Man* expecting candid revelations about the private life of the notorious author of *Portnoy's Complaint* found something else entirely—a novel supposedly made up of the fictional and autobiographical writing not of Philip Roth but of a fictional novelist named Peter Tarnopol.

Tarnopol wrote his two Zuckerman stories as therapy, he told us, in an effort to come to grips with the trauma of his life and, especially, of his disastrous marriage. He undertook his autobiography, he said, "uncertain as to both its advisability and its usefulness." How, he asked in both parts of the novel, did I get from there to here? How did I go from protected Jewish son, star literature student at a small liberal arts college, and promising young author of a collection of stories and a novel that made me a "golden boy of American literature," to wounded middle-aged survivor, unable to write about anything but my pain?

In its form, as in much else, *The Facts* bears an uncanny resemblance to that earlier book. It, too, will disappoint readers looking for gossipy revelations about the author of *Portnoy's Complaint*. It, too, begins with an epigraph that quotes one of its author's fictional characters. It is also made up of two parts. In this case, two letters which begin and end the book—one from Philip Roth to Nathan Zuckerman asking if he should publish this autobiography, the other a reply from Zuckerman to Roth answering in the negative and explaining why—and the autobiographical narrative of a novelist named Philip Roth.

Like Peter Tarnopol, Philip Roth introduces his autobiography by explaining that it is the product of a personal crisis. He reports that in the spring of 1987 he was "all at once in a state of helpless confusion and could not understand any longer what once was obvious to me: why I do what I do, why I live where I live, why I share my life with the one I do." The confusion, he writes, was the product of a "breakdown" that he experienced when "what was to have been minor surgery turned into a prolonged physical ordeal that led to an extreme depression that carried me right to the edge of emotional and mental dissolution."

Roth, like Tarnopol, reports that he abandoned the mask of fiction for the facts of autobiography in an effort to recover his self, to discover how he got from there to here. "In order to recover what I had lost," Roth writes, "I had to go back to the moment of origin." But when he did, "I found no one moment of origin but a series of moments, a history of multiple origins, and that's what I have written here in the effort to repossess life." The events and moments that he goes on to recount in *The Facts* are limited to the first thirty-five years of his life. They include growing up in Jewish Newark during the 1930's and 1940's; moving out into the wider world of Bucknell University and, later, the University of Chicago; meeting, marrying, and struggling for his life with the woman he calls "Josie" in the book; being confronted with the vehement opposition of some segments of the Jewish community because of his early stories, especially "Defender of the Faith"; and arriving at "the high-spirited moment when the manic side of my imagination took off and I became my own writer" with *Portnoy's Complaint*. This is "a novelist's autobiography," then, because its subject is not all of the events that shaped the man but the events that he thinks were particularly important to shaping the writer he became in 1969.

Many of these events and moments will be familiar to readers of Roth's (and Tarnopol's) fiction. The tone of Roth's description of his youth seems suffused with a nostalgia that recalls Tarnopol's story "Salad Days" or the description of the fathers' Sunday morning softball games in *Portnoy's Complaint* but is hardly characteristic of most of his fiction on these same subjects. In fact, it feels as if most of these reminiscences in the book's prologue and early sections are primarily a private act, a final tribute and filial offering to his then ailing father. The treatment of his first wife and of their marriage recalls *My Life as a Man*, although it lacks the hysterical desperation and biting dialogue that made "My True Story" one of the most searing portraits of a mutually destructive male-female relationship ever written.

The triumph and the most original part of *The Facts* is Philip Roth's use of the letters to and from Nathan Zuckerman as a frame for his autobiographical reconstructions. Roth has always been one of our most self-conscious and self-critical writers. And since *My Life as a Man* it has been his habit to include characters in the books themselves who express the views of his critics before those critics have a chance. In an ingenious turn of the novelistic screw, in *The Facts* the critical voices within the book are those of the main characters of Roth's previous novel, *The Counterlife*, Nathan and Maria Zuckerman. The result, in the last forty pages of the book, is a letter from Zuckerman to Roth that raises fundamental questions about truth and autobiography with the verve, wit, and combativeness that we have come to expect from Roth's very best fiction.

Inspired by self-interest—he can only continue to exist, after all, if Roth writes *fiction*—Zuckerman raises all of the objections that a reader might have to the autobiography he has just read and tells Roth not to publish it. It lacks the liveliness of Roth's fiction, he says: "this isn't you at your most interesting." It's too nice: "Where's the anger? . . . And where's the hubris, by the way?" It doesn't tell the whole story: "You try to pass off here as frankness what looks to me like the dance of the seven veils . . ."

He is, of course, distressed to learn of Roth's recent crisis and depression, Zuckerman writes in a postscript to his letter. "But I readily admit that I am distressed as much for me and my future with Maria as for you" (since what happens to Philip Roth often eventually seems to happen to Nathan Zuckerman as well). "This now *too*?" Zuckerman laments. "Having argued against my extinction, in some 8,000 carefully chosen words, I seem only to have guaranteed myself a new round of agony!" Since the books that he has written about Zuckerman have been among Roth's finest, readers of *The Facts* could only end the book hoping that Zuckerman's worst fears would soon be realized.

By framing his autobiography by his correspondence with a fictional character, Philip Roth casts doubt—recasts—all that lies between. Roth's initial description of the personal crisis that prompted him to turn to autobiography sounds "real," "true," "factual." But by including it in a letter to a fictional character he purposely leaves his readers wondering whether there really was such a crisis, whether it was, in fact, real or imagined. The autobiographical sections of *The Facts* seem straightforward enough. If they do not "tell all," what autobiography does? If they do not explain everything, well, Roth has called it "a novelist's autobiography"—that is, an autobiography limited to explaining how he became the writer he is. But rather than allow his readers to leave *The Facts* with the impression that they have now come to know the man behind the fictions, Roth follows the explicitly autobiographical sections of the book with Zuckerman's closing letter, which casts doubt on them and on Roth's veracity. For the description "*novelist's* autobiography" suggests something more. Since we know that the novelist's role is to invent, the description also seems to cast doubt on the "truth" of everything he writes. These doubts are reinforced when Zuckerman charges Roth with leaving out everything that is really important—with substituting reticence for confession, evasion for frankness.

The dummy takes on a life of his own and calls the ventriloquist a liar. Or does he? *Can* he? In the end, readers are left wondering who and what to believe, so that a book called *The Facts* turns out to be closer in spirit and effect to a novel called *The Counterlife* than it first appeared.

VI

Deception takes up some of these same questions in yet another form. Here a novelist famous for his narrative voice and descriptive power totally eliminates narration and description. Dialogue is all. In what its main character claims is not a novel but a writer's notebook for a novel that sounds very much like *The Counterlife*, Philip Roth presents us with fourteen chapters of conversation. Half of the chapters consist of dialogues between a married Jewish American writer named "Philip" and his unnamed English mistress. These dialogues alternate with Philip's conversations with seven other people—with a Czech woman who wants him to help her turn her experiences as a kept woman and call girl into a book; with another Czech woman he met on a visit to Prague; with a Czech man who accuses Philip of having had an affair with his wife; with a former student and lover; with another former lover, a writer, who is now suffering from cancer; with a Polish woman he meets at a party; and, finally, with his British wife.

The conversations are unadorned and unexplained—Roth does not even provide "he said" and "she said." Each chapter puts the reader in the position of eavesdropping on an intimate conversation where he must identify the speakers by how they speak as well as what they say. That the attentive reader can, in fact, do this is a tribute to Philip Roth's often-praised talent for dialogue. The conversations with others immediately establish the voices, characters, and histories of Philip's interlocutors. The characters of Philip and his mistress emerge more gradually, more subtly, through snatches of conversation ranging from several pages long to just a line or two. These conversations seem pre- or post-coital in their intimacy and ease, and cover problems in her marriage, the ebb and flow of their relationship over several years, the nature of his writing, his sensitivity to English anti-Semitism and to his critics, and the games they play. Most notably one called "reality shift," where she takes on the role of one of his characters in order to help him work through an idea.

Each of the book's conversations is, at base, *about* deception. There are the common deceptions: the deception of others through adultery, the self-deception involved in clinging to relationships that are self-destructive, the romantic deception of thinking of love as a panacea, the verbal and emotional deceptions that lovers practice on one another, the deception involved in believing that one person ever really understands or knows another. And there is the uncommon deception that is the essence of fiction such a Philip Roth's: the deception through which a writer combines reality and fantasy, fact and invention, to create his semi-autobiographical tales.

When Philip's wife discovers his notebook and accuses him of having the affair it traces, all these strands of deception are skillfully drawn together. Philip denies the charge, arguing as his creator has so often done, for the freedom to imagine. "I write fiction and I'm told it's autobiography," he tells her. "I write autobiography and I'm told it's fiction, so since I'm so dim and they're so smart, let *them* decide what it is or isn't." In the notebooks, he explains, "I have been imagining myself, outside of my novel, having a love affair with a character inside my novel"—as if Leo Tolstoy had imagined himself in love with Anna Karenina or Thomas Hardy had imagined himself in love with Tess. "It is *not* myself," he insists, echoing Roth's comments in the *Paris Review* interview. "It is *far* from myself—it's play, it's a game, it's an *impersonation* of myself!"

The novel's final conversation between Philip and his mistress provides yet another twist to this argument by indicating that this defense to his wife was probably just another deception. His mistress is a critic of his fictional method, too, but from another perspective. "I object greatly to writing down exactly what people said," she complains. "I object greatly to this taking people's lives and putting them into fiction. And then being a famous author who resents critics for saying he doesn't make things up." But "I made you up," Philip responds, "you *never* existed." To which she answers "then who was that in your studio with my legs over your shoulders? Please, no more of this highbrow nonsense."

With Philip Roth, however, "this" is always much more than highbrow nonsense. What would be postmodernist esoterica in another writer's hands becomes—by virtue of his humor, his ear, and his sense of self-irony—another in a long line of novels that blends intelligence and felt life, his obsessions and his readers'. That some readers will actually mistake this carefully crafted novel for the collection of drafts and scraps from *The Counterlife* that it pretends to be, rather than the sequel on the same themes that it is, may be part of Roth's game—and ultimate proof of the success of his wickedly deceptive form.

VII

After more than forty years, it is not easy for a writer to continue to surprise us. Yet Philip Roth has managed to do so again and again. Consider, for example, the six books he published in the decade after *The Counterlife*. After *The Facts* and *Deception* came *Patrimony*, another autobiographical excursion, a deeply moving memoir and tribute that tells the story of his father's life, illness and death from a brain tumor. *Operation Shylock*, like *The Counterlife*, is a brilliant Chinese box of a book in which Philip Roth claims to be telling us the true story of his confrontation in Israel in 1988 with a fan who adopted his name and identity to lead an exodus of the Jews from Israel to Europe—and of his (the real Philip Roth's) being recruited by the Mossad for a secret mission as a spy. The book, subtitled "A Confession," blends autobiography, real people and a variety of verifiable incidents with events whose truth—

like the truth or fictionality of the dialogues in *Deception* or many of the episodes in *The Facts*—cannot be definitively determined by anyone but its author. With *Sabbath's Theater*, which appeared in 1995, Roth's work again took an unexpected turn as he disappeared as a character and was replaced by his first new fictional hero in nearly twenty years, a furious aged puppeteer named Mickey Sabbath whose rants, venom, vitriol and sexual provocations knew no bounds.

Two years later *American Pastoral* arrived and, for a change, the publicity copy was not an exaggeration. "From the beginning of his long and celebrated career," it said, "Philip Roth's fiction has often explored the human need to demolish, to challenge, to oppose, to pull apart. Now, writing with deep understanding, with enormous power and scope and great storytelling energy, he focuses on the counterforce: the longing for an ordinary life." Those who have read Roth closely over the years will recognize that the struggle between these forces has actually been central to most of his best writing. But the jacket copy was right to suggest that this novel's focus on "the longing for an ordinary life" is not what many readers expect from him. And coming as it did immediately after *Sabbath's Theater*—a novel wholly devoted to a character obsessed with sex and death whose impulses to shock, taunt, demolish, challenge, oppose, and pull apart make Alexander Portnoy seem like a model of decorum and restraint—this shift in focus was nothing short of breathtaking.

American Pastoral is also an exceptional book because, while it shares a great deal with the novels and memoirs that came before it, it is also an ambitious new departure in which a mature writer reaches beyond anything that he has ever attempted before—and succeeds brilliantly. The narrator of the novel's opening pages, which recall how the star high school athlete Seymour "Swede" Levov became "the household Apollo of the Weequahic Jews" during World War II, sounds a lot like the Philip Roth of *The Facts*, *Patrimony*, and *Operation Shylock*. But it soon becomes clear that Nathan Zuckerman is back, and that he will be the one who tries to understand and tell the story of the rise and fall of his high school hero. He is now sixty-three and, since he last appeared in *The Facts*, he has undergone surgery for prostate cancer that has left him impotent and incontinent, broken up with his English wife, and retreated to the same town in the Berkshires where, at the beginning of his career, he had once visited the reclusive writer E.I Lonoff.

He is still as steeped in literature as ever, so when he first thinks about the Swede's life he finds himself remembering Tolstoy's comments about Ivan Ilych. The life of this leading citizen of St. Petersburg, Tolstoy wrote in *The Death of Ivan Ilych*, had been "most simple and most ordinary and therefore most terrible." Maybe so, Zuckerman thinks. "Maybe in Russia in 1886. But in Old Rimrock, New Jersey, in 1995, when the Ivan Ilychs come trooping back to lunch after their morning round of golf and start to crow, 'It doesn't get any better than this,' they may be a lot closer to the truth than Leo Tolstoy was. Swede Levov's life, for all I knew, had been most simple and most ordinary and therefore just great, right in the American grain."

"I was wrong," he writes a few pages later. "Never more mistaken about anyone in my life." The Swede's life turns out to be "most ordinary" and very much in the American grain but, precisely because it is, it also turns out to be "most terrible." In examining what this means in *American Pastoral*, Philip Roth has again taken up the challenge that has spurred his greatest work. The challenge to write a novel that expresses what the critic Raymond Williams once described as the essence of the realistic tradition: "the kind of novel which creates and judges the quality of a whole way of life in terms of the qualities of persons. Neither the society nor the individual is there as a priority. The society is not a background against which the personal relationships are studied, nor are the individuals merely illustrations of aspects of the way of life. Every aspect of the personal life is radically affected by the quality of the general life, yet the general life is seen at its most important in purely personal terms."

Philip Roth meets this challenge in *American Pastoral*, perhaps better than he ever has before, and in doing so he almost seems to have been inspired by another statement of Tolstoy's, one that Zuckerman does not mention. "All happy families are alike; each unhappy family is unhappy in its own way" Tolstoy wrote in the famous opening sentence of *Anna Karenina*. Maybe in nineteenth-century Russia, Roth seems to say. But, in post-World War II America at least, some unhappy families have been unhappy in ways that are typical, emblematic, exemplary. Roth's ambition in *American Pastoral* is to make the connection, to focus on the story of how *an* American dream went awry and, through it, to understand how *the* American dream was shattered in the years since 1960.

For all I knew ... Thirty-five years after high school, when Zuckerman runs into the Swede and his small son at a Mets game in 1985, he is still starstruck. What he knows then is that the Swede looks great and still seems to be the living embodiment of the American dream. After high school, he joined the Marines but never made it into combat. When he returned home in 1947 he enrolled at Upsala College in East Orange, where he starred on the baseball team, turned down a contract with a Double A Giant farm club to join his father's Newark glovemaking company, and married an Irish beauty queen, the former Miss New Jersey. Eventually, he took over the Newark Maid factory when his father retired and moved out of the city to a fantastic home in the tony country town of Old Rimrock, near Morristown—less than an hour away but socially as far from the streets of Newark as you can go and still be in New Jersey.

Ten years after their brief meeting at the Mets game, the Swede suddenly re-enters Zuckerman's life when he writes Nathan a letter inviting him to dinner in New York City. He says he wants to talk about writing a tribute to his father Lou, recently dead at ninety-six. Nathan eagerly agrees, imagining a scenario where the depths behind the Swede's self-satisfied exterior will finally be revealed to him. But he finds the dinner a disappointment: the Swede hasn't come to bare his soul or share his pain. As he talks about his work, his father, his young second wife and their sons, his recent prostate surgery, Zuckerman is quickly bored. "I was impressed, as the meal wore on," he reports, "by how assured he seemed of everything commonplace he said, and how everything he said was suffused by his good nature." He thinks that "this big jeroboam of self-contentment really was in possession of all he ever wanted. To respect everything one is supposed to respect; to protest nothing; never to be inconvenienced by self-distrust; never to be enmeshed in obsession, tortured by incapacity, poisoned by resentment, driven by anger . . . life just unraveling for the Swede like a fluffy ball of yarn." In other words, nothing about the Swede seizes the novelistic imagination of a writer like Zuckerman, whose work thrives on struggle and conflict.

A few months later, at his forty-fifth high school reunion in Newark, his perspective changes when what Nathan learns from the Swede's brother Jerry makes him realize that the Swede's seemingly perfect life was more complicated than he imagined. When they met for dinner, Jerry tells him, the Swede knew he was dying of cancer, and two days before the reunion he passed away. Jerry—like Nathan, no stranger to emotional turbulence, family conflict, and marital discord—shares his own reading of the Swede's life. He was "a nice, simple, stoical guy," he tells Zuckerman, "In one way he could be conceived as completely banal and conventional. An absence of negative values and nothing more. Bred to be dumb, built for convention, and so on. That ordinary decent life that they all want to live, that's it. The social norms, and that's it. Benign, and that's it." Exactly as Nathan thought.

But, Jerry goes on to reveal that the Swede's life was not what it seemed:

> What he was trying to do was survive, keeping his group intact. . .It was a war for him finally. There was a noble side to this guy. Some excruciating renunciations went on in that life. He got caught in a war that he didn't start, and he fought to keep it all together, and he went down. . . . My brother was the best you're going to get in this country, by a long shot. . . . He had a big, generous nature and with that they

really raked him over the coals, all the impossible ones. Unsatisfiable father, unsatisfiable wives, and the little murderer herself, the monster daughter. The monster *Merry*.

He then tells Nathan that Merry, the Swede's daughter from his first marriage, was "the Rimrock Bomber." In 1968, as a protest against the Vietnam War she planted a bomb behind the post office window of the Old Rimrock general store, and when it exploded it killed a local doctor. She then disappeared underground, where she stayed until her death twenty-five years later in 1993. He was "just a liberal sweetheart of a father," Jerry says. "The philosopher-king of ordinary life." But "there was no way back for my brother from that bomb. That bomb detonated his life. His perfect life was over."

Jerry leaves shortly afterward, but Nathan, the novelist whose life consists of imagining other lives, is now totally hooked. "Who could have imagined that his life would come apart in this horrible way?" he thinks. "A sliver off the comet of American chaos had come loose and spun all the way out to Old Rimrock and him." In the coming weeks Zuckerman will visit all the important sites of the Swede's life, pore over newspaper articles and public records, then decide that "anything more I wanted to know, I'd have to make up." Now, as the reunion winds down with Nathan dancing with an old high school girlfriend to the strains of Johnny Mercer's "Dream," he "pulled away from the reunion, and . . . dreamed a realistic chronicle." And there, on page 89, Nathan Zuckerman dances off the stage of *American Pastoral*, which becomes the story of one ordinary American life as he imagines it.

Much of the realistic chronicle that makes up the remaining 334 pages of *American Pastoral* will be familiar to readers of Philip Roth's other work. "You mustn't forget anything—that's the inscription on his coat of arms," he writes of his father in *Patrimony*. "To be alive, to him, is to be made of memory." Philip Roth has always remained true to his father's motto. "You're our Marcel Proust," Alvin Pepler told Zuckerman in *Zuckerman Unbound*, "you are up there with Stephen Crane. You are the two great Newark writers. . . .It'll be you they turn to in the future when they want to remember what it was like in the old days. In *Carnovsky* you have pinned down for all time growing up in that town as a Jew." In this, at least, Pepler was right. And in *American Pastoral* Philip Roth goes beyond anything that even he has done before, "pinning down" 1940s Weequahic, Newark in the 1960's and 1990's, the Jersey Shore of Avon and Spring Lake and Atlantic City, Morristown and rural New Jersey for all time as completely as James Joyce captured his Dublin in *Ulysses*.

Growing up in Jewish Newark during World War II is evocatively described, once again, with a painful sense of nostalgia for the loss of a remembered paradise. The central characters are, again, two siblings who grew up in that world: one who rebels and lights out for the wider territory of an America beyond Weequahic and one who doesn't rebel, marries, has children, moves to the suburbs but stays close to home. Of course, there is Nathan Zuckerman. And, as in so many of Roth's books—especially *The Professor of Desire, Zuckerman Bound*, and *Patrimony*—a highlight of the novel is its portrait of a gruff but endearing second-generation Jewish American father. Generational conflict, sexual transgression, exploration of the relationship between fiction and reality—all of these elements of earlier Roth novels and stories are, again, essential to the story this novel has to tell.

Like most of Roth's other books, the catalyst that prompts the telling of the tale in *American Pastoral* is a personal crisis suffered by the main character which forces him to confront a chaotic reality that he is unprepared to face. Roth's narrative voice continues to be unique, in complete control of its effects, with a tone that ranges from the heartbreakingly elegiac to the boisterously vituperative and dialogue that is drop-dead accurate.

But *American Pastoral* is also striking for its differences from Roth's earlier work. In all of his previous books, the main characters are childless sons of his age and place; here, for the first time, the focus is on a father of his generation whose love and concern for his daughter is as deeply affecting as it is fully imagined. In all of his previous works the focus has been on generational conflicts between strong-willed fathers and sons, or between those sons and their lovers and wives; here, for the first time, the conflict is between a sweet-tempered, eminently reasonable and loving father and a furious, rebellious daughter. Most importantly, in all of his previous novels the author's primary allegiance was to the rebellious characters who challenge the status quo and received wisdom; here, for the first time, it is to a genuinely good and kind man who is totally conventional in his attitudes and beliefs. In earlier books, transgression was usually a form of personal or artistic liberation; here, it is a perverse and destructive force that shatters values that deserve to be defended and preserved.

And it is exactly here—where the story of Swede Levov and his family is linked to the story of American culture and history over the past fifty years—that *American Pastoral* makes its claim as Roth's first historical novel. Roth's subjects have never been as limited or as self-involved as some of his critics have charged. *The Counterlife* and *Operation Shylock*, for example, grapple with the complexities of contemporary Israel more powerfully than any other novels written by an American. But the extent of Roth's attention to historical forces and lives fundamentally different from his own in *American Pastoral* has a cumulative effect that still seems unprecedented.

He once published a rollicking satire about baseball titled *The Great American Novel* (1973), but *American Pastoral* is a completely serious attempt to write just that, inspired not just by Tolstoy but by Melville and Fitzgerald. His descriptions of Newark Maid's glovemaking process are a *tour de force* reminiscent of Melville's descriptions of the details of whaling in *Moby Dick*. And his descriptions of the details of Dawn Levov's cattle-raising, the Miss America pageant, the revolutionary history of Morristown, and the breakdown of Newark since 1967 are equally impressive. In this novel, Nathan Zuckerman seems a direct descendent of *The Great Gatsby*'s Nick Carraway—an observer who struggles to understand and tell the story of a particularly American dream of success and the particularly American tragedy that destroys it, and ends his tale with a poetic evocation of a dream that lives on in spite of all of the forces ranged against it.

The Swede's dream falls apart, Zuckerman explains, because of a daughter "who transports him out of the longed-for American pastoral and into everything that is its antithesis and its enemy, into the fury, the violence, and the desperation of the counterpastoral—into the indigenous American beserk." Because this passage has been all too common since the 1960's, as a glance at the daily newspaper or the nightly news makes clear, telling the Swede's story means telling a larger one as well. But the Swede's story is his own. He lived by the rules, imagining that he could protect his family from the American chaos without. Then one day the chaos was within his own home and, before he knew what happened to him, his life was changed forever by an act of pointless violence. His sense of responsibility leads him to try to understand, to find causes, to blame himself for the act of a driven adolescent. But how can you understand why the child you have loved and cherished, dreamed and hoped for, has become a murderer? And, once she has, how do you deal with that reality for the rest of your life?

The story of the Swede's family is also exemplary: the story of an immigrant first generation's struggle, the second generation's progress, the third generation's consolidation, and the fourth generation's rebellion against it all. In *American Pastoral*, Roth captures a specific form that exemplary story took in the 1960's, as a decade that began with confidence, hope, and a sense of American exceptionalism fell apart under the pressure of assassinations, the Vietnam War, and, finally, Watergate. A generation of middle-class liberal parents found themselves cast as hypocritical enemies by their own radical children. Tens of thousands of those children dropped out in one way or another, and some never returned. For many young people, protest became revolution; for some, killing became the way to oppose the violence of war. Hundreds of middle-class kids like Merry Levov ended up underground, disappeared from their own lives. And when the god of revolution failed, like her many of them turned to the gods of Eastern religions or religious cults. From revolution to Heaven's Gate in two decades.

Recapturing and trying to comprehend this aspect of recent history is no small task. And telling his version of this story will not make Philip Roth popular with those whose ideology insists that there was never really an American dream to lose. But, like his father, Philip Roth remembers what he remembers and he is not about to be told that an idyllic American moment did not exist for him and tens of millions of others. At sixty-four, understanding when things stopped making sense, when the values that he believes once bound a large segment of American society together were shattered, was the task that Philip Roth set for himself in *American Pastoral*. The fact that he succeeds in capturing his version of the American past and present in an historical novel of such ambition and scope is just one more proof that he remains in the first rank of contemporary American novelists.

True Impressions
Saul Bellow

"Just because your soul is being torn to pieces doesn't mean that you stop analyzing the phenomena," Charlie Citrine observes early in *Humboldt's Gift* (1975). His comment could serve as an appropriate epitaph for many of contemporary American fiction's dangling men and their creators, and for all of Bellow's own heroes, but he is thinking here of himself and the subject of his memoir, the poet Von Humboldt Fleisher. The story of their relationship is the core of Bellow's sprawling *roman a clef*, a novel that invites us to consider both how and why he, like Philip Roth, has chosen to base works like *Humboldt's Gift* and *Ravelstein* (2000) on fictionalized autobiography and biography.

In an article that appeared in the *New York Times Magazine* just after Bellow was awarded the Nobel Prize, Richard Stern reported that *Humboldt's Gift* began as a nonfictional memoir of Bellow's friend Delmore Schwartz, shortly after Schwartz's death in July 1966. Though the memoir quickly turned fictional, Bellow was at first unable to find the right narrator for his story. Frustrated, he moved on to other projects, including *Mr. Sammler's Planet* (1970), before finally returning to the Humboldt book as the character of Charlie Citrine began to emerge. Through Citrine the novel began to coalesce because Bellow came to realize that remembering Delmore would only be part of his subject: "who remembered and why, who survived and why" would be of even greater importance.

In the novel we now have, Humboldt, modeled on Schwartz, is

Bellow's representative of the long line of destroyed and/or self-destructive American artists—a line whose ranks swelled to include another old friend, John Berryman, before the book was finished. Citrine, the one who remembers, is modeled on Bellow himself and represents the shorter line of American writers who have, somehow, survived to create significant works over long careers. At base the novel is a series of notes toward a definition of that "somehow," based on Bellow's own experience, which leads him to realize just how thin the line between one fate and the other can be.

Why must I remember? Why have I survived? How have I, so far at least, avoided self-destruction in a culture that expects and encourages me to act out its myth of martyred genius? These are the questions that Saul Bellow must have asked himself as he worked on the memoir that became a *kaddish*, and his answers to them are in the novel, implicit in a comparison of Delmore/Humboldt's biography and Bellow/Citrine's autobiography.

At first glance, Citrine's biography of Humboldt seems a painstakingly exact and detailed replica of Schwartz's life and death. Like Delmore Schwartz's, Von Humboldt Fleisher's very name combines the high and the low, the inflated and the common, and suggests the conflict and dichotomy that were at the base of its bearer's downfall. Both poets were named by neurotic Jewish-immigrant parents—parents who were emotionally estranged from one another for as long as their sons could remember. The mothers seemed "mad" from some "powerful female grievance" that their sons could never fathom; the fathers, men who "plunged into America," took advantage of the pre-Depression real estate boom in Chicago to make a fortune, but left nothing to their heirs.

Bellow gives Humboldt Delmore's personality as well as his parents. From all accounts, Schwartz was like Humboldt, "a wonderful talker, a hectic nonstop monologist and improvisator" and a brilliant mimic. Each was a manic-depressive, an insomniac who tried to erase the night's terrors with pills and alcohol. ("History is a nightmare during which I'm trying to get a good night's rest," Delmore said, paraphrasing James Joyce.) Both were perpetual schemers who saw themselves as schemed against and cheated by everyone who ever cared for them. Each combined the philosophical and the mundane, high and popular culture, "symbolism and street language" in his conversation: "into this mixture," says Citrine, "went Yeats, Apollinaire, Lenin, Freud, Morris R. Cohen, Gertrude Stein, baseball statistics and Hollywood gossip. He brought Coney Island into the Aegean and united Buffalo Bill with Rasputin." Like Delmore, Humboldt was at the center of New York intellectual life in the 1930's and 1940's; and during their declines in the

1950's both still managed to pack the White Horse Tavern with listeners when they "performed."

Physically, each was a handsome man who later gained enough weight to become "shuffling comedy" below the waist, "princeliness and dignity" above. Each was finally destroyed by the later stages of a paranoia which convinced him that the Rockefellers were conspiring to drive him mad with voice rays emanating from the top of the Empire State Building, that his wife was unfaithful with, first, Nelson Rockefeller and then an art critic ("Magnasco"/Hilton Kramer), that his friends were all turning against him. In the end, each had become one of the "big-time solitaries"; and, in the end, each had "no old friends, only ex-friends."

"Poet, thinker, problem drinker, pill-taker, man of genius, manic depressive, intricate schemer"—yes; but also "a success story" who once wrote "poems of great wit and beauty." For before his decline into sadness and instability, each had been a pioneering, Jewish-American literary *Wunderkind*. Each published his first book of poetry in 1938 and was hailed by T.S. Eliot, Yvor Winters and the Gentile literary establishment. Like the lyrics in Schwartz's *In Dreams Begin Responsibilities*, the poems in Humboldt's *Harlequin Ballads* were "pure, musical, witty, radiant, humane . . . Platonic." In the late 1940's, after about a decade of poetic life, each "started to sink." There were frequent critical contributions to *Partisan Review* and other periodicals, a reputation as a prominent anti-Stalinist, and subsequent books of poetry, but the gift seemed to have been lost somewhere along the way. (Each was fond of quoting Wordsworth's haunting lines, "We poets in our youth begin in gladness/ but thereof come in the end despondency and madness.") And there is no more apt description of the quality of mind and imagination which distinguished Schwartz's best lyrics, or the lack which made his poorer poems fail, than Citrine's observation that "Humboldt wanted to drape the world in radiance . . . but he didn't have enough material."

In the early 1950's, both Schwartz and Humboldt moved to rural New Jersey with a new bride; and each taught at Princeton for a year as a replacement for a well-known critic ("Martin Sewell"/R.P. Blackmur). At the same time that each attempted to maneuver the chairman of the Princeton English department ("Ricketts"/Carlos Baker) into a permanent appointment, each had numerous other sinecures: as poetry editor of a literary journal (*"Arcturus"/Perspectives U.S.A.* and *Partisan Review*), as consultant on the staff of an avant-garde publishing house ("Hildebrand & Co."/New Directions), and as a paid advisor to a major foundation ("Belisha"/Ford). Each invested his hopes for a more enlightened America in Adlai Stevenson, and each was devastated by his defeat in 1952.

And then, three decades after *Harlequin Ballads* made him famous,"

Humboldt "died of a heart attack in a flophouse in the West Forties, one of those midtown branches of the Bowery" called the Ilscombe, when he decided to take out the garbage at 3 a.m. and collapsed in the elevator. "At the morgue there were no readers of modern poetry . . . So he lay there unclaimed, another derelict." Schwartz died precisely the same way early in the morning of July 11, 1966, at the Columbia Hotel on West 46th Street. His body lay unidentified in the New York City morgue for two days. Humboldt died "seven years ago," Citrine tells us—in the opening section of the novel, which was written seven years after Schwartz's death and published in the January 1974 issue of *Playboy*.

Just as Schwartz's personality and career are reflected in Humboldt's, Bellow's personality and career are limned in Citrine's. Like Bellow, Citrine was raised in the Humboldt Park section of Chicago in a close-knit family of Russian-Jewish immigrants. Each spent part of his eighth year in the public ward of a tuberculosis sanitarium; each lost his mother when he was very young and remembers his father—a sometime onion dealer, bootlegger, and coal merchant—fondly. Each is his family's youngest son, and each has a financially successful older brother now living in the South. Each is wracked by nostalgia, preoccupied with memories of his "significant dead."

Like Bellow at the time he was writing *Humboldt's Gift*, Citrine chooses to live in Chicago in spite of the fact that he sees the city as totally indifferent to genuine culture. Like Citrine, Bellow made a point of keeping in touch with childhood friends from the old neighborhood. ("I was attracted to these noisy bumptious types," Citrine comments, "they did something for me.") In 1975, both were divorced and lived in the Hyde Park neighborhood, near their former wives and children, in a high-rise apartment overlooking the University of Chicago, furnished with a "broccoli green" sculptured love seat and Persian rug in the living room.

Each is noted for his sartorial extravagance: striped suits from Armando's, shirts from Burlington Arcade, cashmere socks, and those Hermes ties that Moses Herzog so loved. At the time the novel was published, each practiced yoga for an arthritic neck and played paddleball every week at a Chicago health club with an old friend who was a Gary, Indiana contractor. Like Citrine, in 1975 Bellow was interested in the anthroposophical ideas of Rudolph Steiner (he even attended weekly Steiner Society meetings in Chicago). Each is a combination of street kid and intellectual, both a critic of and a sucker for the common life that he is not completely able to accept or participate in. And Bellow's views of the artist and society at the time the book was published—as expressed in a *Salmagundi* interview and an essay in *Critical Inquiry*—are repeated, at times verbatim, by Citrine.

Their professional careers also mirror one another's. Both attended Midwestern universities as undergraduates, and each left graduate studies at the University of Wisconsin in 1938, inspired by the older Jewish writer's success. Both headed for the literary life and a visit to Greenwich Village. Each served as a regular reviewer for the *New Republic* through the 1940's and 1950's; and each early displayed a sense of his special mission as a writer. "I had a funny feeling sometimes," Citrine observes, "as if I had been stamped and posted and they were waiting for me to be delivered to an important address. I may contain unusual information." In his memoir *New York Jew*, Alfred Kazin recalls Bellow at the beginning of *his* career—even before the publication of *Dangling Man* (1944)—as carrying "around with him a sense of his destiny as a novelist. He was going to take on more than the rest of us were." Both Citrine and Bellow taught at Princeton for a year in the early 1950's, in a position partially arranged by the older poet, and neither liked it. Both gained national recognition and renown in 1953: Citrine, with his play *Von Trenck*, and Bellow with *The Adventures of Augie March*.

Both Citrine and Bellow are prominent intellectuals with international reputations, the French Croix de Chevalier des Arts et Lettres, and invitations to the White House. Like Bellow, Citrine is commissioned by *Life* magazine to do a piece on Robert Kennedy in the late 1960's. As Citrine begins his memoir, he tells us that his last book, *Some Americans—the Sense of Being in the USA*, had been a failure which was subjected to a great deal of negative criticism. Bellow's previous book, *Mr. Sammler's Planet*, was also vehemently attacked, in spite of its National Book Award, by many critics who saw its fundamental weakness as a limitation in Bellow's neoconservative vision of "some Americans"—blacks, the young, the sexually liberated—as a limitation in his "sense of being in the USA" in the 1960's.

The break between Humboldt and Citrine is caused by an accusation of theft: Humboldt charges Citrine with "stealing" his character for *Von Trenck*. Bellow's break with Schwartz was prompted by the poet's accusing him of stealing money that had been collected for his hospitalization—money that Bellow himself had solicited from their friends. Just before Humboldt died Charlie Citrine saw him on the street in Manhattan: "he was gray stout sick dusty, he had bought a pretzel stick and was eating it." But Citrine didn't have the heart to talk to him in his decayed condition. "It was impossible," he writes. Shortly before Schwartz's death, Bellow told James Atlas, he saw *him* in Manhattan—he was "East River gray"—and Bellow also turned away.

Bellow further emphasizes the connection between himself and his alter-ego in *Humboldt's Gift* by having Citrine's memoir recapitulate characters, episodes, and themes from his own earlier writings. Like *Dangling*

Man's Joseph and all of Bellow's subsequent protagonists, Citrine and Humboldt are both "dangling men," suspended, as John Updike noted in his *New Yorker* review of the later novel, "in sheer dishevelment of mind." Like the style of Bellow's writing since *The Adventures of Augie March*, Citrine's is what Irving Howe once called "neo-Baroque." Like Bellow's other fictions, Citrine's story—with its picaresque cross-country adventures and comic inventions, many of which serve as elaborations of the novel's themes rather than necessary incidents—could, theoretically, go on forever. The baths of *Seize the Day* (1956) and *Herzog* (1964) are here, and so is the focus in these and Bellow's other novels on the three M's: Money, Marriage and divorce, and Machiavellian reality instructors. Like *Seize the Day*'s Tommy Wilhelm, Humboldt is a bear of a man reduced to living in a run-down hotel; like Tommy, Citrine is counseled to "seize the day" (as well as eternity) in Humboldt's letter/legacy; and, like Tommy, he tries to live in spite of his fatal attraction for *schnorrers* like Thaxter.

Citrine's description of his expedition in search of African diamonds with George Schweibel is clearly an allusion to and parody of *Henderson, the Rain King* (1959)—Bellow's own parody of epic quests into the heart of darkness, which was written before he took such a trip with his friend the Gary contractor Dave Pelz. Like Henderson, Humboldt and Citrine are preoccupied with thoughts of death; for Citrine, a biographer, the dead are "bread and butter," as well as ghosts to be apprehended and exorcised. Like Arthur Sammler, who turned to Meister Eckhart's mysticism as an escape from a world too much with him, Citrine seeks a way to see beyond the quotidian, a means to cast aside the veil of Maya, in anthroposophy. Like Bellow's other urban landscapes, Citrine's Chicago is a deteriorating wasteland, smothered by steel-smoke and flames, where the Cantibiles rule.

But the closest and most significant parallels between Citrine's story and Bellow's previous works are with *Herzog*, Bellow's most autobiographical novel before *Humboldt's Gift*. For *Herzog*'s Romona, read Renata; for Madeleine, Denise; for Shura, Ulick; and for Herzog, *both* Citrine and Humboldt. Like Bellow and Herzog, Citrine sees himself as a man with a mission to understand what others have failed to comprehend. Both are plagued by the enmity of their ex-wives and the manipulations of lawyers. Both constantly explain themselves "in full to people who couldn't have cared less." Each rails against accepting "the Wasteland outlook" and posits, instead, a humanism based on acceptance of life in all its frustrating and exhilarating diversity and a spirituality that is not hesitant to speak of the fate of the soul. Like Herzog before him, Citrine is surrounded by reality instructors—by Humboldt, Cantibile, Longobardi, Schweibel, Ulick, and Denise. Herzog and Citrine are, like

Humboldt, wrapped up in thought, buffeted by reality, challenged to yoke the two. Like Herzog, Citrine writes letters that he doesn't mail (to his daughter) and acts the Peeping Tom (in Appleton, Wisconsin instead of Chicago). Where Herzog spies on his ex-wife Madeleine after she leaves him for Valentine Gersbach and steals Romona from her former lover, who then shadows them about the city and haunts the street outside her apartment in dejection, in *Humboldt's Gift* Citrine is cast as the rejected suitor on the outside looking in. After Renata leaves him for an Italian undertaker he haunts the places where she has been and wanders around Madrid with her cloak around his shoulders and her mother at his side.

In his isolation and madness, Humboldt also reminds us of Herzog. Both try to achieve a grand intellectual synthesis; both fail. Herzog's thoughts and conversation, his letters to the great and near-great, living and dead, echo Humboldt's conversation as Citrine reports it. Like Herzog, Humboldt tried to "think himself clear away from this American world." In the depths of his confusion and dismay, one day Herzog notices an old friend, Nachman, on a New York City street and flees rather than face him. His situation is Humboldt's. (And this scene is one of several that suggest that Schwartz may have been one of the inspirations for Herzog long before he became the inspiration for Humboldt.)

The parallels between Delmore and Humboldt, Bellow and Citrine, are extensive then—I have actually only scratched the surface here— and they range from major events in their lives, to trivial details, to personality traits and character quirks. But Bellow's fictional creations *are* fictional, and they also differ from their inspirations in significant ways. And recognizing these divergences as well as the parallels helps to point us toward Bellow's intentions and achievement in *using* biography and autobiography in *Humboldt's Gift*.

Citrine presents Humboldt as a paradigm: "crystallizing many evils in himself, he died as an example, his legacy a question addressed to the public," he tells us. But to make Humboldt an example Bellow ignores or exaggerates crucial points about Schwartz's character and career. Although it is true, for example, that Schwartz's career, like Humboldt's, started to sink in the 1940's, Schwartz's decline was certainly not the precipitate downhill slide to artistic oblivion after his first book that Humboldt's was. After *Harlequin Ballads* Humboldt becomes a psychological case; we follow his various exploits, listen to his conversation, watch his schemes built and shattered, but we learn nothing more about his *writing*. It ceases to exist.

While certainly not as successful as *In Dreams Begin Responsibilities*, Schwartz's subsequent works—*Shenandoah* (1941), *Genesis* (1943), *The World Is a Wedding* (1948), *Vaudeville for a Princess* (1950), and stories such as "The Track Meet"—were each recognized as experiments touched with flashes of genius that were worthy of serious critical consideration in spite of their failings. And his *Summer Knowledge: New and Selected Poems 1938-1958* (1959) was awarded both the Bolingen Prize in Poetry and the Shelley Memorial Prize. The honors were not prompted by nostalgia or sympathy, for the collection clearly demonstrates that Schwartz's poetic achievements did not end in the early 1940's. In some of the later poems included in *Summer Knowledge*—poems like "Baudelaire," "The Kingdom of Poetry," "I Am a Book I Neither Wrote nor Read," "The Foggy, Foggy Blue," "Once and for All," and even "The True-Blue American" and "The Would-Be Hungarian"—Schwartz displayed a confessional power which, while quite different from the power of his early lyrics, was still moving, original, and noteworthy.

In addition to simplifying the actual course of Schwartz's poetic career, Bellow's portrait of Humboldt also ignores Delmore Schwartz's considerable achievements as a critic. In his criticism, as Louis Simpson has noted, Schwartz was elegant, incisive, and perceptive until the end. Reading *The Selected Essays of Delmore Schwartz* (1970), however, does suggest reasons other than personal ones for Bellow's choosing Schwartz as his model for the failed artist. For from the beginning, his essays reveal, Schwartz found his art and his self split. While as a man he was omnivorous in his interests, as an artist enamored of T.S. Eliot he felt compelled to remain intellectual and formal. Psychologically, the result was a disassociation of sensibility that sabotaged his art and thereby helped to bring about his eventual breakdown.

In Delmore Schwartz's psyche, Heinz Politzer argued in an extraordinary 1950 essay in *Commentary* that the poet certainly read,

> there is a world of experience, as constituted by his biography, memories and immediate feelings. This he has fixed in time and called childhood; he has also fixed it in space, in Brooklyn. . . . Beyond this sphere of real life, there lies the world of his education, full of names of books, famous men, and images taken from books: an abstract universe of intelligence where he developed his consciousness . . . The incompatibility of experience and consciousness—the contradiction between the banality and ugliness of daily life and the truth and beauty of intellectual existence—has remained ever-present in Schwartz.

In his own essay on "The Isolation of Modern Poetry," Schwartz saw the predicament caused by such incompatibility as *general,* not personal, and concluded that "in cultivating his own sensibility, the modern poet participated in a life which was so far removed from lives of other men who, insofar as they could be considered important characters, were engaged in cultivating money or building an industrial society." As a result, he argued,

> It became increasingly impossible for the poet to write about the lives of other men; not only was he removed from their lives but, above all, the culture and sensibility which made him a poet could not be employed when the proposed subject was the lives of human beings in whom culture and sensibility had no organic function.
>
> Since the only life available to the poet as a man of culture has been the cultivation of his own sensibility, that is the only subject available to him, if we may assume that a poet can only write about subjects of which he has an absorbing experience in every sense. . . writing about poetry and in general works of art is the most direct way of grasping one's sensibility as a subject. But more than that, since one can only write about one's sensibility, one can only write lyric poetry. Dramatic and narrative poetry require a grasp of the lives of other men, and it is precisely these lives, to repeat, that are outside the orbit of poetic style and poetic sensibility. An analogous thing has, of necessity, happened in the history of the novel; the development of the autobiographical novel has resulted in part from the inability of the novelist to write about anyone but himself or other people in relation to himself.

These quotations tell us much about Schwartz, his strengths and debilitating limitations, as well as about the roots of both the confessional poetry and the autobiographical fictions that have become a major strain of the serious writing of our day. But they are also especially useful in providing a lens through which to examine Saul Bellow's novelistic achievement. For the conflict between consciousness and experience that Politzer observed in Schwartz's writing is also at the heart of Bellow's fiction. And Bellow's most characteristic strength is that he has done exactly what Schwartz could not do because of both his temperament and his aesthetic theory: connected and contained both parts of his experience—the intellectual and the mundane, the past and the present, Hyde Park and Humboldt Park—and found the formal strategies necessary to make this connection both believable and entertaining. In other words, Bellow has made the connection in his *work* which Schwartz and Humboldt could only make in their *conversation*—and has done so, in part, by making his work a series of conversations.

The abdication of the world outside himself, the insistence on the artist's own special consciousness as his only possible subject, the condescending and oversimplified attitude toward the lives of the vast majority of men and women which we find in Schwartz's essay express modernist attitudes that Saul Bellow has consistently challenged in both his fiction and his public statements. And recognizing the contrast between Bellow's attitudes and Schwartz's helps to explain why Bellow was drawn to a form that blends fiction, biography, and autobiography in *Humboldt's Gift*.

Since *The Victim*, a number of critics have observed, a consistent element in Saul Bellow's fiction has been his use of doubles, characters who act as foils to his heroes and who, through their failings, suggest the dangers and weaknesses the heroes must somehow overcome. Humboldt is one of the most important in this long line of doubles. Citrine and Bellow *must* remember Humboldt and Delmore—because forgetting the lesson of their lives would be artistic suicide. Humboldt is the funhouse mirror-image that shows them themselves with all the flaws magnified. "As time went on," Citrine says, "I found myself becoming absurd in the manner of Von Humboldt Fleisher. By and by it became apparent that he had acted as my agent. I myself, a nicely composed person, had had Humboldt expressing himself wildly on my behalf, satisfying some of my longings."

Without Humboldt, Citrine must learn to do without this "psychological delegation." And doing so requires that he, like Bellow, must come to terms with the destructive elements that the other represented for him in the past. He must also come to recognize the elements in his own character that have allowed him to avoid his other's fate. Where Citrine strives to roll with the punches contemporary reality constantly delivers—can contemplate the eternal while trapped in a bathroom stall with a defecating Mafioso—Humboldt most certainly could not. When Humboldt rambled on about Carl Jung and Marilyn Monroe, his ramblings often lacked a coherent center; but when Citrine and Bellow do the same thing there (usually) is such a center, shaped by conscious artistry. "His talent had gone bad," Citrine thinks of Humboldt, "and now I had to think of what to do about talent in this day, in this age. How to prevent the leprosy of souls. Somehow it appeared to be up to me."

Just as Schwartz counseled the abdication of the public life in favor of the private in "The Isolation of Modern Poetry," Humboldt once told Citrine that "poets ought to figure out how to get around pragmatic America". But both Bellow and Citrine reject their advice. Rather than "get around" American life, they argue through their writing and their example, the artist must *confront* and *assimilate* contemporary life in his art. "Mankind must recover its imaginative powers," Citrine writes, "recover living and thought and real being, no longer accept these insults to the soul, and do it soon. Or else! And this is where a man like Humboldt, faithful to failed ideas, lost his poetry and missed the boat."

The solution, Citrine and Bellow argue, is to create an art that can compete with Sperry Rand or IBM or RCA for the attention and the souls of men and women. For the lesson of Humboldt's life is that "you don't make yourself interesting through madness, eccentricity, or anything of the sort, but because you have the power to cancel the world's distraction, activity, noise, and become fit to hear the essence of things." Bellow said much the same thing in his Nobel Lecture. It may be more difficult, he said, "to reach the whirling mind of a modern reader, but it is possible to cut through the noise and reach the quiet zone. In the quiet zone we may find he is devoutly waiting for us." To Bellow, writing is about communicating with "the reader," with "us," not with a small elite of other writers or intellectuals. "The essence of our real condition," he said

> The complexity, the confusion, the pain of it, is shown to us in glimpses, in what Proust and Tolstoy thought of as "true impressions." This essence reveals and conceals itself. When it goes away it leaves us again in doubt. But our connection remains with the depths from which these glimpses come. . .
> The value of literature lies in these intermittent "true impressions." A novel moves back and forth between the world of objects, of actions, of appearances, and that other world, from which these "true impressions" come and which moves us to believe that the good we hold on to so tenaciously—in the face of evil, so obstinately—is no illusion. . .
> The novel can't be compared to the epic, or to the monuments of poetic drama. But it is the best we can do right now. It is a latter-day lean-to, a hovel in which the spirit takes shelter. A novel is balanced between a few true impressions and the multitude of false ones that make up most of what we call life.

Like Saul Bellow, Charlie Citrine recognizes the difficulty of this task. For while Bellow has consistently produced novels which meet the standards Citrine and he outline, Citrine has been unable to meet them himself, has been unable to complete his major work. If Citrine also spends too much time trying to think himself away from this American world instead of seeking the "true impressions" that will save both him and his readers, he *recognizes* this tendency in himself *as* a difficulty. He, like Bellow, chooses to live in Chicago, where his Mercedes can be demolished and his pride can continually be assaulted, rather than in an artificial Arcadia like Humboldt's and Schwartz's. He makes this choice not because he is a perennial victim bent on self-destruction but because he is exactly the opposite. He senses that "Chicago in its gigantesque outer life contained the whole problem of poetry and the inner life of America," and "in raw Chicago you could examine the human spirit" under modern conditions. In other words, he realizes that he *needs* Chicago, and the American reality it represents for him and Bellow, because he refuses to allow his writing to become disassociated from the world of common experience as Humboldt and Schwartz did.

In the version of himself Bellow has named Charlie Citrine he presents his view of an artistic survivor—perhaps foolish at times, perhaps pompous, sometimes unloving, often inept—but a man struggling to become aware of the realities about him *and others* and dedicated to encompassing them in all their absurdity within the circle of his moral art. In the version of himself that Bellow calls Von Humboldt Fleisher he presents his view of the other path—the one from which he, and any artist who would survive, must turn away. The path that leads to surrendering to a belief in the inevitable destruction and ineffectuality of the artistic sensibility in philistine America; the path that leads to retreat into an art preoccupied with self-examination and isolated alienation, to making contact with the world only to act out "The Agony of the American Artist."

That both versions of the artist are ones Bellow feels in himself is clear from comments he made to *Newsweek* when the novel first appeared. He described himself as far from unfamiliar with "the temptation to torpor," lack of attention to the world's business. "I feel I've fallen short of my talents," he said. "Always, in this book too . . . Charlie feels he's snoozed through his life, missing the significance of the real events of his time. I've fallen short of wakefulness too." And because he feels he's fallen short, Bellow can see himself in Humboldt as well as Citrine, and also in his friend Delmore Schwartz. So, at the end, Delmore Schwartz must have appeared to Bellow as a shadow self, a double met on the street rather than the page. One so like an aspect of the self that he realized he, too, had the potential to become that Bellow could not face Schwartz in his final decline. The pain was, at least in part, the pain of self-recognition.

A comment John Berryman once made about Robert Lowell's "Skunk Hour" suggests the larger implications of Bellow's portraits. "I would call it virtually certain that Lowell had in mind and at heart during this poem not only his own difficulties, whatever they may be or have been, but the personal disorders to which other poets of his age and place have been so furiously subject," he wrote. Saul Bellow's achievement in *Humboldt's Gift*—like Philip Roth's in his later novels, Robert Lowell's in *Life Studies*, John Berryman's in *The Dream Songs*—is that he has learned to use his preoccupation with his self-consciousness. Like them, he has escaped the fatal flaw of the merely autobiographical which Schwartz described and too often displayed. Like them, he has recognized the worst in himself, recognized the dangers that his life and art are liable to, and then overcome those dangers through a talent which makes the personal a comment on the general predicament. If, again like them, Bellow has sometimes been unable to move far beyond the autobiographical, has had trouble in creating and identifying with protagonists unlike himself, he has nevertheless managed to overcome the limitations inherent in the autobiographical mode. We are drawn into his self-consciousness because, through his art, it touches our own.

II

Like *Humboldt's Gift*, many of Bellow's later works are based in both biography and autobiography and present recognizable portraits of friends who are now gone. Victor Wulpy of "What Kind of Day Did You Have?" is modeled on the critic and Bellow colleague Harold Rosenberg. "Zetland: By A Character Witness" is a character sketch of Bellow's childhood friend and literary rival Isaac Rosenfeld. *Ravelstein* is cast as another chronicle of a friendship by a survivor. Chick, the chronicler, is as clearly based on Bellow as Abe Ravelstein, the subject, is on Allan Bloom, Bellow's colleague at the University of Chicago's Committee on Social Thought and the author of the surprise 1987 bestseller *The Closing of the American Mind*. Like *Humboldt's Gift*, which included characters modeled on friends and acquaintances such as R.P. Blackmur, Carlos Baker, Dwight McDonald, Hilton Kramer, Robert Maynard Hutchins, Edward Shils, and Studs Terkel, *Ravelstein* includes fictionalized portraits of members of Bellow's and Bloom's Chicago circle such as Shils, Leo Strauss, and Mircea Eliade.

In the long run, of course, this will not really matter. When the gossip of the moment has subsided and readers of the future pick up the book they will see it as fiction, not thinly disguised fact, and they will recognize it for what it is: another in the long line of Saul Bellow's raids on the inarticulate, another of his efforts to use words to capture what he sees as the essentials of human experience.

"I had a funny feeling sometimes," Charlie Citrine says in *Humboldt's Gift*, "as if I had been stamped and posted and they were waiting for me to be delivered to an important address. I may contain unusual information." Saul Bellow has felt this way since he was a boy. When he was eight years old, Solomon Bellows spent six months in the children's ward of Montreal's Royal Victoria Hospital with an attack of tuberculosis. He still remembers having the sense when he was released that he had been somehow spared, saved because there was something special that he was expected to do. When his Russian-Jewish immigrant parents moved him and his three older siblings to Chicago the next year, he set out both to remake his body and his self. In Chicago, he carried coal scuttles, holding them at arm's length, and followed the then popular exercise regimens of books such as *How to Get Strong and Stay So* to build his body. He also immediately found himself drawn in several directions at once: toward the streets, where he sensed the excitement and possibilities of a new world; toward the Humboldt Park branch of the Chicago Public Library, where he found yet another kind of new world in the books of Poe, Twain, Dreiser, London, and Anderson; and toward the synagogue, where his orthodox parents hoped he would begin his path to becoming a rabbi. Years before he published his first story and changed his name to Saul Bellow, the streets and the library had won out, and by the time he went to Tuley High School, he had already decided that he wanted to be a writer.

He enrolled at the University of Chicago as an English major in 1933 but found little encouragement of his ambitions there. "It was made clear to me when I studied literature in the university that as a Jew and the son of Russian Jews I would probably never have the right feeling for Anglo-Saxon traditions, for English words," he recalled in his 1966 *Paris Review* interview. He transferred to Northwestern University after his sophomore year and switched his major from English to anthropology, but he didn't change his mind. Two years later, he earned his B.A. from Northwestern and began graduate work in anthropology at the University of Wisconsin. But he stayed less than a year—every time he tried to work on his thesis it turned into a story—before marrying and returning to Chicago. Soon he was making a living by writing biographies of Midwestern writers for the WPA Writers Project, teaching at Pestalozzi-Froebel Teachers College, and serving as an editorial assistant with the Encyclopedia Brittanica's Great Books Project.

Within a few years, Bellow was living in New York and getting to know the writers associated with *Partisan Review*, which published his first story, "Two Morning Monologues," in 1941. *Dangling Man*, a short novel inspired by Dostoevsky's *Notes from Underground* and Rilke's *Journal of My Other Self*, appeared in 1944, and in its opening paragraphs there were already clear signs of the voice and vision that would emerge full-blown in *The Adventures of Augie March* and fundamentally change the style of the American novel in the second half of the century:

> There was a time when people were in the habit of addressing themselves frequently and felt no shame at making a record of their inward transactions. But to keep a journal nowadays is considered a kind of self-indulgence, a weakness, and in poor taste. For this is the era of hardboiled-dom. Today, the code of the athlete, of the tough boy—an American inheritance, I believe, from the English gentleman—that curious mixture of striving, asceticism, and rigor, the origins of which some trace back to Alexander the Great—is stronger than ever. Do you have feelings? There are correct and incorrect ways of indicating them. Do you have an inner life? It is nobody's business but your own. Do you have emotions? Strangle them. To a degree, everybody obeys this code. And it does admit of a limited kind of candor, a closemouthed straightforwardness. But on the truest candor, it has an inhibitory effect. Most serious matters are closed to the hardboiled. They are unpracticed in introspection, and therefore badly equipped to deal with opponents whom they cannot shoot like big game or outdo in daring.

If you have difficulties, grapple with them silently, goes one of their commandments. To hell with that! I intend to talk about mine, and if I had as many mouths as Siva has arms and kept them going all the time, I still could not do myself justice. In my present state of demoralization, it has become necessary for me to keep a journal—that is, to talk to myself—and I do not feel guilty of self-indulgence in the least. The hardboiled are compensated for their silence; they fly planes or fight bulls or catch tarpon, whereas I rarely leave my room.

Bellow has regularly dismissed *Dangling Man* and *The Victim* (1947), describing them as like M.A. and Ph.D. theses in which he was trying to establish his credentials. "When I wrote those early books," he has said, "I was timid. I still felt the incredible effrontery of announcing myself to the world (in part I mean the WASP world) as a writer and an artist. I had to touch a great many bases, demonstrate my abilities, pay my respects to formal requirements. In short I was afraid to let myself go." In *The Victim*, he explained in his *Paris Review* interview, he was trying to live up to a "Flaubertian standard." But he felt that this style was "repressive"—"because of the circumstances of my life and because of my upbringing in Chicago as the son of immigrants, I could not, with such an instrument as I developed in the first two books, express a variety of things I knew intimately. Those books, though useful, did not give me a form in which I felt comfortable."

The Victim now feels every bit as repressed and arch as Bellow suggests. But although the subject of *Dangling Man* is claustrophobia and angst, so much that we associate with Bellow's mature achievement is already present in this little book that it deserves more attention than it usually gets. The Bellovian voice, a mixture of formality and slang, is already audible. The stance, in stubborn opposition to fashionably advanced thinking and dominant ideas, is already apparent. The focus, on an individual's consciousness and perceptions of the public and private worlds, is already there. The characteristic style, which blends the street and the library, straight talk about personal crisis with references to great books and cultural history, is already visible. And the inclination toward comedy—"whereas I rarely leave my room"—is already evident as well.

Bellow's comments about these books, of course, are based on the perspective that he gained after the stylistic breakthrough of *The Adventures of Augie March*—a breakthrough that Philip Roth once characterized as closing the gap between Damon Runyon and Thomas Mann. Certainly no one would ever associate the word "repressed" with Bellow's sprawling, exuberant, six hundred-page third novel; in fact, rejecting the whole idea of repressing anything is exactly where the novel begins. And there is no doubt that its famous opening is as important to the history of the American novel as *Moby Dick*'s "Call me Ahab":

I am an American, Chicago born—Chicago, that somber city—and go at things as I have taught myself, free-style, and will make the record in my own way: first to knock, first admitted; sometimes an innocent knock, sometimes a not so innocent. But a man's character is his fate, says Heraclitus, and in the end there isn't any way to disguise the nature of the knocks by acoustical work on the door or by gloving the knuckles.

This is a style that opens the door to picaresque adventures, to endless digressions, to high and low speculation, to great ideas and petty grievances—and while Bellow would modify and refine it in the books that would follow, it has served him and his readers very well for nearly fifty years. It has also liberated hundreds of writers who have come after him—not just other Jewish American writers, but writers from every ethnic group and every region—by offering a model of what can be done by being faithful to their own voices and their own experiences of the American scene.

In *The Adventures of Augie March*, which earned him the first of three National Book Awards, Bellow did more than throw off the burden of trying to be proper and discover his own voice, he also began to explore his characteristic concerns and personalities. Augie is the first of Bellow's many seekers, and he ultimately realizes that he must do more than bounce around from adventure to adventure, that he must search for an *amor fati*, a fate good enough. In some ways, Augie is a character out of an eighteenth-century English novel—a Tom Jones or Joseph Andrews, Chicago born and bred. But like Bellow's later heroes, Augie is more complicated—both observant and blind, canny and naïve. And like those later heroes, he is constantly running into big-time "reality instructors" who think they need to wise him up about the way things are in the real world.

Although *Seize the Day* seems in retrospect to be a kind of anachronism—more like *Dangling Man* or *The Victim* than *Augie March* or the novels that would follow in its tone of depression and victimization—it, too, reflects Bellow's fondness for these reality instructors in the character of Dr. Tamkin. *Henderson the Rain King* is probably the novel closest in spirit to *Augie March*. A burlesque and parody of epic quests in Frazer and Jung, in Conrad, *Don Quixote*, and *Gulliver's Travels*, it is the story of another large character with spiritual longings. Henderson takes off for Africa in search of something he can't quite define—"things got worse and worse and pretty soon they were too complicated," he says. He ends on frozen tundra, holding a child not his own, having learned the difference between living as a "becomer" and as a "beer," between only listening to the voice that says "I want" and recognizing that being human means understanding that "he wants, she wants, they want" too.

When Bellow is asked which of his characters he feels closest to or is fondest of, he usually answers "Henderson—the absurd seeker of higher qualities." But his fondness for Henderson may also be connected to two of the refrains that appear in the novel and continue to be touchstones in his later fiction. "Truth comes with blows" is one of those refrains; "I do remember well that hour that burst my spirit's sleep" is the other.

Herzog was Bellow's first popular success as well as his second National Book Award winner. Moses Herzog is an intellectual who finds that books, ideas, and letters to the great and near-great can't help him cope with the mundane realities of betrayal, infidelity, and injustice that life presents to him. In the course of shaping Herzog's confession, Bellow says, he discovered that comedy would allow him to express himself more freely than complaint. To Bellow, the comedy of *Herzog* grew out of the insight that Herzog has been "educated out of his senses. He has received an utterly useless education and breaks down as soon as he faces a real crisis." Only when Herzog has discovered this, when he has finally come to the point where he can sit quietly, cancel the world's distractions and preconceptions, does he seem ready to begin a new and potentially better life. What the novel says about Herzog's personality and approach foreshadows a narrative style that would increasingly welcome digression. Herzog was "a person of irregular tendencies," we are told, "he practiced the art of circling among random facts to swoop down on the essentials. He often expected to take the essentials by surprise by an amusing stratagem."

There is very little that is amusing about *Mr. Sammler's Planet*. Like *The Dean's December* (1982), it is a somber novel written in anger and anguish, packed with overtly social and political ideas, full of opinions Bellow had stated in other places, and driven by a sense of an ending, of things running down and out of control in contemporary life. Artur Sammler barely survived the Holocaust, and he knows that the world, the way human beings treat one another, has been unalterably changed for the worse by modern history. He is an outsider who is never truly at home in America. And the New York City he inhabits, the family he sees around him, the people he meets on the streets and the subway, all seem to him to be bound for destruction, caught up in the headlong pursuit of immediate gratification because they have not learned to come to terms with the most important spiritual truths. Mr. Sammler seeks understanding in Meister Eckhart; others seek it in science. "The real problem is the problem of death," Bellow told an interviewer when the book first appeared. "If people don't know how to come to terms with it, and souls have no preparation, then the only thing is to be externally young and in pursuit of pleasure and further sexual and hedonistic horizons."

In describing his objectives in creating the monologue that underlies

Mr. Sammler's Planet, Bellow explained the technique that would characterize all of his later work. He set out, he said, to create "the thinking of such a person never disconnecting the thought from the person, so that these things are not presented in the book as sermons, but rather as a monologue. . . It seems to me—and it seemed to me when I wrote it—that it was sustaining itself through the passion of the thinker or the passion of the speaker and that it was justified, that there was no superfluous word or movement in the book." If Bellow is successful, in other words, the monologist's character justifies his monologue's digressions, opinions, or quirks.

"Many American writers cross the bar in their 60s and 70s and become Grand Old Men, gurus or bonzes of the Robert Frost variety," he told *Newsweek* when *Humboldt's Gift* was published.

> This is how society eases us out. Sees us off on the immortal train, with waving and cheering and nobody listening. Just as well, because there's nothing but bombast coming from the rear platform. If I last long enough, I assume this will happen to me too. And then there are two possibilities. Either you've run out of imagination . . . Or your imagination keeps cooking, in which case you're lucky. You're among the blessed. No man knows which way he's gonna go. He can only hope.

It now seems clear that Saul Bellow has been one of the lucky ones. In the thirty-one years between *Dangling Man* and *Humboldt's Gift*, Bellow published ten books: six full-length novels; three novellas or collections—*Dangling Man*, *Seize the Day*, and *Mosby's Memoirs* (1968); and a play, *The Last Analysis* (1964). The year *Humboldt's Gift* appeared he turned sixty; the following year he was awarded the Nobel Prize for Literature. And in the twenty-five years since his sixtieth birthday he has published ten more books: three novels—*The Dean's December*, *More Die of Heartbreak* (1987), and *Ravelstein*; five novellas or collections of stories—*Him with His Foot in His Mouth* (1984), *A Theft* (1989), *The Bellarosa Connection* (1989), *Something to Remember Me By* (1991), and *The Actual* (1997); and two works of nonfiction, *To Jerusalem and Back* (1976) and *It All Adds Up* (1994). But he has not just continued to publish into his ninth decade—rare enough in itself—he has also continued to struggle with questions that matter and create characters worth meeting.

Writing in the year that *Mr. Sammler's Planet* won him his third National Book Award, Jane Howard observed that "ideas always outweigh plots in Bellow's novels. His people tend to be brooders, musers, and writers of letters more than they are doers. Of such action as there is they are witnesses and victims, who always resemble, in some way or another, their creator." Beginning with *Humboldt's Gift*, which was awarded the Pulitzer Prize, Bellow's fiction has usually treated these characters within a particular form. Most of his later books are presented as a witness's story about one or more larger-than-life figures. Sometimes the narration is in the first person, sometimes it's in the third, but regardless of this formality the fiction usually reflects the consciousness of the witness, who is always a seer, an observer, and someone other characters are trying to improve. Each of these witnesses sets out to tell us about another person but constantly digresses to tell us about himself and self-consciously comment on his narration. (In Bellow, the main characters are usually men, but Clara Velde of *A Theft* and Katrina Goliger of "What Kind of Day Did You Have?" are interesting exceptions to this rule.) Each story, in other words, is as much about the witness as it is about the ostensible subject.

Charlie Citrine sets out to tell us the story of the poet Von Humboldt Fleisher—"poet, thinker, problem drinker, pill-taker, man of genius, manic depressive, intricate schemer," but also "a success story" who wrote poems "of great wit and beauty." Shawmut, the letter-writer in "Him with His Foot in His Mouth," who intends to explain himself to a librarian he once insulted, describes himself as "a reverberator" who responds to what he senses in other people and ends up telling us about his friend and colleague Walish, his brother Philip, and his brother-in-law Hansl. Katrina Goliger, the divorced suburban matron and mother of two whose point of view dominates the novella "What Kind of Day Did You Have?" tells us about Victor Wulpy, "a major figure, a world-class intellectual, big in the art world" who "often struck people as being a king." "Zetland: By a Character Witness" is a fragmentary account of its narrator's talented young friend. In *More Die of Heartbreak*, Kenneth Trachtenberg tries to explain his uncle, Benn Crader, "the real thing," a botanist of a "high level of distinction," who he says is so special that he thinks of him as having "the magics." In *A Theft*, Clara Velde, "the czarina of fashion writing," spends much of her time talking and thinking about her friend and former lover Ithiel (Teddy) Regler, "a Wunderkind in nuclear strategy" whom "world figures had found . . . worth their while." The unnamed narrator of *The Bellarosa Connection*, the retired founder of the Mnemosyne Institute in Philadelphia, would like to "forget about remembering"; instead he tells the story of his cousin Harry Fonstein, Harry's wife Sorella, and the Broadway producer Billy Rose. In *The Actual*, Harry Trellman, "a first-class noticer," recounts a story that involves the Chicago "notables" the Adletskys and his friends Jay and Amy Wustrin. And in *Ravelstein* a Chicago writer named Chick tells the story of Abe Ravelstein, a "magnificent," "great-souled" man whose "intellect had made a millionaire of him."

Big ideas, big talkers, big thinkers—characters of distinction, comfortably situated—populate each of these books. The location is usually a named or unnamed Chicago or New York. As always, there are recognizable character types: narrators who are constantly told about their weaknesses and faults at the same time that they are acknowledged to be "first-class noticers," scheming lawyers, unfaithful wives and ex-wives, tough-talking relatives, big time pontificators, hard-headed reality instructors, and womanizers Bellow has taken to describing as *homme a femmes*. The form is loose, allowing for a kind of higher garrulousness where the talk is, itself, the main point.

Like Bellow, the witnesses and subjects of his later works are much concerned with questions of death, spirit, and the soul. Bellow described *Humboldt's Gift* as a comic novel about death, telling Joseph Epstein shortly after it appeared that "I have exercised my imagination . . . working out obsessions about people I loved who are now dead." When an interviewer asked him several years later if he saw himself as a survivor, like Sammler and Citrine, Bellow said much the same thing. "No," he replied, "I think of myself as horribly deprived of people whom I loved and who are dead."

Questions about the existence and nature of the soul have also become constant concerns in these later books. Humboldt's legacy to Charlie Citrine was a message—"Remember: we are not natural beings but supernatural beings." "Our immortal hopes we know," Bellow said in 1977. "We understand what they are. We don't dismiss them out of hand. And it's not just because of ancient superstition, it's because there is some unacknowledged information that we have. It's about time we simply dealt with it directly and without being evasive." And in his essay "Mozart: An Overture" (1992), he returned to the subject again. "Ideas of transcendence are associated with crankiness or faddism—even downright instability and mental flabbiness. These are the charges and the guilts you open yourself to when you confess that you find it impossible to dismiss such speculations."

"The rule for the dead is that they should be forgotten," Chick tells us after his friend Abe Ravelstein dies. "After burial there is a universal gradual process toward oblivion. But with Ravelstein this didn't altogether work." Partly because ideas of transcendence were among the topics that Chick and Abe discussed often during Ravelstein's final months. Partly because since Chick agreed to Ravelstein's demand that he write his biography he can't be free of his friend's memory until his memoir is done. And partly because by the time he actually writes his biography of Ravelstein Chick has his own reasons for thinking seriously about whether immortal longings promise something besides oblivion at the end of our lives.

"You don't easily give up a creature like Ravelstein to death," Chick tells us in the novel's last sentence. And *Ravelstein* is his explanation of that statement. The novel actually contains three related stories: Chick's portrait of the character and last days of Abe Ravelstein, his account of the end of his marriage to a Romanian physicist, and his description of his marriage to a much younger woman and the brush with death that he has soon after.

"You could do a really fine memoir," Ravelstein tells Chick. "It's not just a request. I'm laying this on you as an obligation. Do it in your after-supper-reminiscence manner, when you've had a few glasses of wine and you're laid back making remarks." "In approaching a man like Ravelstein," Chick tells us, "a piecemeal method is perhaps best." In fact, it may not be. These statements are meant to explain and justify, not just describe, *Ravelstein*'s style. But they don't really convince since it's hard not to finish the book with the feeling that, in this case, shorter would have been better. *Ravelstein* has a moving story to tell, but it might have been better told in another of Bellow's fine novellas, rather than in a looser, more episodic longer form that is marred by far too much rambling and repetition.

Ravelstein is one of those "noisy bumptious types," the larger-than-life figures that Bellow's readers expect to meet in his fiction. A big, bald, chain-smoking man, both a stutterer and a champion talker, a big-time operator and genuine character, he's a creature of excess and extremes. He loves expensive and beautiful things, and in his day-to-day living he's a materialist of the first order. When we first meet him he's staying at the Crillon in Paris; he buys his clothes at Hermes, Lanvin, Sulka, and Gelot's. His shirts are custom made on Jermyn Street by Turnbull & Asser and he air mails his silk ties to Paris to be cleaned. He talks about his Spode, his Quimper, his Jensen silver, his Pratesi linens. His apartment is in a beautiful old building, and is furnished with

> big antique (sometimes threadbare) Oriental carpets, wall hangings, classical figurines, mirrors, glass cabinets, French antique sideboards, the Lalique chandeliers and wall fixtures. The living-room sofa was deep, wide, low. The glass top of the coffee table in front of it was about four inches thick. On it, Ravelstein sometimes spread his effects—the solid-gold Mont Blanc fountain pen, his $20,000 wrist watch, the golden gadget that cut his smuggled Havanas, the extra-large cigarette box filled with Marlboros, his Dunhill lighters, the heavy square glass ashtrays....

The apartment also includes a high-tech sound system, CDs he orders through catalogues from around the world, a restaurant-style espresso machine so large that the only place he can put it is in his kitchen sink, and a telephone console that Chick calls his "command post."

Ravelstein is also a homosexual who likes to take risks and relishes "*louche* encounters"—a man of "idiosyncrasies and kinks, of gobbling greed for penny candies or illegal Havana cigars." But he would not be of interest to Chick—or Bellow—if he were not much more. For Ravelstein combines these excesses with an equally obsessive devotion to the world of ideas. The big questions—about love, friendship, politics, education, the Jews, life, death, the spirit, and the soul—also fill his days. And though Chick repeatedly tells us that he will leave explaining Ravelstein's ideas to others who are better qualified, he keeps coming back to those ideas throughout his memoir. Ravelstein is also an extraordinary and caring teacher, a charming and challenging friend, an independent thinker, and a mentor to whom his students (Chick calls them "disciples") turn for advice long after they've gone on to the larger world beyond the university. And when he finds himself facing death—he's HIV positive and begins to suffer from one illness after another—he ends up teaching Chick how to live.

Chick is one of Bellow's familiar witnesses. A narrator who constantly questions his own narration, he's a successful writer and "serial marrier" who's quite a conversationalist himself. He's also another of Bellow's highly educated and high-minded men who find themselves struggling to survive in the real world. Ravelstein often compliments him on his intelligence and character—such compliments about the alter egos in Bellow's novels have, by now, become as common as they are in the later Hemingway—but Abe thinks Chick's too innocent for his age, too willing to be used and taken advantage of by his unfaithful and uncaring wife and her friends. Since love, Eros, was Ravelstein's "perennial interest" and Chick is his friend, the state of Chick's marriage to Vela, the physicist, becomes one of the central topics of their conversations. Ravelstein sees what Chick doesn't: that Chick has allowed himself to become involved in a relationship that does not even come close to meeting his needs, and that his spirit is being destroyed by the absence of love.

Although Chick is seventy-eight, Ravelstein's senior by fifteen years or so, and although Ravelstein brought together and reshaped his lecture notes into the critique of American higher education that became a bestseller and made him a millionaire at Chick's urging, Abe Ravelstein turns out to be another of Bellow's reality instructors. The difference between him and his predecessors, however, is that being a reality instructor is his vocation, and Chick is just one of his many students.

In *Ravelstein*'s first two thirds, Chick shares anecdotes about Ravelstein in Paris, in his apartment, on the phone with his former students, in the hospital recovering from one of many serious illnesses, back in his apartment after his hospitalization where he has to struggle to get back on his feet and back into the classroom, visiting Chick's summer place in New Hampshire. In the last third of the novel, which takes place after Abe dies, Chick tells us about the difficulties he faced in trying to keep his promise to Ravelstein and then recounts how he and his new wife Rosamund, one of Abe's former students, took a Thanksgiving vacation to St. Martin that almost killed him.

Chick eats a red snapper for dinner at an outdoor restaurant on the beach and the fish turns out to be toxic. Within a few days he finds himself in the intensive care unit of a Boston hospital suffering from pneumonia, cardiac arrest, and a rare tropical disease that devastates the nervous system. At first, the disease incapacitates him so fully that he can't even draw a circle or sign his name, much less write. And for a while it isn't clear whether, or how fully, he will recover. He eventually does, with Rosamund by his side and the memory of Ravelstein as his inspiration, and then he is finally able to write the memoir that is *Ravelstein*.

Early in the book Chick describes walking around the neighborhood where he spent fifty years of his life. "On every one of the surrounding streets," he says, "there were front rooms where friends had lived—and at the sides, the windows of bedrooms where they died. There were more of those that I cared to think about." At his age, he explains, "you don't want to be too tender-minded. It's different if you lead an active life. And I am active, on the whole. But there are gaps, and these gaps tend to fill up with your dead."

One of the subjects that Ravelstein and Chick debate is the question of immortality, of whether there is an afterlife and whether the soul will continue to exist after death. While he's in intensive care, Chick has several nightmares and dreams. One of them seems to tie the two parts of *Ravelstein* together. "During these weeks I was heavily dosed with Verset," Chick explains. "One effect of this drug is to suspend all mental life. I didn't consider whether I was dead or alive. All appearances (the external world) were canceled. My late brothers, both of them, drew near, once. They wore their customary shirts, neckties, shoes, the suits their tailors made for them. My father was in the background. He didn't come forward. My brothers indicated that they were satisfied with their condition."

This feels very much like an epiphany. From Ravelstein's example, Chick learned how to face illness and the prospect of death by living every day as fully as possible, with dignity and spirit. From this dream, he learns that his immortal longings may not be misplaced after all.

Bellow, who went through a similar illness and recovery in 1994, gives Chick his memory of a brush with death as an eight year-old. As a writer who has always been deeply concerned with fundamental questions about life and death, eternity and time, the spirit and the flesh, Saul Bellow must have seen struggling with and finally recovering from such a serious illness as yet another close escape, another sign that he had unfinished work left to do. Considering this close call, as well as the loss of many of his contemporaries and closest friends to illness and age, regaining both his health and his ability to write must have seemed an extraordinary gift to Bellow. That he is still writing, still creating memorable characters who take important questions seriously, is certainly a gift to all of us.

A Novelist's Revenge

E.L. Doctorow

"Essentially I believe you have to reinvent fiction with each and every book," E.L. Doctorow told one interviewer; "you've got to take the conventions and break them down, reconstitute them." The strongest impulse in twentieth century literature, he told another, has been "to assault fiction, assault the forms, destroy it so it can rise again. You let go of the tropes one by one. You get rid of the lights, you get rid of the music, you forego the drum roll, and finally you do the high-wire act without the wire." In practice, what the attitudes expressed in these comments have meant is that Doctorow's work has combined an aversion to repeating himself with a persistent intention. The aversion has made versatility and daring distinguishing marks of his fiction; the intention has made his individual books seem parts of an ongoing project.

Each Doctorow book seems a new departure. With each he creates a different narrative voice, focuses on a different time, experiments with a different style, and explores a different aspect of American experience. In *Welcome to Hard Times* (1960), the time is the nineteenth century, the setting is the Old West, and the narrator is a cowardly mayor plagued by existential angst. In *The Book of Daniel* (1971), the time is the Cold War 1950's and the explosive 1960's, the focus is on the Old Left's legacy to the New, the narrator is an angry, self-mocking graduate student whose life story incorporates the radicalism of both eras. In *Ragtime* (1975), the time is the turn of the century, the style mixes real and imagined figures, and the narrative voice is the verbal equivalent of ragtime music.

In *Loon Lake* (1980), the time is the Depression, the form combines the Horatio Alger story and the proletarian novel, and the multiple narrators include the main character, a failed poet, and a computer. In *Lives of the Poets* (1984), the time is the 1980's, the form is a series of related stories, and the narrative voice is a pastiche of the sounds of contemporary American fiction. In *World's Fair* (1985), the time is, again, the Depression, the setting is the Bronx, the form blends fiction and memoir into a *Bildungsroman*, and the narration is shared by a young boy, his older self, his mother, and his brother.

Beneath this variety and versatility, each of Doctorow's books represents another contribution to a continuing project. That project has focused on testing the limits of genre, blurring, and so challenging, the accepted boundaries between the real and the imagined, the historical and the fictional, the serious and the popular.

In the middle of the summer of 1975's annual publishing doldrums—a period which many readers of contemporary American fiction had expected to divide between trying to finish Joseph Heller's *Something Happened* and waiting for Saul Bellow's *Humboldt's Gift*—Doctorow's fourth novel appeared and quickly became a literary phenomenon. The signs were unmistakable: featured excerpts in *American Review*, designation as a Book-of-the-Month Club Main Selection, a front page review by a major critic in the *New York Times Book Review*, Jill Krementz photographs of the author in all the leading newspapers and magazines, a contract for a Robert Altman film adaptation, and, finally, a $1.8 million sale of the paperback rights to Bantam just as the book reached the top of bestseller lists all across the country.

More interesting than *Ragtime*'s status as a masterfully orchestrated and packaged publishing venture, however, was its status as one of those anomalies of American letters: a serious work of fiction that is greeted with both popular and critical acclaim. Typically, in twentieth-century American culture a writer's popular success has virtually guaranteed critical disdain. The critic knows that the sacred works of the modernist imagination, works like *The Waste Land* or *Ulysses*, are unread by the general public; that when an important American author has reached a broad audience it has most frequently been through one of his lesser works—*Typee* and *Omoo* not *Moby Dick*, *This Side of Paradise* not *The Great Gatsby*, *Sanctuary* not *The Sound and the Fury*. There have always been exceptions, of course, writers like Ernest Hemingway or Kurt Vonnegut who have managed to cultivate both critical and popular followings, but they are unusual enough to prove not invalidate the rule.

So when a novel like *Ragtime* comes along, bucks the trend and breaks the mold, we are confronted with a cultural case which invites us to consider several interesting questions about art and the contemporary audience for fiction in America. What is there about *Ragtime* that allowed it to cross the border and close the normally unbridgeable gap between "high" and "popular" culture when the same author's previous novels—like those of most serious novelists—could not? What, if any, artistic compromises were involved? What does the novel's popularity tell us about the tastes of the audience whose imagination it apparently captured so completely?

The answers are to be found in both the form and content of *Ragtime*: a form that is experimental and accomplished enough to appeal to critics who demand innovation and yet familiar enough to attract the common reader; a content that grapples with fundamental issues confronting contemporary fictionists yet never ceases to entertain and engage. This is a combination which Doctorow's previous novels lacked.

His first, *Welcome to Hard Times* is an apocalyptic fable presented as a variation on Western formulae familiar to readers of Bret Harte's "The Outcasts of Poker Flat." Set in the Dakota Territory during the late 1800's, it records the efforts of a small community of "lost souls"—a cowardly mayor named Blue, an inarticulate Indian, a nearly-autistic orphan boy, a Swedish pimp, and several whores with hearts of varying veins of gold—to build up and maintain a town against the ravages of the frontier violence of men and nature. Its plot, grounded in a cyclical movement from destruction to rebirth to destruction, is tightly-knit and narrated in an almost cinematic style by Blue (the book eventually became a B movie starring Henry Fonda). Underlying the story, a memoir of a survivor with sections titled "ledgers," is a characteristically 1950's concern with debts and sorrows, moral accounts outstanding that must be repaid over time. Though its characters are generally well-drawn, there is finally little to distinguish it from other books written at the same time on similar themes and remaindered, as it was, within a few short months.

Doctorow's third novel, *The Book of Daniel*, on the other hand, is most certainly an exceptional book worthy of the National Book Award nomination that it received. A critic's delight because of its structural complications, its use of multiple points of view, the complexity of its character development, its imaginative juxtaposition of reality and fantasy, and its political stance, it can be frustrating to many common readers—for exactly these reasons. They find it difficult to keep the threads of the narrative straight (and they demand narrative above all else, as any Sunday's bestseller list will attest); they are confused by the novel's abrupt and seemingly arbitrary shifts in viewpoint and find much that the critics praise as experimental to be merely distracting self-consciousness. Brilliant set pieces like the "Bintel Brief"—which introduces material developed at greater length in *Ragtime*—often get lost in the confusion.

Instead, the reader tends to remember self-indulgences like the narrator's exclamation as we finally realize that Daniel is the son of a Rosenberg-like couple who are executed for treason: "Oh baby, you know it now. We done played enough games for you, ain't we. You a smart lil fucker. You know where it's at now, don't you big daddy. You got the picture. This is the story of a fucking, right? You pullin' out yo lit-er-ary map, mutha? You know where we goin', right muthafuck?"

The story of Daniel Isaacson's radicalization develops against the background of the political turblulence of the late 1960's, and the connection Doctorow suggests between the treatment of dissent during both periods, like many of the other connections in the novel, is especially apt. But the novel's politics were as alien to the popular mind that re-elected Richard Nixon in a landslide in 1972 as its techniques, so in spite of its many virtues and its critical reception it made no impression on the broader culture.

On rereading, both of these books display a great many strengths and delights, and their most memorable achievements clearly foreshadow the achievements of *Ragtime*. From the first, Doctorow had a knack for seizing on the telling detail, for mentioning exactly the right brand name and cultural artifact to capture an era, for juxtaposing images from different times in a way that surprises and compels attention, for creating and re-creating American myths through his use of familiar images of our shared past, and for describing the events of personal lives from a perspective that calls attention to social forces. In *Ragtime* Doctorow found both a story and a technique that would allow him to capitalize on these strengths and reach a broader audience as well. *Ragtime*'s point of view is stabilized. And there is, to make the point simply, something for everyone in the story of three families caught up in the events of the first decade-and-a-half of the twentieth century—the era when America lost her innocence and suddenly found herself naked in the modern world.

One of the primary reasons for the novel's broad appeal is that, whoever we are, we can see ourselves reflected in its images. The personages of our shared past whose names fill the pages of our history books are here—Henry Ford, J.P. Morgan, Emma Goldman, Harry Houdini, Teddy Roosevelt, Admiral Perry—side by side with three families who represent figures in each of our personal histories. These families are an incarnation of the millions of people who lived and died without being named in the history books, but who are our most personal links to the American past. My immigrant grandparents are represented here, with their babushkas and broken English, in the family of Mameh-Tateh-Daughter. And yours are likely here too, either in them, in the WASP family from New Rochelle, or in the black family of Coalhouse Walker. Though these three families are the only "fictional" characters in the book, they are also the most real because they are our own.

To the reader weary of contemporary American fiction's self-conscious explorations of the individual psyche, then, *Ragtime* offers an exuberant journey through the storehouse of our common memories. To the reader intimidated by the increasingly common use of unfamiliar mythological references in contemporary fiction, it offers the creation of a new mythology out of the familiar images of our shared past. To the reader inundated with novels of complicated character, it offers a return to narrative and story; to the reader confused by contemporary experimentation, accessible innovation; to an age in the grip of nostalgia, another time; to an audience captivated by the rhythms of Scott Joplin's "The Entertainer," a verbal equivalent of ragtime. And at the same time that *Ragtime* attracts the popular reader because of all these elements, it satisfies the critic because of its style and the architectural complexity created by the manipulation of its central metaphor of ragtime music.

In ragtime, as James Lincoln Collier has explained, "the syncopated melodies in the right hand are set over a repeating bass in the left . . . There are call-and-answer figures and repetition . . . A rag is made up of a sequence of three, four, or even five strains, one of which is repeated. These do not develop out of one another but are more or less independent." In *Ragtime*, as the left hand provides a bass line of historical events and narrative movement, the right hand furnishes the repetitions, improvisations, and call-and-answer figures that give the book its distinctive style and texture. The several sets of characters—Mameh-Tateh-Daughter, Grandfather-Father-Mother-Brother-Son, Coalhouse Walker-Sarah-child, Stanford White-Evelyn Nesbitt-Harry Thaw, Harry Houdini—are the equivalent of ragtime's musical strains. They appear and reappear throughout the narrative, each time slightly altered. Again and again the narrative seems to be veering toward conventionality and sentimentality; again and again it is saved by a surprising improvisation. Consider Grandfather's reaction to the coming of spring. First the conventional chord:

> Spring, spring! Like a mad magician flinging silks and colored rags from his trunk the earth produced the yellow and white crocus, the fox grape, the forsythia flowering on its stalks, the blades of iris, the apple tree blossoms of pink and white and green, the heavy lilac and daffodil. Grandfather stood in the yard and gave a standing ovation. A breeze came up and blew from the maples a shower of spermatazoic softheaded green buds. They caught in his sparse gay hair. he shook his head with delight, feeling a wreath had been bestowed. A joyful spasm took hold of him and he stuck his leg out in an old man's jig,

and then the syncopation:

> lost his balance, and slid on the heel of his shoe into the sitting position. In this manner he cracked his pelvis and entered a period of declining health from which he would not recover. But the spring was joyful and even in the pain he wore a smile.

There are verbal call-and-answer figures, as in the novel's early description of Houdini's exploits:

> He went all over the world accepting all kinds of bondage and escaping. He was roped to a chair. He escaped. He was chained to a ladder. He escaped. He was handcuffed, his legs were put in irons, he was tied up in a straight jacket and put in a locked cabinet. He escaped. He escaped from bank vaults . . . he escaped from a zinc-lined Knabe piano case . . . He escaped from a Siberian exile van. From a Chinese torture crucifix. From a Hamburg penitentiary. From an English prison ship. From a Boston jail. He was chained to automobile tires . . . and he escaped.

"Today," this passage ends, "nearly fifty years since his death, the audience for escapes is even larger." Houdini gradually emerges in the narrative as an artist-figure, and through him Doctorow comments on two of the central issues confronting the contemporary American writer: the place of the artist in society and the challenge reality presents to the writer's imagination.

Like the contemporary fictionist, Houdini feels the burden of his audience's demands for escape and innovation. "His success had brought . . . a host of competitors," he thinks. "Consequently he had to think of more and more dangerous escapes." Like the contemporary American writer, Doctorow's Houdini recognizes that reality is constantly topping his inventions: "Houdini had high inchoate ambition and every development in technology made him restless. On the shabby confines of the stage he could create wonder and awe. Meanwhile men were beginning to take planes into the air, or race automobiles that went sixty miles an hour." Houdini realizes that "There was a kind of act that used the real world for its stage. He couldn't touch it. For all his achievement he was a trickster, an illusionist, a mere magician. What was the sense of his life if people walked out of the theater and forgot him? The headlines on the newsstand said Peary had reached the Pole. The real-world act was what got into the history books."

Faced with the competition of the real world, Houdini, like the novelist, tries more and more dangerous tricks. At first, people are intrigued and captivated by them, but he himself remains unsatisfied; eventually, the tricks begin to alienate them and isolate him. The last time that we see him, he is performing with such intensity that he begins to lose his audience: his performances had "such a strange and disquieting effect on them, that in some cases children were hurried out before the end of the performance. Houdini never noticed." And then, ironically, in the midst of his wildest act reality overshadows him anyway. The theater is shaken and the performance is stopped because of the bomb set off by Coalhouse Walker at a nearby firehouse.

Competing with "the real-life act" has obsessed American novelists at least since the end of World War II, and they have responded to the challenge in a variety of ways. Doctorow's method in *The Book of Daniel*, *Ragtime*, and later works—like William Styron's in *The Confessions of Nat Turner*, Thomas Pynchon's in *Gravity's Rainbow*, Philip Roth's in *The Great American Novel*, *Our Gang*, or "Looking at Kafka"—is to blur the distinctions, to place fictitious characters in real situations with real (i.e., historically identifiable) characters, or to place real characters in fictional situations. The tendency in these fictions, Roger Sale wrote in a review of *Ragtime* in the *New York Review of Books*, "is to insist that these more purely or openly imagined versions are truer than those historical fictions that always give facts where facts are known. Reading these books, one is constantly dared to doubt that the essential truth is being told, to draw some dividing line where truth is separated from fiction."

The author makes the issue a central element in his fiction, reconstructs reality through the force of his imagination. The method is not really new, of course. Its roots go back to the beginning of the English novel in Daniel Defoe's first fictions, where imaginary and real characters intermingle in order to assert the validity of the vision. But in the hands of a talented writer like E.L. Doctorow such a method manages to both satisfy the public's desire for nonfiction and allow the author's imagination to run free.

Doctorow described *Ragtime* as "a mingling of fact and invention, a novelist's revenge on an age that celebrates nonfiction." And he and many of his contemporaries have come to see the novel's method as a means of expressing the central perception expressed by the boy in his New Rochelle family, that "the forms of life are volatile," that "everything in the world [can] as easily be something else," that the interpenetration of reality and fantasy in contemporary life can be an imaginative opportunity as well as a problem.

II

In *Lives of the Poets* Doctorow again experiments with narrative voice to produce a stylistic and moral portrait of the contemporary scene and the contemporary imagination. Like Samuel Johnson's *Lives of the English Poets*, which is the inspiration for its title, this book is, in part, a series of biographical sketches of contemporary writers by a writer who is their contemporary. But there the similarity ends. For the writers Doctorow tells us about are fictional; and he tells us about them in the long title story through another fictional character, the writer Jonathan, who narrates the first and last of the seven stories in the book.

Doctorow's subject here is not just the lives his fictional characters live, but the lives they imagine in their own fiction—about the lives they create for themselves and for their characters; and about the imaginary transformation that turns the events of a writer's life into the images and conflicts of his work. It is a book about the way we live, and the way we write, now.

At first reading, *Lives of the Poets* seems just a collection of stories framed by the autobiographical first and last stories by the writer Jonathan. In the first, "A Writer in the Family," Jonathan recalls how his aunt convinced him to write letters to his grandmother in his dead father's name so that the old woman would not know that her son had died. In the last, Jonathan is a fifty year-old wrier in crisis ruminating on the decline of New York City and the unhappiness, the malaise, the sexual betrayals and marital wrangles, that characterize the lives he and his fellow writers lead in America today.

In the five stories separating these autobiographical ones, the characters and setting vary widely. "The Water Works" is a brief, mysterious sketch describing the discovery of a child's mangled body at a waterworks. (It would become the germ of Doctorow's 1994 novel of the same name.) "Willi" describes a boy's discovery of his mother's adultery, and the consequences of his revealing that discovery to his father. "The Hunter" portrays the unraveling of the life of a young woman who teaches in a desolated hill town after she is shot at—perhaps by mistake, perhaps not—by a hunter. "The Foreign Legation" takes us to the suburbs, where a recently divorced man jogs into the middle of an act of terrorism. And "The Leather Man" presents the outlines of a theory of "dereliction"—of the bag ladies and homeless wanderers of the city—as a lecture by an agent of the powers-that-be.

These are cryptic, elliptical stories of fragmentation, isolation, desperation, anxiety, rootlessness and betrayal. Each has the power to disturb, to lodge in the memory like the strains of a sad song that won't leave you alone. But *Lives of the Poets* is more than a random collection of stories.

Doctorow has said that the stories are meant to express a "continuous mentality," that the Jonathan of the first and last stories is to be seen as the author of the rest. The themes, images, conflicts and characters of the five stories, in other words, are the themes, images, conflicts and characters of the autobiographical stories turned into art. But there is yet another way to read the book. On one level, a simple collection; on another, a group of stories created by the writer whose own story frames them. On still another, *Lives of the Poets* may be read as a survey of the styles, themes and voices of Doctorow's contemporaries.

The Jonathan of "A Writer in the Family" and "Live of the Poets" echoes the confession and complaint, the obsession with physical and psychological aches and pains, of the writers in Saul Bellow's *Humboldt's Gift,* Philip Roth's *My Life as a Man,* or Bernard Malamud's *Dubin's Lives*. "The Water Works" is reminiscent of the morbid, gothic, Kafkaesque tales of Joyce Carol Oates or Jerzy Kosinski. "Willie" combines Isaac Bashevis Singer's evocation of an Eastern European Jewish culture destroyed by the Holocaust with the highly charged, lyrical and impressionistic language with which John Hawkes treats sexual betrayal. "The Hunter" imitates the flat, gritty realism of failed hopes and thwarted possibilities that marks the stories of Raymond Carver or Jayne Anne Phillips. "The Foreign Legation" takes us into the upper middle class suburbs touched by frustration, fantasy and terror that we recognize as John Cheever and John Updike country. And "The Leather Man" combines the existential speculations of Norman Mailer with the fragmented forms of Donald Barthelme.

It is as if Robert De Niro were to offer an evening of perfect impressions of Laurence Olivier, Humphrey Bogart, Marlon Brando, Gary Cooper and Richard Pryor—and then close the evening with a stream-of-consciousness monologue about his life and the lives of his co-stars. In other words, it's an absolutely astounding performance.

III

World's Fair is a novel in the guise of a memoir. By labeling it a novel and then presenting it as a memoir in which his and his family's names are assigned to the characters, Doctorow focuses his reader's attention on the ways that both personal and collective histories are, at best, selective reconstructions built of fragmentary memories.

The book ends with its nine year-old hero burying a personal time capsule, in imitation of the one that he has seen on display at the 1939 World's Fair in Flushing Meadow. The capsule at the Fair had been designed "to show people in the year 6939 what we had accomplished and what about our lives we thought meaningful." The fictional Edgar buries his Tom Mix decoder badge with a spinner shaped like a pistol, his four-page handwritten biography of Franklin Delano Roosevelt, his M. Hohner Marine Band harmonica, two Tootsy Toy lead rocket ships, one of his mother's torn silk stockings, and a pair of prescription glasses with a cracked frame that belong to a friend. (He withdraws his copy of *Ventriloquism Self-Taught* from his capsule at the last minute and walks off in the book's last paragraph, practicing.)

World's Fair is another time capsule, by another Edgar, which combines mementos of the public and private experiences of a Bronx boyhood during the Depression. For this Edgar, ventriloquism—projecting one's thoughts, feelings, and words through imagined characters—is not a hobby but a calling. Like the boy's capsule, Doctorow's book is made up of both objects from the popular culture and personal, highly charged, images; like the capsule, the book is meant to provide a foundation for understanding the meaning of an era through cherished, carefully selected memories of a representative individual. By mixing the boy's limited, child's-eye view of experience with those of Edgar as an adult and the oral testimonies of his mother and older brother, Doctorow renders those memories multi-layered and appropriately complex.

Much of the pleasure of *World's Fair* lies in its lovingly recorded images of an era's sights and sounds. Edgar's world includes treats from the Sweet Potato Man; visits to Irving's Fish Store and Rosoff's Drugstore; excursions to Times Square for the frenzied rites of the "Flinging of the Textiles" and the "Try-On"; summer evenings by the radio, listening to shows such as "Easy Aces," "The Chase and Sanborn Hour," "The Royal Gelatin Hour," "Jack Benny," "Traces of Lost Persons," "Information Please," "Green Hornet," and "The Shadow," and commentators such as Fulton Lewis, Jr., Boake Carter, H.V. Kaltenborn, Father Coughlin, Gabriel Heatter, and Walter Winchell; Giants' games at the Polo Grounds; film serials such as *The Lone Ranger*, *Dick Tracy*, *Flash Gordon*, and *Zorro*; Little Blue Books; the Ringling Brothers, Barnum and Bailey Circus at Madison Square Garden; and, of course, the 1939 World's Fair.

Against the background, Edgar's private family history unfolds as a saga of two adored parents increasingly alienated from one another by conflicting temperaments and disappointed expectations. His father is a lively, charming character full of schemes that never succeed. His mother, embittered by her husband's irresponsibility and failure, grows old in the struggle to have the life that she imagined when they first met. Edgar, adoring them both, at first vaguely and then clearly aware of the gulf dividing them, takes on the role of mediator.

At the same time, Doctorow records the growth of Edgar's consciousness of the world beyond his family. He tags along behind his older brother and begins to learn about friendship, sports and sex. He enters school and begins to discover a route to success and acceptance through writing. He meets a girl and, through her and her mother, is introduced to romance and adventure. He begins to explore other neighborhoods.

His public and private lives converge at the Fair. Doctorow's World's

Fair is not the fair of vanity and facade of James Joyce's "Araby." It is, instead, a place where past, present and future coexist for a while in a harmony that is extraordinary. Edgar enters a writing contest sponsored by the Fair, and when his essay "The Typical American Boy" is awarded honorable mention, he gets free tickets for his family. Together they enter the wider world of the Fair and share a glimpse of the wonders its contains, setting aside for a day the tensions that divide them.

For the young Edgar, it is a lesson about the power of words and of art to change lives—if only for a while—a lesson about the power of imagination to shape history and reality. The lesson is one that another Edgar—Edgar Laurence Doctorow—has never forgotten.

Old Friends
John Updike

"We read to confront reality as mediated to us by another human mind," John Updike once told a Washington audience. But, he went on to say, all too often the contemporary American writer seems "baffled and disgusted by what would seem to be his prime subject, the daily life of his society . . . he flees to the woods, to abroad, to the psychiatrist's couch, to opium under one name or another, and seeks to shock, dazzle, taunt, or save his audience—anything, almost, but engage it in conversation."

Anyone who reads contemporary American fiction can make up a rather long list of the shockers, dazzlers, and taunters among our writers, but a list of the consistently engaging conversationalists who bring us meaningful perspectives on the way we live now would be much shorter. Updike, of course, would be on it. Like a witty and treasured friend who passes through town once or twice a year and stops by for an evening of drinks, dinner, and talk, since he first appeared in 1958 Updike has become a regular visitor. Like a friend he's had his off nights—but not very many. And even when he's been off he's usually still more enjoyable to be with than most of the people we know. In part that's because while, like any friend, he has his own interests and preoccupations, those interests and preoccupations aren't simply personal; we share them. When he visits, he always has something provocative to say about what's going on around all of us. And though he can be as relentlessly autobiographical as the rest of us, he never seems to forget that good conversation is a dialogue—that what we're thinking and feeling deserves his attention too. Finally, he's a great storyteller. Every time he visits he has new stories to share about people like ourselves; often, he fills us in on the latest happenings in the lives of characters we've come to know through tales he's told us about them before—characters like Harry Angstrom, Richard and Joan Maple, or Henry Bech.

For Updike, one of fiction's primary concerns is "the inner lives of hidden men." As he sees it, "the collective unconscious that once found itself in the noble must now rest content with the typical." And Harry "Rabbit" Angstrom is his typical man, the man he might have been if his talent during his Pennsylvania youth had been basketball instead of art.

He first introduced us to Rabbit in *Rabbit, Run* (1960). Then Rabbit was a twenty-six year-old unemployed ex-basketball player trying to come to terms with civilization and its discontents as they were experienced in Brewer, Pennsylvania in the late 1950's. Rabbit was torn by the conflict between self and society and felt himself about to be hemmed in by the life he was expected to grow up and live. He reacted as he'd learned to do when he played ball: when "they put two men on you and no matter which way you turned you bumped into one of them and the only thing to do was pass. So you passed and the ball belonged to the others and your hands were empty and the men on you looked foolish because in effect there was nobody there." Double-teamed by his wife and his mistress, by his desire for freedom and society's demands that he grow up and accept responsibility, by his sense of injured innocence and his sense of guilt, he passed off—he ran.

By the time Updike returned to his story a decade later in *Rabbit Redux* (1971), a lot had changed. While the Apollo astronauts are taking their first steps into outer space, Rabbit is firmly tied down by the limits of lower middle class life. He and his family have moved to a quiet suburb, Mt. Judge. But moving out of the city doesn't bring an idyllic life or save his family from becoming caught up in the maelstrom of the 1960's. Now it is his wife Janice who runs away in search of herself and Rabbit who defends society's values against the onslaught of demands for liberation and change. For in Mt. Judge Rabbit soon finds himself caught up in the decade's conflicts as he becomes involved with a young hippie named Jill and a small-town Black Power Messiah named Skeeter in a relationship that almost destroys him. A relationship that ends in violence and death. *Rabbit Redux* is a dark and depressed book, Updike's *Mr. Sammler's Planet*, and like Bellow's controversial novel, in retrospect it seems much more sensitive and complex than it did when it first appeared.

As *Rabbit Is Rich* (1981) begins, another decade has passed. It has treated Rabbit well. He and Janice are relatively happy, and their intimacy is one built up over years of shared pain as well as joy. Although Janice's father left Springer Motors to her when he died, he left Rabbit in charge of the Toyota dealership. In the novel's now—1979, in the middle of the gas crisis—the place has become a gold mine. Rabbit is making fifty thousand dollars a year, belongs to the country club, the Rotary, and the Chamber of Commerce, and his high school press clippings are yellowing on the wall of his office. "Life is sweet," he thinks. Of course, "he avoids mirrors, when he used to love them" and he can't help feeling that "running out of gas . . . the American ride is ending." But he also feels good about becoming a figure in the community again, about "casting a shadow."

Updike's preoccupations with sex, death, and religion are still present—but their immediacy is muted. Rabbit still has sex on his mind, but most of the time that's where it stays. He can't help but think of the dead—"Jesus, they were multiplying, and they look up begging you to join them, promising it is all right, it is very soft down here. Pop, Mom, old man Springer, Jill, the baby called Becky for her little time, Tothero. Even John Wayne, the other day." But mostly Rabbit is happy just to be alive. As for religion, the intimations of God that Rabbit once felt on a golf course are almost totally absent from the mind of his middle-aged self.

Instead, the crises he faces in this comedy are the crises of a prosperous twentieth-century American man in his prime: how to invest his money so as to outfox inflation, how to get his son to live up to his expectations of him, how to move to a better, more prestigious neighborhood. Few people remember Rabbit as he once was—in fact, most people call him Harry now. But his son Nelson refuses to forget or forgive Harry for the past. And ten years after the traumatic events of *Rabbit Redux* he seems ready to recapitulate the worst mistakes of his father's life—without the saving grace of his father's spirit. Harry is convinced that Nelson is bent on doing this to spite him, because of Jill, the hippie who died in their home. Like his father, Nelson marries a girl who's pregnant; and, like his father, he then runs when things get tough. But this is a quieter, more peaceful book than its predecessors. No one dies, and the worst dangers are caused by Nelson's minor accidents with the family cars.

If the tone in *Rabbit Is Rich* is more subdued and comic, Updike's eyes, ear, and voice are as impressive as ever. There is more of America in the first ten pages of this novel than in volumes published by other novelists, historians, and sociologists. The Iranian hostage crisis, the invasion of Afghanistan, the oil crisis, inflation, the "me" generation's turn inward—all are made vivid through their touching Rabbit's life. As he had once looked back on his years as a basketball star as a golden age, Harry now vaguely senses that, in spite of his prosperity, things around him are getting worse, not better. Here's what he sees when he looks out of the front windows of his showroom, for example:

> Across the highway, the four concrete lanes and the median divider battered by many forgotten accidents, stands a low building faced in dark cinder brick that in years since Harry watched its shell being slapped together of plywood has been a succession of unsuccessful restaurants and now serves as the Chuck Wagon, specializing in barbecued take-outs. . . Beyond its lot littered with flattened take-out cartons, a lone tree, a dusty maple, drinks from a stream that has become a mere ditch. Beneath its branches a picnic table rots unused, too close to the overflowing dumpster the restaurant keeps by its kitchen door. The ditch marks the bound of a piece of farmland sold off but still awaiting its development. This shapely old maple from its distance seems always to be making to Harry an appeal he must ignore.

Where Rabbit looked to the Mickey Mouse Club for advice on how to live his life in *Rabbit, Run*, in *Rabbit Is Rich* Harry turns to *Consumer Reports*. Where Rabbit once fled the ties that bound on an all-night drive to West Virginia, Harry now seeks the daughter he thinks he had by his old mistress, Ruth, in furtive drives to the neighboring town of Galilee. Everything is running down. And yet, by the end of the novel Harry has a grandchild, a new home in a better neighborhood, and a sense of peace about his life.

Ten years after *Rabbit Is Rich* Updike completed his saga in *Rabbit at Rest* (1990). Published in an Everyman's Library edition as *Rabbit Angstrom: The Four Novels* (1995), the tetralogy belongs in any time capsule designed to capture post-World War II American life and will be remembered as one of the most important achievements of twentieth-century American literature.

II

The Rabbit books alone assure John Updike a place in the first rank of American novelists. With his other books, they represent one of the most prodigious literary careers of our time. Counting the five books that he's written for children and the Everyman's Library edition of the four Rabbit novels, Updike published fifty books over the forty years between his first, the poetry collection *The Carpentered Hen* (1958), and *Bech at Bay* (1998). *Fifty.* And in his novels, stories, poems, essays, reviews, and art criticism, he has created a body of work that has indisputably established him as contemporary American literature's foremost "man of letters." No major writer in the history of American literature has even come close to this record of productivity, and very few have ranged as widely or written as many books worthy of a serious reader's attention.

Updike called his first collection of episodes in the life of Henry Bech "a book," referred to his second as "a semi-novel," has subtitled his third "a quasi-novel," and has labeled the audiobook made up of excerpts from the series *Bech at Bay and Before: Three Bech Novels*. However you describe the individual volumes—and they've given this reader so much pleasure over the past three decades that Updike can call them whatever he likes as far as I'm concerned—there is no doubt that the Bech trilogy includes some of the finest and funniest writing of Updike's career.

If the farewell gesture in the final paragraph of *Bech at Bay* means what it appears to mean—that with this book Updike is saying goodbye to Henry Bech as he earlier said goodbye to Richard and Joan Maple in *Too Far to Go* (1979) and Rabbit Angstrom in *Rabbit at Rest*, we can only respond with a sigh of regret and a grateful backward glance.

His creator's productivity is something that notoriously blocked Henry Bech, who has published eight books in the fifty-six years since he published his first story, can only envy. For as Bech knows all too well, facing the blank page is never easy and often terrifying. How do you resist the distractions and temptations of a media-saturated, celebrity-obsessed culture and find the silence and solitude that writing requires? How do you cancel out the voices of your past and future critics so that you can hear yourself think? How do you start again, and again? What do you have to say that has not already been said? If you've written dozens of books, as Updike and some of his most important contemporaries have, what do you have to say that *you* have not already said?

Looking back over Updike's career, it is clear that—like Balzac and Trollope, Faulkner and Roth and Vonnegut, not to mention a host of popular mystery writers—one of the ways that he has faced the challenge of the blank page has been to revisit familiar characters and locales for inspiration. By the end of the 1960's, in fact, Updike had already discovered all of the returning characters who would keep him and us company for the next thirty years. Two of his earliest works, the poem "Ex-Basketball Player" and the story "Ace in the Hole," led him to *Rabbit, Run*, published in 1960. Richard and Joan Maple, who became the subjects of a series of semi-autobiographical stories tracing the arc of a marriage in *The Music School* (1966), *Museums and Women* (1972), *Problems and Other Stories* (1979), and ultimately *Too Far to Go*, were first introduced in the 1958 story "Snowing in Greenwich Village."

Bech at Bay is the latest result of a fictional journey that began when Henry Bech first appeared in the 1965 short story "The Bulgarian Poetess." Writing that story, Updike obviously found that Bech offered him a congenial way to explore aspects of the contemporary writing life that he had not had access to through his other characters. "What I saw through Rabbit's eyes was more worth telling than what I saw through my own, though the difference was often slight," he writes in his introduction to *Rabbit Angstrom: The Four Novels*. "His life, less defended and logocentric than my own, went places mine could not." Bech, on the other hand, is fun, he once explained in an interview, because the character allows him to write about someone more like himself, "permits me to write without holding back, without compensating for the character's mind."

Taken together, the trilogy follows Bech from his early forties to the age of seventy-six. Each of the collections includes both previously published stories and stories written specifically for the volume; each is anchored by a novella. Written as a sequence, they include internal cross-references, images and allusions that add to the pleasure for those who have read the previous books, yet each includes enough of the "backstory" to stand on its own.

Bech: A Book (1970) is probably the funniest in the series and may well have been the most enjoyable to write. The character and the premise are new. And the book, begun in the mid-1960's at the height of the vogue of contemporary Jewish-American writing, is a self-conscious act of literary *chutzpah*. Updike, the Gentile from Cheever country, invades the territory of his Jewish contemporaries and their creations, imagining himself as a deracinated, well-known but blocked, New York Jewish-American writer. From the foreword (a letter from Bech to Updike that trumps critics by stating many of their expected objections before they have a chance to comment) to the concluding bibliography (which wittily fleshes out the career described in the stories and also includes hilariously apt citations of imaginary reviews and essays by all of the major critics of the era), *Bech: A Book* is full of high spirits and low comedy, parodies and puns.

When we first meet Bech in "Rich in Russia" he thinks of himself as "artistically blocked but socially fluent," his reputation "grown while his powers declined," his life falling "deeper and deeper into eclectic sexuality and bravura narcissism." Instead of writing, he spends his time acting the part of a writer on State Department tours to Russia and Eastern Europe, during visits to college campuses, and at literary cocktail parties in London and New York. By the end of the decade covered by the book, he's traveled, had liaisons on several continents, suffered a breakdown, given pot a try, become expert at self-deprecating humor ("Am I blocked? I'd just thought of myself as a slow typist."), and failed to write another book.

In "Bech Enters Heaven," the last story in *Bech: A Book*, Bech recalls the reverence and awe with which he viewed the artistic vocation as a young man, describing how his mother took him to the heights beyond Harlem to watch from the balcony as a family friend became a member of the American Academy of Arts and Letters. In "Three Illuminations in the Life of an American Author," the first story in *Bech Is Back* (1982), Henry Bech attends another ceremony at the Academy, this time as a member who is receiving the Melville Medal, "awarded every five years to that American writer who has maintained the most meaningful silence." In the first half of this volume Bech continues his travels—to Korea, Ghana, Kenya, Nigeria, Tanzania, Venezuela, Australia, Canada, Israel, and Scotland—but Updike's inventiveness and interest in him occasionally flag.

In "Bech Weds," the novella at the center of the collection, however, Bech is revived. He marries the sister of his former mistress, moves out of the city into her mock Tudor home in Ossining and, two years later, delivers his fourth novel, *Think Big*, to his astonished publisher. The advertising campaign reads "BECH IS BACK . . . Fifteen Years in the Making"; the book, a melodramatic potboiler, quickly becomes a bestseller and makes Bech a millionaire at fifty-six. Of course, such success cannot go unpunished: his marriage immediately falls apart and he returns to the city alone.

Bech at Bay resumes the account of Bech's adventures in 1986 when he is sixty-three. In the seven years separating the episodes in this volume from those in *Bech Is Back*, Bech has published two books: a collection of sketches and stories called *Biding Time* and *Going South*, a novella. (Although it lacks the obligatory B's, "Going South"—in the vernacular, going wrong, falling apart, running down and out of control, nearing the end, dying—would be an apt title for *Bech at Bay*.)

The first story, "Bech in Czech," finds Bech on the road again. In pre-1989 Prague he again meets with approved and dissident writers; again he briefly falls in love with a young writer, as he had in "The Bulgarian Poetess"; again mocks the State Department officials whose largesse he enjoys. But Bech does, in fact, seem not only older but somewhat wiser. The Jewishness that he earlier dismissed weighs on him as he visits Kafka's grave and recognizes an anti-Semitism he always ignored before. And so does his sense of his own character. "More fervently than he was a Jew, Bech was a writer, a literary man," he thinks, "and in this dimension, too, he felt cause for unease."

> He was a creature of the third person, a character. A character suffers from the fear that he will become boring to the author, who will simply let him drop, without so much as a terminal illness or a dramatic tumble down the Reichenbach Falls in the arms of Professor Moriarty. For some years now, Bech had felt his author wanting to set him aside,

to get him off the desk forever. Rather frantically hoping still to amuse, Bech had developed a new set of tricks, somewhat out of character—he had married, he had written a best-seller. Nevertheless, and especially as his sixties settled around him, as heavily as an astronaut's suit, he felt boredom from above dragging at him; he was . . . an experiment whose chemicals were about to be washed down the drain.

In each of the remaining stories, Bech continues to try to develop new tricks, somewhat out of character, in order to amuse both his readers and his creator. In the end, they allow him to delay, but not escape, his fate.

The two novella-length stories "Bech Presides" and "Bech Noir" are the comic highlights of the book. In "Bech Presides," Bech can no longer read other writers for more than a page or two, and every time he enters a room he scans its bookshelves for his own works. At bottom, he thinks, "he didn't like any of his contemporaries' work."

> It would have been unnatural to: they were all on the same sinking raft, competing for dwindling review space and demographic attention. Those that didn't appear, like John Irving and John Fowles, garrulously, Dickensianly reactionary in method seemed, like John Hawkes and John Barth, smugly, hermetically experimental. O'Hara, Hersey, Cheever, Updike—suburbanites all living safe while art's inner city disintegrated. And that was just the Johns. Bech would not have minded if all other writers vanished, leaving him alone on a desert planet with a billion English-language readers.

Although he has always seen himself as an inveterate outsider and critic of social pretension, Bech agrees to serve as president of a sclerotic Academie Francaise-like group called the Forty which is in the process of falling apart. Bech's brief term in office, together with his rivalry with a prickly and prolific contemporary, Izzy Thornbush, give Updike the chance to make lighthearted comedy of the backbiting and pretension that characterize so much of the cultural scene. "There are no more composers," one old member of the Forty declares. "There is only electronic tapes! That is all the young musicians care about! To elect one of them would be to elect a machine." "Painting now is all crap," declares another, "victim art with stick figures. Ever since Kiefer and Kienholz hit it big, atrocities are all you get." "How do you feel, Bech?" a writer asks when the subject of fiction comes up. "I confess, ladies and gentlemen . . . that new fiction makes me tired. All that life that isn't mine."

"Bech Noir" is an over-the-top wish-fulfillment fantasy in which Bech and his latest young woman, nicknamed Robin, become caped and masked avengers dedicated to ridding Gotham—and beyond—of the critics who have done Bech wrong over the years. All of the creativity that he has been unable to channel into his art is suddenly unleashed on his enemies (the aptly named quartet Featherwaite, Frueh, Cannon, and Cohen) and on adopting the language and attitudes of the hard-boiled detective stories, B movies, and comics of his youth. As the story ends, four critics have been given their just rewards and Bech, now seventy-five, is reinvigorated and ready to begin a new life with Robin.

"Bech and the Bounty of Sweden," which rounds out the collection and the trilogy, appears to be Updike's fond farewell to his long-suffering character. Now the doting father of eight-month-old Golda, Bech is stunned to learn that he has been awarded the 1999 Nobel Prize for Literature. A tremendous honor, he thinks, in spite of the nearly-universal critical outrage . . . if only he weren't required to write an acceptance speech. A writer cannot denigrate his own characters, Updike once said, he can only love them. In "Bech and the Bounty of Sweden," and especially in its last pages, Updike is true to his word.

At first glance, Henry Bech and John Updike would seem to have little in common. Bech seems more anti- than alter ego. One is tied to the city, the other has lived for forty years in rural and suburban Massachusetts. One is notoriously blocked, the other notoriously prolific. One is Jewish, the other is a Gentile. One has spent most of his life single, the other has spent most of the past forty years married. One began his career identifying with the writers of *Partisan Review*, the other with the writers and cartoonists of the *New Yorker*. One is largely unschooled, the other went to Harvard and the Ruskin School of Drawing and Fine Arts at Oxford. One seldom reads, the other never stops. One is famously unfocused and undisciplined, the other has famously husbanded his time and talent. One writes melodrama, the other mainly domestic realism. One is incapacitated by his critics, the other is not.

Where Bech's first novel, *Travel Light*, is in the spirit of Kerouac's *On the Road*, Updike's second and third, *Rabbit, Run* and *The Centaur* (1963), were explicitly written to oppose that spirit: one portrayed the consequences of taking off, the other celebrated the virtues of hanging in. Where *Think Big* is a melodrama filled with gratuitous sex and violence, Updike's bestseller *Couples* (1968), which was also criticized as a potboiler, was much more: a treatment of the effects of the sexual revolution on mid-century marriage, family and social fabric.

Yet despite all these differences, Updike has also always seen Bech as a kind of alter ego. "Well, if you must commit the indecency of writing about a writer, better I suppose about me than about you," Bech wrote thirty years ago in his foreword to *Bech: A Book*. "Except, reading along in these, I wonder if it is me, enough me, purely me." After reading these accounts of his adventures, Bech says, he finds traces of Mailer, Bellow, Singer, Malamud, Henry Roth, Daniel Fuchs, Salinger and Alexander Portnoy. And also "something Waspish, theological, scared, and insulatingly ironical that derives, my wild surmise is, from you."

"Perhaps I share his faults," Updike told that interviewer years ago, "he wants his work to be absolutely right, and he frequently worries that nothing he does is ever quite good enough." Most of the critical comments applied to Bech's writing are drawn from those of Updike's detractors. ("He was afraid that his critics were right," Bech thinks in *Bech Is Back*. "That his works were indeed flimsy, unfelt, flashy, and centrifugal.") Both have been faithful to one publisher throughout their careers while upheaval and musical chairs have characterized the publishing scene around them. Both have traveled abroad and throughout America; both have overcome their reservations to make the media rounds when required, veering, as Bech puts it, "between the harlotry of the lecture platform and the torture of the writing desk." Both continue to see writing as a high calling. Both are steeped in American popular culture. And both write on Updike's army-green metal desk.

"By the way," Bech said at the conclusion of his foreword, "I never—unlike retired light-verse writers—make puns. But . . .I don't suppose your publishing this little *jeu* of a book will do either of us drastic harm." To the many readers for whom the 656 pages of the completed trilogy are a special part of the long shelf of Updike's books, this turns out to have been one of Henry Bech's few understatements.

III

In an imaginary interview that he gave to Henry Bech when *Memories of the Ford Administration* appeared in 1992, John Updike confessed that "Some time ago I reached the age when everything I did was, more or less, a sequel to something I had done earlier." Certainly this is true of *Licks of Love* (2000), a collection that consists of a series of remembrances of things past, of new stories on familiar themes in equally familiar settings.

"We have one home, the first, and leave that one," Updike wrote in his early poem "Shillington." "The having and the leaving go on together." Throughout his more than forty-year career, the rural Pennsylvania home that he left behind when he headed off to Harvard at eighteen has remained tremendously vivid to Updike, furnishing him with a physical landscape and a moral geography, a cache of memories and a cast of characters that have shaped some of his best work. In *Licks of Love*, the hometown that he christened Olinger and several of the alter egos that he invented in his earliest Pennsylvania stories reappear. "Lunch Hour" and

"The Cats" bring back David Kern, the character introduced as a boy in the title story of his second collection *Pigeon Feathers* (1962) and presented as an adult in the collection's concluding story "Packed Dirt, Churchgoing, A Dying Cat, A Traded Car." Allen Dow, the young protagonist of "Flight," one of the most powerful stories in that early collection, reappears as the unnamed narrator of one of this collection's most effective, "My Father on the Verge of Disgrace."

Characters from Updike's later work also return in these stories. Martin Fredericks, who was originally introduced in "Killing" (in the 1987 collection *Trust Me*) and returned in "The Journey to the Dead" in *The Afterlife* (1994), is the rueful reminiscing narrator of *Licks of Love*'s first story, "The Women Who Got Away." Don Fairbairn, of "How Was It, Really?" is the latest in the series of aging, nostalgic men whose names all begin with "F" who have populated a group of stories that Updike has written since the mid-1970's—men like Ferris of "Guilt Gems" and Fraser of "Domestic Life in America" in *Problems and Other Stories*, or Foster of "Still of Some Use," Fegley of "Learn a Trade," and Fulham of "The Wallet" in *Trust Me*. "His Oeuvre" is a Bech story that appeared in the *New Yorker* after *Bech at Bay*. ("Licks of Love" seems like a Bech story in disguise, with Henry Bech recast as a famous banjo player and renamed Eddie Chester, but still acting out his familiar roles of cultural ambassador and celebrity.)

Other stories in the new collection, such as "New York Girl," "Natural Color," "Scenes from the Fifties," and "Metamorphosis," do not revive former characters. Instead, they return to the New York City, suburban Boston, and Back Bay locales of most of his non-Pennsylvania stories, and treat subjects such as marriage, infidelity, and divorce among the middle and upper classes that Updike long ago claimed as his own in collections such as *The Music School* and *Museums and Women* and novels like *Couples*.

Aside from "Oliver's Evolution," an experiment in "snapfiction," each of the stories in the first half of *Licks of Love* offers the satisfactions that Updike's readers expect of his short fiction. "My Father on the Verge of Disgrace" and "The Cats" are among his best. The novella *Rabbit Remembered*, however, which makes up the second half of the book, is definitely the highlight of this charmlessly named collection. (It should have been titled *Rabbit Remembered and Other Stories*.) For the real news about *Licks of Love* is that Updike has begun his fifth decade as a novelist as he began each of the last four: by surveying the American scene in a novel about the world of Harry "Rabbit" Angstrom.

Since Harry died at the end of *Rabbit at Rest*, this is no small feat. When he published that book, which was described as the final installment of the series, Updike justified his decision to end Harry's story in a

Florida hospital as a product, in part, of his own intimations of mortality. Fortunately, at sixty-eight his energy and imagination show no signs of flagging: in the eighteen months between the middle of 1999 and the end of 2000 he published three books, including the 856-page *More Matter*, the ingenious and provocative *Gertrude and Claudius*, and *Licks of Love*. Since he had turned to Harry at the end of each decade of his writing life, when he reached 1999 in good health he naturally began thinking about him again. But how do you write a novel about a dead man?

Rabbit Remembered is Updike's audacious answer to that question. First, he realized that in the Rabbit novels he had imagined more than a life: he created a vivid tapestry of names, dates, places, characters, relationships, and family histories. A tapestry that did not fall apart when Rabbit died. In *Rabbit Remembered* he decided to write an appendix to the tetralogy, a coda in which he would revisit Brewer, Pennsylvania ten years after Rabbit's death and weave the final threads of the stories of the characters whose lives had been most intimately bound up with Rabbit's. Perhaps the most extraordinary aspect of this novella, however, is the second idea that Updike hit upon. Since Harry is unforgettable, larger than life, to those who knew him, Updike imagines him affecting his survivors' thoughts and feelings after his death as powerfully as he did when he was alive. So powerfully, in fact, that in an extravagant sleight of hand he makes sure that Harry appears—usually explicitly, occasionally implicitly—on every single page of *Rabbit Remembered*.

At the conclusion of *Rabbit at Rest*, Harry's wife Janice had just become a widow; his son Nelson had managed to lose the family's business, Springer Motors, through his drug addiction; Nelson's wife Pru had betrayed both her husband and her mother-in-law by spending a night with Harry—the episode that led to his fleeing Brewer for Florida and his last days; and Nelson, Pru, and their children—eight year-old Judy and four year-old Roy—were living with Janice in the Springer family home at 89 Joseph Street in Mt. Judge.

Rabbit Remembered opens in that house in September 1999, with two words that readers of the earlier novels will find a shock. "Janice Harrison," it begins, and it is immediately clear that Rabbit is not just dead: his place at Joseph Street has been taken by Ronnie Harrison, his rival for forty years. While the reader is still adjusting to this shock Janice gets one of her own. A young woman named Annabelle Byer appears at her front door to announce that she is Harry's daughter by Ruth Leonard Byer, the woman with whom he had his first affair in *Rabbit, Run*. Soon, Nelson reappears, and the novella unfolds through Thanksgiving, Christmas, and the millennial New Year from the point of view of these three survivors.

Nelson is now forty-two, just four years younger than Harry was in *Rabbit Is Rich* (1981). In the last two books of the tetralogy Nelson became an increasingly annoying and self-destructive figure who inherited all of Harry's narcissism and none of his grace. By the time *Rabbit Remembered* begins, however, he has grown up. Less petulant, less selfish, less self-pitying, more reflective and self-aware, he is now a more sympathetic, even intriguing, character. Since Harry's death he's left drugs behind, earned a counseling certificate from the local community college, and become a mental health counselor at the Fresh Start Adult Day Treatment Center in Brewer. (Nelson's becoming a counselor to others is nearly as shocking a development as Janice's second marriage, but Updike makes it believable.) Although he and Pru are separated, and she has taken their two children and returned to her hometown of Akron, Ohio, Nelson remains connected to them through the e-mails he exchanges with his now fourteen-year-old son Roy. When Annabelle appears, he is the one who accepts her as a sister and a link to Harry and tries to protect her as he was unable to protect his drowned sister Becky.

All of the recurrent stylistic and thematic elements of the Rabbit novels reappear in *Rabbit Remembered*. The story is told in the same present tense, and marked by the same form of interior monologue, as the earlier books. The locations are the same. The focus is once again on children and parents, on immediate and extended families, on domestic entanglements and conflicts. Allusions to the news at the time that the book is set are, again, pervasive—in this case, they include references to the Clintons, the Lewinsky scandal, the death of John F. Kennedy, Jr., Elian Gonzalez, the crash of an Egypt Air flight, the Y2K panic, Hurricane Floyd, *The Vagina Monologues*, and more. Cultural changes—the spread of ATM's, the emergence of e-mail as a form of communication, the Internet, the rise of dot.com companies—are, as always, duly noted. Like their father, Nelson and Annabelle defend the President against all detractors. Sex and death are still on the characters' minds, while infidelities, divorces, and separations—here as memories and topics of conversation, rather than as current events—again shape the action. The offhanded bigotries of Harry and his circle echo in the comments and attitudes of their children.

Internal references to incidents and motifs of the four novels are extensive and often subtle. In *Rabbit Is Rich* and *Rabbit at Rest*, for example, Nelson's recklessness and rebellion lead to a series of car accidents—episodes that are ironically echoed for the reader who remembers them in the near-fatal crash at the end of *Rabbit Remembered*. *Rabbit, Run* began with an epigraph from Pascal that suggested the contradictory elements that would animate the series: "The motions of Grace, the hardness of heart; external circumstances." Just before he meets Ruth for the first time Rabbit feels as if he's at one with the universe: "*He* is the Dalai Lama," he thinks. *Rabbit Remembered* ends with Nelson quoting the first page of another book, *The Art of Happiness*: "The very motion of our life is toward happiness." The words are the Dalai Lama's. The journey from the first quote to the second is the path that the five Rabbit tales recount.

Updike has now rewritten the ending of the Rabbit series, concluding it on a note of comedy, and this feels right, in keeping with the tone of all the earlier books except *Rabbit Redux*. By the final section of *Rabbit Remembered*, titled "And Beyond," everyone is forgiven, romance flourishes, lovers are reunited, a wedding is imminent—and the characters the reader has come to care about are all left as hopeful and safe as can reasonably be expected in a world of flawed human beings and constant contingency.

"The misery of the world," Nelson tells Annabelle. "That's what I kept thinking during my group this morning—the pity of everything, all of us, these confused souls trying so pathetically hard to break out of the fog—to see through our compulsions, our needs, as they chew us up." The fog is certainly still there at the end of both *Rabbit Remembered* and most of the stories in *Licks of Love*. Souls are still confused. But in these mellow stories the misery has been replaced—at least temporarily—by John Updike's sense of the consolations of memory and the surprising possibilities of even the most mundane life.

II

A Father's Words
Richard Stern

When the American Academy and Institute of Arts and Letters selected Richard Stern as the recipient of its Medal of Merit in February 1985, most of the body of work for which he was being honored was out of print. Two years later, when the University of Chicago Press issued a Phoenix Fiction reprint of *Golk* (1960), the majority of his novels—including *In Any Case* (1962; reissued as *The Chaleur Network*), *Stitch* (1965), *Other Men's Daughters* (1973), *Natural Shocks* (1978), and *A Father's Words* (1986)—were once again available both to those who have admired his work for years and those who were just discovering it. And how much there is to admire and discover.

"Novelists count only as they are distinct from other novelists," Stern once wrote. "Everything that is different about them becomes their stock in trade." The republication of *Golk* invites us to consider what the distinctive character of Richard Stern's own fiction has been; and re-reading *Golk* in relation to his other novels makes that character clear.

Golk is a first novel, and it shows. While it introduces a narrative voice that will shortly become recognizable, that voice is not yet fully under control; while it sketches what will become Stern's recurrent themes, conflicts, and character types, these have not yet been given their mature forms. So in *Golk* we can see Stern struggling to create a voice that will allow him to mix the street and the library, what he has seen and heard and what he has read and thought. That distinctive narrative voice is already largely here and largely successful. But the struggle is apparent in the novel's few false notes—in what now appears offensive in the treatment of the black woman, Elaine, and artificial in the love scenes of Hondorp and Hendricks. By his third novel, *The Chaleur Network*, such false notes will have disappeared entirely.

What will emerge as the persistent concerns of Stern's mature fiction—the challenges of change, the burdens of moral responsibility, the nature of fatherhood and the emotional entanglements of the domestic life, a fascination with power—are also already evident. But in *Golk* these concerns are uncharacteristically combined with a wildly comic satire of television. And the satire is so good that it all but overwhelms Stern's focus on the Hondorps and Golk.

In *Golk*, these characteristic concerns and this satire are interwoven from the novel's opening pages, where Stern's first hero Hondorp, an unemployed observer of life and pampered son, is suddenly drawn into the world of the popular television program "You're On Camera" and its creator, Golk. But the wit and insight of Stern's treatment of what was then the relatively new medium of television often makes Hondorp's conversion from an observer of life into a participant seem secondary. In fact, twenty-seven years after its initial publication, *Golk* remained noteworthy as one of the first—and, with Jerzy Kosinski's *Being There*, still one of the few—treatments of the character and impact of television in serious American fiction. Its moving and hilarious portrait of Poppa Hondorp, mesmerized in front of the screen; its black comic treatment of the world of ratings battles, midlevel media managers, and godlike network moguls that would later be captured in the film *Network*; its witty demonstration of how this powerful new medium quickly began to create its own language; its exploration of Golk's and Hondorp's Faustian bargains with the medium—all retain their freshness.

While the satire of television dominates *Golk*, Stern's first novel nevertheless provides an introduction to the concerns that would follow it. In its fascination with power—the power of television, of Golk and, on an infinitely higher level, of Parisak, the empire builder who sits atop the midtown Manhattan skyscraper that bears his name in an office hermetically sealed and fully, magically, automated—it touches on a subject that will continue to intrigue Stern throughout his career.

In *Golk* we can also detect Stern's first treatment of other themes that will emerge to dominate his subsequent fiction. All of Stern's novels focus on characters confronted with jarring changes—changes that disrupt their equilibrium and challenge their sense of themselves and their closest relationships. "Life surprised me," his Professor Merriweather will explain to the father of the young woman with whom he is having an affair in *Other Men's Daughters*. "Life still had surprises up its sleeve. (Sometimes it seemed all sleeve.)" Cy Riemer will echo in *A Father's*

Words. And what will be true for these later heroes is also true for Hondorp, from the moment that Golk finds him browsing in a bookshop until the novel's final pages.

In Hondorp's case, life's surprise is an unexpected chance to be somebody and do something after years of floating aimlessly. For him, as for the later heroes, that surprise quickly turns into a moral challenge. How far will Hondorp be willing to go in pursuit of the main chance? How will he respond when his newly-discovered desires and ambitions come into conflict with what he owes to his father and to Golk?

As Fred Wursup will put the recurrent question in *Natural Shocks*, "How much of life do you owe to another person?"—"If you're a father, a husband, a son, a lover, a worker, how divide yourself, your sympathy, energy, time, money? Is the act of division itself treason?" "How much was one supposed to do?" Cy Riemer will ask as he lets his son walk away from him on a Manhattan street. "Sometimes I feel I'm nothing but my bonds," Riemer thinks in words that express what all of Stern's heroes feel at one time or another.

In Stern's fiction, the most important bonds are always those of fatherhood. Where Philip Roth's heroes are, above all, sons and Saul Bellow's heroes are, above all, ex-husbands, Stern's are most often and most importantly fathers. Like John Updike's or John Irving's, his novels are full of a parent's heartrending doubts and fears, a father's sometimes inarticulate but always profound feelings toward his children. And if *Golk* is atypical in that it focuses on a son's emotions rather than a father's, the book's father, Poppa Hondorp, and its other father figure, Golk, light up every page on which they appear in a way that often leaves Hondorp himself in the narrative's shadows.

The father-son relationship, Poppa Hondorp explains as he himself is being "golked" (by Golk himself), is "noble." Noble, but "packed to the margins, packed, impacted, with heartbreak.... The matter is not treason, just—how shall I say it?—a carelessness, inattention, lack of thought, but terrible, all terrible. Worse might be better. You would be stiffened to resist. But against so soft a thing, who can push?" And he goes on to compare a father's heart to an hourglass, in which filial love runs out "the thin neck of old age."

Poppa Hondorp is a classic of fatherhood, an unforgettable combination of warmth and self-pity, of affection and need, of possessiveness and manipulation. Although none of Stern's later fathers will be quite as funny, all will share his emotional attachments. "I was a terrible father to my son, at least until it was too late for him to know otherwise," *The Chaleur Network* begins. (If Hondorp had had more self-awareness, *Golk* might have ended with the place of father and son in the opening clause reversed.) "For me, family counted," Riemer explains in *A Father's Words*,

"Though I am not much of a son (and perhaps not much of a father)...."
The Chaleur Network traces a father's odyssey across post-World War II Europe in an effort to rehabilitate his dead son's reputation; in *Stitch*, Edward Gunther carries his twenty-two month-old son across a Venetian square, "kissing him on the cheeks and under the ear, muttering his name. This," he thinks, "is what counted." Merriweather describes holding his young son in bed as a purer moment of love than any other he has ever known; after his separation from them, Wursup climbs to the roof of his new apartment building to watch his children move about in the apartment across the street. And Riemer, Stern's masterpiece of fatherhood, sets off on a cross-country plane trip to see and try to make peace with each of his children.

But the fatherhood of Stern's heroes is complicated, as Poppa Hondorp's relation with his son is, by their own egos and desires. Like Gunther, each is faced with the question of why he "couldn't lose himself in what counted, what belonged to him, what was his human duty to assist and care for." Each, like Hondorp, finds himself struggling to accept his responsibility to those he loves. Each, like Gunther, seems stymied by the sense that "first he had to understand what he was" and realizes that "a rusty, backfiring, clotted ego" will not serve; that he must "clean out the heart." The cleansing is never easy, and Stern's novels are a record of its complications.

These complications may be traced, in part, to the fact that Hondorp and Stern's subsequent heroes are, like Gunther, "an unstable mixture of sensitivity and opacity"; that, like Wursup, each struggles with a sense that there are "glacial rifts" in him, "times when he was as unfeeling as the chemicals which made him." And each, again like Gunther, must struggle with "the irreconcilability of his attachments." For they are not only fathers, after all, but fathers met in the midst of or just after the breakup of marriages, about to be or just recently separated from their children. More often than not, they are already involved with, but unable to commit themselves to, another woman. And after his fathers and their children, the most important characters in Stern's novels are these new women and ex-wives. *Golk*'s Hendricks is a first version of the type: attractive, talented, strong-minded, yet somehow thwarted. Her sisters in the later novels will also be insecure and unbalanced by their lover's or husband's self-involvement. The dissolution of Hondorp's marriage, his failure to establish a relationship to which he can fully commit himself, sets the pattern for the many estrangements that will follow.

The familial struggles, paternal feelings, and moral quandaries of Stern's novels take on their distinctive character because of the particular nature of his settings—cities like New York, Chicago, Paris, Venice, Rome—and of his heroes. Urbane, witty, garrulous, highly educated, reflective, self-conscious, they allow him the broad range of cultural allusion his own erudition requires. Hondorp the autodidact is succeeded by Gunther, the failed theoretical physicist and amateur man of letters; by Merriweather, the physiologist and Harvard professor; by Wursup, the globe-trotting nationally-known journalist; and by Riemer, author and editor of a highly-respected newsletter. And their thoughts and observations, their voices, are the foundations upon which Stern's novels and their conflicts are built.

Like Bellow's heroes and Roth's, each of these men confronts the fact that familiarity with the great ideas of world culture does not necessarily make handling the mundane problems of the world's daily business of living and loving any easier. But because of their characters, their confrontations always turn out to be both engaging and revealing. Beginning with Hondorp, each of Stern's heroes grows, changes, learns. How they grow and change, what they learn, is what Stern's novels from *Golk* on have mainly been about.

"To be decent," Wursup thinks. "Just to be decent." This is no small ambition, Stern keeps telling us, but what ambition matters more?

II

Some novelists publish collections of their occasional prose because they can; others, because they actually have something to say. Reading the former we are subjected to a display of ego; reading the latter we are treated to a display of versatility in which a novelist's virtues of intellect and art make ephemeral essays and reviews worthy of renewed attention. Richard Stern's collections, which he has called "Ordered Miscellanies," fall into the second category. For while they may not be as memorable as his novels or his story collections *Teeth, Dying and Other Matters* (1964), *1968—A Short Novel, an Urban Idyll, Five Stories and Two Trade Notes* (1970), *Packages* (1980), or *Noble Rot: Stories 1949-1988* (1989), they are shaped by the same character and care.

"There is an omitted story in every miscellany," Stern wrote in the opening of *The Books in Fred Hampton's Apartment* (1973): "that of the observer-reporter(s) and its assembler(s). In some miscellanies much of the story gets told, and the result is autobiography." Though *The Invention of the Real* (1982) is much less directly autobiographical than either its predecessor or its successor, *The Position of the Body* (1986)—we learn something about where Stern has been and whom he has met over the past thirty years, but even the journal excerpts included in the book are mainly those of an observer rather than a diarist—it provides a portrait of its author nonetheless. Or rather, it demonstrates on every page the intellectual sensibility that makes Richard Stern the novelist he is.

The Stern who emerges as we read *The Invention of the Real* is a judicious critic, a man serious and passionate about books and ideas, personally reticent and witty; he is also a writer of fiction whose talents for isolating the telling detail and establishing a meaningful juxtaposition make all of his work a pleasure to read. The collection in which these qualities are displayed is anything but miscellaneous, in spite of Stern's label. Much of Stern's prose since *The Books in Fred Hampton's Apartment* is not included, while a number of pieces written earlier are. What is included is as carefully selected, arranged, and orchestrated as the scenes in one of his novels in order to present a series of variations on the book's title theme of the relationship between the written and unwritten worlds. Like a seasoned slugger, Stern comes to bat, blasts one long and hard, and rounds the bases with style, only to end where he began. He sprints to first with portraits of literary inventors like Pound, Bellow, Borges, Mailer, and Faulkner; takes off for second with pieces on the relationship between the literary and political worlds in Malraux and DeGaulle, C.L Sulzberger and Beckett, Nixon, Kissinger, and the Mandelstams; stumbles a little on the way to third with some straight political polemics on Jimmy Carter, inflation, the bicentennial, and the post office; and comes home strong with another, more personal, series of pieces on the art of fiction and his own writing. The Cubs should only do as well.

His critical judiciousness strikes this reader first. In the piece on Saul Bellow, for example, which originally appeared in the *New York Times Magazine* shortly after Bellow received the Nobel Prize for Literature, Stern brilliantly succeeds at staying on the right side of the thin line between providing unique insights into his old friend's character and revealing the confidences of friendship. In "Bellow in Five Hundred Words or Less," he succeeds just as well in isolating the special character of Bellow's fiction when he observes that "Balzac's heroes fight their way in and out of intrigues. Dostoevsky's tangle with ideological madmen. The Bellow hero fights windmills which look not like giants but like philosophers and wives." In the first sentence of an essay on Norman Mailer he writes that Mailer "is to American mental life what jet planes are to transport: familiar, remarkable, ubiquitous, powerful, rapid, noisy, and not altogether free of hot air." In a short review of one of Mark Harris's autobiographies he again captures the essence of his subject's character—a character that would later form the comic center of Harris's own book on Bellow, *Drummlin Woodchuck*—when he writes that "Harris is always being tipped off, educated, shown the way . . . . The biggest drama is the Harris strip show. Harris strips and strips." Every essay and review in *The Invention of the Real* has lines equal to these in insight and style.

Stern approaches political memoirs with a literary critic's eye and a concerned citizen's skepticism. As a result, he can appreciate and justly evaluate Henry Kissinger's literary ambitions in *The White House Years* at the same time that he recognizes his limitations as a policymaker and power politician. He can offer the telling observation that Nixon and Kissinger appear in Kissinger's mind as Don Quixote and Sancho Panza. He can investigate why Nixon's own memoirs are not the tragedy Nixon would have liked them to be, and then end his review with the memorable lines "Is *RN: The Memoirs of Richard Nixon* a good book? Does the earth have a good moon? It's the only one we have." His understanding of his own art and the art of his contemporaries comes through just as clearly in one of the best pieces yet written on the use of autobiography in modern fiction, "Inside Narcissus," and in a wicked and witty parody of contemporary experimental writing called "Prose-Thumbing."

For meaningful and original juxtaposition, readers need only consider "Fundamentals, Symmetries and the Germans." Stern begins by describing how he listened to the physicist Werner Heisenberg lecture at the University of Chicago while "Nixon's Germans" were resigning in Washington. And where he takes that coincidence is almost as fascinating as where he takes a chance encounter with a sad little black boy in Hyde Park in an essay called "The Nixinger Doctrine." In both cases, and throughout this collection, a turn of mind, a shift in attention, leads to insights as striking as those which mark Stern's best fiction.

His passion for books and ideas underlies the entire collection, but it is perhaps most striking in the short introduction to an interview he conducted with Jorge Luis Borges. The interview itself is fascinating, but Stern's description of visiting Borges in his Buenos Aires apartment is what this reader will remember as characteristic of the mind behind *The Invention of the Real*. "I returned to the little apartment on Maipu to read Browning and Rosetti to him," Stern writes. "The reading excited us immensely. He called out lines, said, 'You see, you see, it's the Devil,' or gripped my arm and cried *'Que lindo, que lindo.'* The poem that rocked us was 'Childe Roland to the Dark Tower Came.' . . . When an old lady walked into the room, I did not, would not, stop. We were within the poem and couldn't break out. Together, Borges and I chanted the last line."

Passionate Partiality
Susan Sontag

Susan Sontag is an enthusiast and an explorer, a partisan and a provocateur. She is also a constant challenge and disconcerting anomaly to those who want their writers easy to pigeonhole, tag, and file. A film critic and filmmaker, literary critic and experimental fictionist, historian of ideas and cultural journalist, social critic and political activist, she has as much—perhaps more—in common with writers like Roland Barthes and Walter Benjamin, of whom she has written with such sympathy and understanding, as she does with the New York intellectuals with whom she is usually linked. She has cultivated an eclecticism that is rare among American writers. And although she carries an American passport, her most profound allegiance has always been to the tradition of the cosmopolitan European intellectuals who have been both her models and her most congenial subjects.

She has written so much, and about so much, that no single selection of her work has fully displayed the breadth of her interests or the subtle and not so subtle modulations that the key terms in her thought—*style* and *sensibility*, *mind* and *consciousness*, *passion* and *intellect*, *morality* and *modernism*—have undergone since she first attracted attention with the essays collected in 1966 as *Against Interpretation*. Since then there have been many Sontags. The Sontag whose flashy early essays on happenings, science fiction, the "new sensibility" of the Sixties, and "camp" helped to make popular culture an acceptable subject for serious critical discussion in journals such as *Partisan Review*, *Commentary*, and *The*

Nation. The Sontag who established her reputation by attacking the substitution of interpretation for experience and intellect for emotion, and went on to become one of America's most passionate interpreters and intellectuals. The Sontag who seemed to begin as an aesthete who dismissed the importance of morality in art, but turned out to be a critic for whom aesthetics and morality are inextricably linked. The Sontag whose early essays on camp, happenings, and the "new sensibility" earned her a reputation as an exponent of popular culture, but whose most characteristic essays have been appreciations of high culture heroes and "exemplary sufferers" such as Simone Weil, Antonin Artaud, Benjamin, Elias Canetti, Barthes, Jean-Luc Godard and E.M. Cioran. The Sontag who has practiced what she has preached—called for a new fiction and written it; expanded our understanding of film, and written and directed films herself. The Sontag whose politics made her a leading voice of the American Left in the Vietnam era and its pariah following her Town Hall speech in 1982. The Sontag whose principles led her to speak out immediately in defence of Salman Rushdie in the wake of the Ayatollah's *fatwa* and to spend a large part of several years of the war in Bosnia living and working in Sarajevo.

Election to the American Academy and Institute of Arts and Letters; MacArthur, Guggenheim, Rockefeller and other distinguished fellowships; a National Book Critics Circle Award; the presidency of the PEN American Center—all testify to her status as one of America's most influential and honored intellectuals. Constant references to her work by other critics over the last thirty-five years—some positive, some negative, all impassioned—reinforce this judgment. And popular culture has echoed these assessments through its own references: in feature articles everywhere from *Time, Newsweek,* the *New Yorker,* and *U.S. News and World Report,* to *People, Vanity Fair, New York Woman,* and *USA Today*; and in films like Woody Allen's *Zelig* and Ron Shelton's *Bull Durham.*

The essay written in response to a book, a film, a photograph, a play, an event—as many of Susan Sontag's early essays were—has a notoriously short half-life. And a critic like Sontag, whose commitment has been to the avant-garde, is always in danger, and often accused, of mistaking the new for the important. One way of evaluating such a critic's intelligence and imagination is to reread her work to see how it stands up after the occasion that prompted it has faded; one way of assessing her importance is to reread her work to see whether the trends she has been drawn to examine, the figures she has been the first (or one of the first) to identify as significant, seem in retrospect to have been the ones really worthy of attention. On both counts, Susan Sontag's work cannot help but impress us.

Of the twenty-six pieces collected in *Against Interpretation*, for example, only one—a theater chronicle—now seems dated. Though she has since modified and complicated many of the views expressed in those famous early essays, even the briefest of them still has the power to surprise and engage. And no one has been better at spotting the trends and figures that those who care about contemporary culture need to note. She brought news from Paris of structuralism, Levi-Straus, and Roland Barthes long before they became the foundations of a new academic orthodoxy; she defined and explored the postmodern sensibility before it had a name. Twenty years before Ihab Hassan's *Paracriticisms*, her "Notes on Camp" experimented with a more playful form of criticism. When John Barth was still writing *The End of the Road*, she was already writing and writing about experimental fiction. When Elias Canetti received the Nobel Prize in 1981, one of the few pieces of major criticism on him in English was her "Mind as Passion." And many of her essays—"Syberberg's Hitler" and "Fascinating Fascism" come to mind—were not only the first but remain the definitive treatments of their subjects. Again and again, in other words, she has brought her readers the genuine news, not just the novelties, of contemporary Western culture.

After fifteen books, several dozen uncollected essays and stories, three films, and more than three decades of publication, Susan Sontag is still probably best-known as the author of *Against Interpretation*. The book remains one of the more stunning critical debuts in American literary history. By the time it appeared in 1966, several of the essays it collected—"Notes on Camp," "Against Interpretation," "On Style"—had already attracted attention and begun to establish Sontag's reputation as one of the most important and most controversial critics of her generation. When the collection was published, Ted Solotaroff recalls, "almost every reviewer seemed compelled to stand up and be counted as to whether Miss Sontag was a culture hero or villain, the lovely, brave Minerva of a genuine new underground/avant-garde or the glib bootlegger of the latest wave of French modernism, East Village Pop, and other modes of the higher unseriousness."

Attitudes toward her and her subsequent work still divide along similar lines and, as often as not, are rooted in the commentator's attitude toward the positions she stated—or is viewed as having stated—in the most famous of these early essays. Of all the book's first reviewers, Benjamin DeMott and Jonathan Baumbach now seem the most prescient. "At the end of the sixties," DeMott predicted, *Against Interpretation* "may well rank among the invaluable cultural chronicles of these years." The book, Baumbach said, should be viewed as "an autobiography of a sensibility."

In her note to the first paperback printing of the collection, Sontag revealed how perceptive Baumbach's description had been. The essays collected in the book, she explained, were mainly written between the time when she finished *The Benefactor* (1963) and began her second novel, *Death Kit* (1967). "The energy, and the anxiety, that spilled over into criticism had a beginning and an end," she wrote; and "that period of search, reflection, and discovery already seemed somewhat remote" to her at the time of *Against Interpretation*'s initial American publication. She did not view most of the essays as "criticism proper," she said, but as a kind of "meta-criticism." In them, she recalled, she was writing "with passionate partiality, about problems raised for me by works of art, mainly contemporary, in different genres; I wanted to expose and clarify the theoretical assumptions underlying specific judgments and tastes. Although I did not set out to devise a 'position' about either the arts or modernity, some kind of general position seemed to take shape and to voice itself with increasing urgency no matter what particular work I wrote about."

Although she admitted that she already disagreed with some of what she had written several years earlier, she explained in the note, she decided not to make revisions for the paperback edition because she felt that whatever value the essays had, "the extent to which they are more than just case studies of my evolving sensibility, rests not on the specific appraisals made but on the interestingness of the problems raised." She wrote the essays as "an enthusiast and a partisan," she explained, and, for her, at least, they had "done their work" because her conception of her tasks as a novelist had radically changed. "Before I wrote the essays I did not believe many of the ideas espoused in them; when I wrote them, I believed what I wrote; subsequently, I have come to disbelieve some of these same ideas again—but from a new perspective, one that incorporates and is nourished by what is true in the argument of the essays. Writing criticism has proved to be an act of intellectual disburdenment as much as intellectual self-expression."

The autobiographical impulse behind the essays in *Against Interpretation* links the collection to her other books—each of which has grown out of similar sources. And the tentativeness with which she viewed her own formulations just a year after the collection appeared has continued to be a crucial element of her sensibility. But her readers, both then and now, must be forgiven if her tentativeness is not what strikes them most about the essays in *Against Interpretation*.

The flash of her rhetoric, the breadth of her knowledge of and references to American and European art, literature, and film, the pugnaciousness of her attitude, the quotability of her aphorisms, the willfully intemperate tone of many of her assertions, the unique mixture of learning and wit apparent in her choice of subjects and her approach to those subjects—these are the elements of Sontag's early style that account for *Against Interpretation*'s initial impact and continuing interest. While that style immediately established her as a highly individual critical voice, it also firmly linked her to the tradition of the New York intellectuals associated with the *Partisan Review*.

Like the older generation of New York intellectuals, she was an exponent of radical politics and avant-garde art, viewed literature and the other arts as elements of a single culture of modernism, looked to Europe for her cultural heroes, demonstrated little interest in American writing and little patience for the close reading of literary texts favored by the New Critics, clearly enjoyed a good cultural fight, and saw herself as a free-lance intellectual unfettered by the specialization of the academy. But her perspective was also significantly different from that of most of the older generation of *Partisan Review* intellectuals, such as Philip Rahv, Lionel Trilling, Irving Howe, Dwight MacDonald and Mary McCarthy. For, unlike them, she exhibited no obsession with the political battles of the 1930's Left, was drawn to rather than put off by the new political radicalism of the 1960's, was intrigued rather than repelled by the "new sensibility" emerging among the young, refused to dismiss popular culture as wholly unworthy of critical reflection, and obviously did not feel that moral or political seriousness was always the only critical value. The differences between these two perspectives—between the older generation of New York Intellectuals and the younger, between the "Old" and "New" Lefts, between the culture of high modernism and the counterculture that later became known as postmodernism—became the basis for one of the central intellectual debates of the last decades of the twentieth century. As it did, Susan Sontag—whose sensibility seemed to combine both perspectives in an uneasy harmony—would emerge as an exemplary cultural figure instead of just another critic.

Though it included essays mainly written on assignment and published over a four-year period between 1961 and 1965, *Against Interpretation* also made an impression because it was unusually coherent for a collection. Its coherence grew out of both the individuality of its voice and the consistency of its intellectual position. The polemical character of that position was signalled by the book's title; its coherence was underlined by the collection's careful organization. Although *Against Interpretation* differs from her subsequent collections, each composed of a small number of long essays, it does not include everything Sontag published in the period of writing it covers; nor does it simply present the essays it includes in the chronological order of their initial publication. Its first section consists of two of the last essays to be written—"Against Interpretation," originally published in *Evergreen Review* in 1964, and "On Style," which first appeared in *Partisan Review* in 1965. The general argument they expound is then elaborated and exemplified in the collection's four remaining sections—one devoted to "exemplary sufferers" and literature, one to theater, one to film, and one to cultural attitudes and trends—and echoed, further refined, and concluded in the last two essays, "Notes on Camp" and "One Culture and the New Sensibility." In each of these sections, too, the order is thematic rather than chronological, so that one essay elaborates on or contrasts with the ideas explored in the next. And each of the four sections contains two kinds of pieces: essays that enthusiastically introduce the new, and essays that provide iconoclastic and fresh readings of the familiar.

Each essay on a book, a play, a film, an event or trend becomes an occasion for Sontag to examine the broader cultural questions that would preoccupy her throughout her career: questions about the relationship between form and content in the arts, the place of extremity in modernism, the nature of surrealism, the premises and possibilities of the novel, the proper standards for aesthetic judgment, the relationship between morality and art, the state of contemporary thought on the intellectual and political Left, the psychology of sexual and religious attitudes, the art of film. These questions and related ones thread their way through *Against Interpretation*, making each appreciation and each attack a part of a larger exploration of the ideas and issues raised in the four notorious assertions of critical and aesthetic principle that frame the collection.

II

In the midst of what Randall Jarrell once called the "Age of Criticism," Susan Sontag launched her collection and her reputation with a scathing attack on the state of contemporary critical commentary. In retrospect, it seems clear that at a time when the New Criticism dominated most literary discussion, the underlying premise of her book's first two essays—that separating form from content, and focusing on the latter rather than the former was a disservice to art—was hardly either revolutionary or controversial. The intellectual fireworks in "Against Interpretation" and "On Style" were caused, instead, by the authority and distinctiveness of Sontag's voice, the complexity of her views on the form/content distinction, and the way that she seemed to turn her discussions of this old critical chestnut into a wholesale challenge to both the fundamental values of Western liberal culture and the very enterprise of criticism itself.

Sontag's first voice lacks even a trace of humility or ambivalence. Instead, it insists on and establishes its authority through the extraordinary range of its specific and general references to literature, to art, to philosophy, to cinema, and to criticism. This range is apparent in the diversity of artists and subjects she treats, both in the collection as a whole and in its individual essays. Within the dozen pages of "Against Interpretation," for example, she refers to Homer, Dante, Wilde, Kafka, Mann, Beckett, Proust, Joyce, Lawrence, Faulkner, Gide, Rilke, Eliot, Pound, Robbe-Grillet, and Tennessee Williams; to cave paintings and DeKooning; to Plato, the Stoics, Philo of Alexandria, Aristotle, Marx, and Freud; to Jean Renoir, Cocteau, Bresson, Resnais, Truffaut, Godard, Bergman, Antonioni, Olmi, Ozu, D.W. Griffith, Cukor, Walsh, and Hawkes; to Auerbach, Barthes, Benjamin, Jarrell, Erwin Panofsky, Northrop Frye, Pierre Francastel, Manny Farber, and Dorothy Van Ghent. Almost every one of the other twenty-six essays demonstrates a comparable range of reference. The effect is staggering, and clearly distinct from cultural name-dropping. For while it is true that many of these references are simply mentions of a name, together with those that are not—references to a particular film by a director, a particular essay by a critic—they suggest that Susan Sontag is not simply familiar with the work of all of these figures, but knows them thoroughly enough to select exactly the right work from the *oeuvre* of any one of them to make her point.

The authority of Sontag's critical voice in these two essays—as well as in the later essays in this and her subsequent collections—is also the result of the same talent for memorably aphoristic phrase-making that she would later note and admire in writers such as Walter Benjamin and Elias Canetti. "Interpretation is the revenge of intellect upon art," she asserts; or "interpretation is not simply the compliment that mediocrity pays to genius"; or contemporary American novelists are "writing the literary equivalent of program music"; or "in place of a hermeneutics we need an erotics of art"; or "Art is seduction, not rape"; or "A work of art, so far as it is a work of art, cannot—whatever the artist's personal intentions—advocate anything at all"; or "Style is the principle of decision in a work of art, the signature of the artist's will."

Her own style vacillates between strictly controlled, logical statement and a pyrotechical rhetoric that obviously revels in its own hyperbole. "From now to the end of consciousness," she writes; or the doctrines of Marx and Freud "actually amount to elaborate systems of hermeneutics, aggressive and impious theories of interpretation"; or contemporary forms of interpretation are "reactionary, impertinent, cowardly, stifling"; or the "idea of content is today mainly a hindrance, a nuisance, a subtle or not so subtle philistinism." (In these first essays, "philistine" is her favorite epithet for those who do not share her views.) "Like the fumes of the automobile and of heavy industry which befoul the urban atmosphere," she writes, "the effusion of interpretations of works of art today poisons our sensibilities." While C.P. Snow's idea of two cultures rests upon "an uneducated, uncontemporary grasp of our present cultural situation. It arises from the ignorance of literary intellectuals."

"I get impatient with linear forms in which you go from a to b to c," Sontag explained in a 1988 interview with Richard Lucayo. "It takes too long. I love to go faster." The form of "Against Interpretation" reflects this characteristic of her distinctive critical voice. Unlike the usual critical essay, then or now, "Against Interpretation" does not pretend to present a seamless argument. Instead, like much of modern art, it consists of fragments. It is divided into ten numbered sections, ranging in length from several pages to a single sentence. Each of these sections develops an aspect of the subject, so that the effect is of a series of variations on a theme, jazz riffs, rather than the sequential exposition of a logical argument. In "Against Interpretation" the exposition is, in fact, sequential; but the form says that the young critic is in too much of a hurry to be interested in following the established conventions of the critical essay. The consequence is an immediacy that captures and holds the reader's attention. Several of the other essays in Against Interpretation—"Spiritual Style in the Films of Robert Bresson," "Godard's *Vivre Sa Vie*"—follow exactly the same formal model, as do later essays such as "The Aesthetics of Silence" or "Fragments of an Aesthetic of Melancholy." Most of Sontag's other essays in *Against Interpretation* and her subsequent collections incorporate variations on it. "On Style" uses basically the same form, but its sections are unnumbered and its exposition is much less sequential. "Notes on Camp" carries the form to its furthest extreme—a series of brief numbered points, with narrative connections between them totally abandoned. And in between on the formal spectrum there are essays like "Marat/Sade/Artaud," "The Imagination of Disaster," or "One Culture and the New Sensibility," in which shifts in tone or jumps in thought in an essentially traditional essay are expressed through unmarked divisions created by white spaces on the printed page.

The argument in "Against Interpretation" is consistent with its form. For Sontag does not simply attack the tendency of contemporary critics to focus on content rather than form, she attacks interpretation itself, the very essence of the critical project as it is usually understood. The kind of interpretation she feels art needs to be defended against, she writes, is "a conscious act of the mind" whose goal is "translation." The interpreter chooses pieces of the whole work and says "Look, don't you see that X is really—or, really means—A? That Y is really B? That Z is really C?" While interpretation began with the Stoics as an effort to "reconcile ancient texts to 'modern' demands," she argues, in our own time their piety toward the work of art has been replaced by an "open aggressiveness," by the same overt contempt for appearances embodied in the theories of Marx and Freud. The act of interpretation, she insists, "must itself be evaluated, within a historical view of human consciousness. In some critical contexts, interpretation is a liberating act. It is a means of revising, of transvaluing, of escaping the dead past. In other cultural contexts"—such as ours—"it is reactionary, impertinent, cowardly, stifling."

In the modern context, interpretation has become "the revenge of intellect upon art . . . upon the world." Real art—especially the modern art which most interests her—is difficult and challenging; in fact, it may be characterized by its capacity to make us nervous. Interpretation focuses on the content of a work of art, "explains" and "tames" it, thereby making the intentionally difficult and challenging "manageable, comfortable" and reducing an experience to an intellectual statement. Such interpretation violates art by making it "an article for use, for arrangement into a mental scheme of categories," instead of respecting its autonomous existence and often willed complexity.

In Sontag's view, the power of such interpretation has become so great that much of modern and contemporary art can be seen as shaped by it. Its influence drives avant-garde and arriere-garde alike. In response to it, avant-garde artists have sought to foil interpretation through parody, or abstraction, or mere decoration, or creating works that seem to be non-art, or increasingly radical experiments with form. Thus abstract painting attempts to undermine content; and Pop Art uses content so blatant it "ends by being uninterpretable." American fiction and drama, on the other hand, have allowed themselves to be so tied to the accessibility and interpretability of the mimetic tradition that they have largely eschewed formal experiment. As a result, the American sense of what may be done with form in fiction, for example, has remained "rudimentary, uninspired, and stagnant."

It should be possible, Sontag says, "to elude the interpreters . . . by making works of art whose surface is so unified and clean, whose momentum is so rapid, whose address is so direct that the work can be . . . just what it is." It happens in films, she writes, and this is why "cinema is the most alive, the most exciting, the most important of all art forms right now." Because films have been viewed as popular rather than high culture, they have been "left alone by most people with minds"; and because of their technological component, they have required their critics to develop a "vocabulary of forms."

She concludes "Against Interpretation" by briefly describing what a criticism that would "serve the work of art, not usurp its place" might look like. It would pay more attention to form, would develop a descriptive rather than prescriptive vocabulary of forms, and would "dissolve considerations of content into form"; it would supply "a really accurate, sharp, loving description of the appearance of a work of art"; and it would value "the thing in itself."

"Ours is a culture based on excess, on overproduction," she writes in one of the many passages in this first book where aesthetics and politics come together; "the result is a steady loss of sharpness in our sensory experience." And this is the historical context, she believes, in which the task of the contemporary critic must be assessed. Rather than replace works of art with interpretations, rather than turn the experience of art into another intellectual exercise, critics should help us "to *see* more, to *hear* more, to *feel* more," to "cut back content so that we can see the thing at all." Consequently, she concludes, the "aim of all commentary on art now should be to make works of art—and, by analogy, our own experience—more, rather than less, real to us. The function of criticism should be to show *how it is what it is*, even *that it is what it is*, rather than to show *what it means.*"

More than thirty years after it first appeared, "Against Interpretation" is one of the most frequently quoted critical statements of the postwar period. To its credit or to its shame—depending on one's critical allegiances—it is now generally recognized as a harbinger of much that was to come after it. By linking its attack on the nature of contemporary critical discourse to dominant political and cultural ideologies, it presages the movement in critical theory from the New Criticism which dominated literary discussion in the 1940's and 1950's to the structuralist, deconstructionist, feminist, new historicist, and Marxist perspectives that claimed it in the 1970's and 1980's. In its description of the variety of strategies that artists use to foil interpretation, the essay forecasts both the character and the increasingly rapid pace of the succession of movements in the arts that have come to characterize the postmodern sensibility. And by emphasizing sensual experience over logical analysis, it expresses a commitment that would become central to the counterculture which was just emerging, and as yet unnamed, when it first appeared.

Her discussion of film in "Against Interpretation" is also a sign of things to come. Not only does it suggest an interest that would remain with Susan Sontag throughout her career, but it also reflects the emergence of film as a subject of serious intellectual discussion. When she wrote the essay, films were still widely ignored or dismissed as "popular culture" unworthy of serious critical attention by American intellectuals. Characteristically, the challenge of developing a critical vocabulary for examining the formal elements in film and the opportunity to write about an aspect of modern art and culture that intrigued and excited her led Sontag to devote nearly a quarter of *Against Interpretation* to groundbreaking essays on the aesthetics of film. It has also led to her including essays on cinema in each of her subsequent collections; and to her spending nearly six years abroad writing and directing her own films.

"Against Interpretation" also states, as succinctly as possible, elements of Sontag's own critical perspective that have not changed appreciably in the years since she wrote it. Her own work has dissolved

> "all thinking is 'interpretation' and she writes against interpretation, against thinking when applied to art (& perhaps other experiences as well)

considerations of content into those of form; has consisted of sharp, accurate, often loving descriptions of the trends, writers and works that fascinate her. Most often, this has led her to discussions of form and style as expressions of an artist's particular consciousness, and of the artist's consciousness as an expression of the particular intellectual context of modernity. What she calls the "classical dilemma" of modern Western culture—the conflict between mind and body which Freud explored in *Civilization and Its Discontents*—has remained one of the central concerns of her fiction, her essays, and her films. And so has her allegiance to the modernist aesthetic of difficulty that the essay defends.

"All thinking is interpretation," she would later acknowledge in *Aids and Its Metaphors* (1989). "But that doesn't mean it isn't sometimes correct to be 'against' interpretation." While she doesn't disclaim the essay today, Sontag did tell Charles Ruas that she now finds its argument "too assertively stated." (In fact, when they were compiling *A Susan Sontag Reader* in 1982 she reportedly suggested to Roger Straus that they leave "Against Interpretation" out. "You must be out of your mind," he answered.) Perhaps, she told Ruas, she feels this way because she "couldn't imagine writing it now," since it and most of the other pieces in *Against Interpretation* share a "first voice" from which she feels she has since evolved.

The youthfully brash and combative voice of "Against Interpretation" and her other early essays has been replaced in most of her later essays—*Illness as Metaphor* (1978), *AIDS and Its Metaphors*, and "Fascinating Fascism" are exceptions—with a more contemplative and appreciative, often even elegiac, one. And she has gone on to modify some of the views that this early essay expressed to engage in a species of interpretation that includes more than its share of commentary on what writers and works "mean." In fact, to a large extent her distinction as a critic has been to write essays that join what she called the "hermeneutic" and the "erotic." The result has been a body of criticism that the author of "Against Interpretation," reacting against the critical establishment of the late Fifties, might well have found an insufficiently pure compromise; but also one that the author of the rest of the essays in *Against Interpretation* was already practicing.

III

Although Susan Sontag's reputation is primarily based on her essays on modern culture and culture heroes, her first book, *The Benefactor*, was a novel, and she has continued to publish fiction throughout her career. In her second novel, *Death Kit*, the short story collection *I, Etcetera* (1978), and several uncollected stories published in the 1980's, she has been engaged in an ongoing effort to transform the passion and intelligence she has brought to her appreciations of other artists and thinkers into creative achievements of her own.

For nearly thirty years, the common critical opinion has been that she has not succeeded in this effort. Her fiction has been judged as too willed, too experimental, too claustrophobic, and too self-conscious an expression of the aesthetic positions she has taken in her essays. (The aptly titled story "The Way We Live Now," published in the *New Yorker* in 1987, has generally been viewed as an exception. One of her most powerful and accomplished stories, as well as one of the decade's most memorable and important, it captures the pathos and terror of the AIDS epidemic through a fragmented spiral of voices that expresses the emotional and psychological impact of a young man's dying of an unnamed disease on his circle of friends.)

Sontag, however, has never been very concerned with common critical opinion, about her work or anything else, and writing fiction is clearly what she has always most wanted to do. As her reputation as an essayist has grown, she has never stopped developing her own fictional voice; periodically, she has even expressed a desire to stop writing essays completely in order to devote herself full-time to fiction writing.

Until the 1990's, she was prohibited from doing so—by her habitual impulse to respond to things that excite, interest, or challenge her by writing about them; and by her situation as a free-lance intellectual who has depended solely on her writing, and occasional lecture fees, for her livelihood. The MacArthur Fellowship she received in 1990, the new four-book contract she signed with her publisher shortly thereafter, and the surprising best-seller status *The Volcano Lover* (1992) seem to have changed her circumstances enough that her first novel in twenty-five years should be seen as more than just another book. It is also a turning point that suggests what will come in the next phase of her career. On the evidence of *The Volcano Lover*, readers can expect a fiction quite different from her earlier novels, yet recognizably hers—a fiction that combines a newfound interest in realistic description, a capacity to engage the external world and explore other lives that *The Benefactor* and *Death Kit* sorely lacked, with the wide-ranging intellect, the literary and cultural allusiveness, and the flair for aphorism that her best essays have always displayed.

The Volcano Lover is the result of two decades of self-criticism and largely unpublished fictional experiments through which Sontag has sought to move beyond the style and perspectives of her earlier work to another kind of fiction. "I want to write fiction which is not solipsistic," she told Charles Ruas in 1982, "in which there is a real world, but I'm not drawn to the conventions of realism." A lot of her fiction, she went on to say, has focused on "different ways of expressing distress, perplexity, and alienation. It assumes too much about the world, and devalues the world in a certain way. One is always inside a head, but I think I can get the world into that head now." When *The Volcano Lover* appeared, she told Leslie Garis that she was "glad to be free of the kind of one-note depressiveness that is so characteristic of contemporary fiction. I don't want to express alienation. It isn't what I feel. I'm interested in various forms of passionate engagement."

Being "inside a head"—and an obsessed, alienated, depressed, distorting, and dream-driven head at that—certainly is an apt description of the experience of reading both *The Benefactor* and *Death Kit*. Both novels have their strengths and virtues as particular kinds of fictional experiments, but neither is remembered for its passionate engagement with anything but the formal possibilities of the genre and its narrator's self-consciousness. *The Volcano Lover*, which overflows with the passions of its author and its characters, is clearly something else entirely. The distance that she has traveled since *Death Kit* is apparent before the reader even opens the book: in the lush painting of Mount Vesuvius erupting before observers dressed in the clothing of an earlier age on the colorful jacket of a book titled in red letters; in the jacket's tongue-in-cheek photo by Annie Liebowitz of Sontag posed in a romantic swoon; and in the very idea that a book by Susan Sontag should be described as "A Romance." All of these aspects of the book seem highly conscious decisions, declarations of independence from both her earlier fiction and her established image as an erudite and intimidating intellectual.

The Volcano Lover lives up to the declarations. Although it is neither a romance that Sir Walter Scott would recognize nor the kind of best-selling bodice-ripper that goes by the name today, it is a story about various forms of passion, set in the past, and brought to life by its author's intense immersion in the life and customs of another time and place. It began in the early 1980's with an emotion: Sontag's excitement when, browsing through a bookstore near the British Museum, she discovered the engravings of Mount Vesuvius commissioned by Sir William Hamilton for a 1799 book on the volcano. She immediately bought sixteen of the engravings and then hung them on the wall of her apartment when she returned to New York. Later, she read a biography of Sir William. As a film buff, she also knew *That Hamilton Woman*, Alexander Korda's 1941 version of the story of Sir William, his wife Emma, and Nelson, which starred Vivien Leigh and Laurence Olivier. Visiting Berlin in 1989, as the Berlin Wall fell and a new revolution swept across Europe, all of this came together as she began a novel that would connect Vesuvius, these lives, and the revolutions of another age.

Her particular sensibility and enthusiasms did not just lead her to this story, they also shaped its form—a form most reminiscent of the novels of Milan Kundera. For Sontag, as for Kundera, the novel has never been synonymous with the tradition of realism. In her earlier novels, she explored its possibilities as confession and dream narrative; in *The Volcano Lover* she adopts a form that is best described by comments Kundera once made in an interview with Philip Roth. A novel, he said, is "a long piece of synthetic prose . . . Ironic essay, novelistic narrative, autobiographical fragment, historic fact, flight of fancy: the synthetic power of the novel is capable of combining everything into a unified whole like the voices of polyphonic music. The unity of the book need not stem from the plot, but can be provided by the theme."

Like Kundera, Sontag is at least as interested in exploring ideas and themes as she is in telling a story. The narrative voice that she has fashioned in *The Volcano Lover* is designed to allow her to range over the many aspects of present and past experience and culture that engage her. In her prologue, she suggests to her readers that beginning the novel will be like entering a flea market: "There may be something valuable, there. Not valuable, exactly. But something *I* would want. Want to rescue. Something that speaks to me. To my longings." Like Kundera's fiction, her novel combines novelistic narrative with a host of other forms—anecdotes, autobiographical asides, diary entries, philosophical speculations, historical notes, biographical essays, monologues, opera stories, and much more. Like her essays, it diplays the breadth of her interests and enthusiasms: through mini-essays on the nature of collecting, the value of antique vases, the lore of volcanoes, love, ways of telling jokes, the fate of beauty, the psychology of making lists, revolution, differences between classic and modern conceptions of art, melancholy, friendship; through allusions to *Tosca*, *Don Giovanni*, and *Cosi fan tutte*; through cameo appearances by Johann von Goethe, Horace Walpole, the Gothic novelist William Beckford, and the painter George Romney.

The novel's unity lies in its theme of the various forms that passion may take, but history also provides Sontag with both characters and a plot that any traditional novelist might envy. The characters are the British diplomat Sir William Hamilton, a dispassionate collector, volcanologist, and antiquarian, who has been posted to the corrupt court of the Kingdom of the Two Sicilies in Naples; Emma, his nephew's former mistress, widely reputed in her youth to be the greatest beauty of the age, who breaks the shell of his reserve, inspires passion for another human being in him for the first time, finds luxury, security, and respect when she becomes his second wife, and then loses everything when her beauty fades and she falls in love with Nelson; and Nelson, the age's most famous admiral and defender of monarchy, who struggles with the conflicting passions of love and duty. Their relationship provides the love affairs and intrigues that any book calling itself a romance must have, but their private story is also enmeshed in the public history of the democratic revolutions that swept over Europe in the late eighteenth century, and in the broader cultural currents of their time. This allows Sontag to move beyond the conventions of traditional romance or traditional realism into the wider intellectual exploration that fully engages her temperament and talents.

The major achievement of *The Volcano Lover* is that all of this works, and works well, because of the narrative voice that Sontag has devised. Throughout most of the novel that voice is her own: the voice of her essays, the voice of a thoroughly knowledgeable contemporary leading the reader through action and reflection, describing what these people looked like, cared about, thought, and said. The voice is comfortable and confident, and the reader follows it through the twists and turns makes, hardly missing the sound of other voices until the very end. Then, in the last section, the reader encounters a vernacular monologue by Emma's mother, Mrs. Cadogan, that is so beautifully conceived and executed, so salty and full of life, that it suddenly makes us feel the absence of other voices in the rest of the novel.

Nevertheless, *The Volcano Lover* clearly signals an exciting new phase of Susan Sontag's career. From its first page to its last, it displays talents that were not evident in her earlier novels and suggests that she has begun to find a novelistic form that is particularly suited to her sensibility and well-stocked mind. It would be great loss to contemporary intellectual life if she were to stop writing her provocative essays, but it will also be exciting to see where her renewed commitment to fiction takes her and her readers next.

IV

Eight years after *The Volcano Lover* readers saw, when she published the National Book Award-winning novel *In America* (2000). The form of *In America* also mixes realistic narrative, anecdotes, autobiographical asides, diary entries, letters, monologues, philosophical speculations, mini-biographies, historical notes, travelogue, and plot summaries of other works of popular and high art into an amalgam that is particularly suited to Sontag's interests and talents. Like *The Volcano Lover*, it is a novel in which she re-imagines the past from the perspective of the present, blending fact and fiction, real and invented characters, actual and imagined events. Again, the story involves a love triangle between a beautiful and famous woman, her husband, and her lover, all of whom are based on— Sontag says "inspired by"—real people. Again, the lives of these characters are revealed to us in a novel that recaptures another time and place; and again those characters' lives touch those of both invented characters and other historical personages who are cast as bit players in their story—in this case, the writers Henry James, Henry Wadsworth Longfellow, Oscar Wilde, and Charles Nordoff, and the actors Edwin Booth and Sarah Bernhardt. Sontag again pays particular attention to the circumstances of women's lives. She again begins and ends her book with bravura set pieces.

In retrospect, Susan Sontag's works seem to be not just a part of an ongoing effort to examine a series of key ideas but an expression of her own evolving sensibility. Certainly this is true of *In America*. It seems to have grown out of three projects that she worked on in the 1980's but eventually abandoned. The first was a novel, *The Western Half*, about Polish and Russian emigres in America that was inspired by her friendships with the poets Czeslaw Milosz and Joseph Brodsky. The second was a novel about divas of the 1920's. The third was a long essay about intellectuals and politics. But a reading of Carl Rollyson and Lisa Paddock's *Susan Sontag: The Making of an Icon* (2000), which appeared several months after *In America*, suggests that *In America*'s sources were even broader and deeper.

For example, Sontag's fascination with acting and the theater—one of the novel's major subjects—dates back at least as far as her college days, when she worked on undergraduate productions with Mike Nichols at the University of Chicago. It has continued to be evident over the years: in her experiments with writing and directing films from *Duet for Cannibals* (1969) to *Unguided Tour* (1983); in her directing theater productions of Pirandello's *As You Desire Me* in Italy in 1980, Kundera's *Jacques and His Master* in Cambridge in 1985, and Beckett's *Waiting for Godot* in Sarajevo in 1993; in her appearing (as herself) in Woody Allen's *Zelig* (1983) and speaking (as Sarah Bernhardt) in Edgar Cozarinsky's documentary *Sarah* (1988); and in her writing the play *Alice in Bed*, which premiered in Bonn, Germany in 1991.

Her interest in Poland is lifelong. Her maternal grandparents were Polish Jews, and as a child she avidly read biographies of Marie Sklodowska Curie, who became one of her first intellectual idols and inspirations. Throughout her career she has been drawn to the works and lives of émigré writers from Eastern and Central Europe like Walter Benjamin, Elias Canetti, Milosz, and Danilo Kis. In the spring of 1980, shortly before the first strikes that led to the creation of Solidarity, Sontag visited Poland for the first time on a State Department-sponsored cultural tour and saw firsthand that the ruling system was morally, socially, and financially bankrupt. And this visit, combined with her reading of Solzenitsyn's *The Gulag Archipelego* and her friendships with Milosz, and Brodsky, led her to reassess the lifelong sympathy for socialism that had led her and many others on the American Left to praise the Communist revolutions of Vietnam, China, and Cuba in the 1960's. Together, these experiences led her to see the rhetoric of revolution as hollow and the Communist system as dehumanizing. A judgment that she boldly and controversially stated at a forum for Solidarity at Town Hall in New York City in 1982, when she described Communism as "fascism with a human face." Finally, in the 1990's she returned again and again to war-torn Sarajevo, a late twentieth-century example of the same kind of ethnic, religious, and national conflict that divided Poland in the nineteenth century.

Sontag has always been a traveler, has always lived a transatlantic life. Her twentieth-century journey has been from the New World back to the Old, from West to East—from North Hollywood to Chicago to Cambridge to New York to Oxford and to Paris. A journey, she says in her autobiographical essay "Pilgrimage" (1987), from an adolescence spent in an American West that she found cultureless and stifling, from a place and time that she had to suffer until a new life—her "real life"—could begin in a cosmopolitan world elsewhere. For *In America*'s Maryna, the dream of a new life is just as fundamental a motivation, but the vectors are reversed: her nineteenth-century journey is from the Old World to the New, and she seeks change and fulfillment by coming to America, heading steadily westward from Warsaw to Bremen to New York to Panama and to Anaheim.

The art of *The Volcano Lover*, Susan Sontag has said, "is that these are real people, but I reinvented them giving parts of myself to each character." The same may be said of *In America*. Maryna shares Sontag's history of marriage at an early age to a much older mentor, of mothering an only son while trying to establish and maintain a career, of early acclaim, celebrity, and myth-making interviews, of surviving serious illness. She also shares Sontag's fondness for risk-taking and her willingness to revel in self-contradiction and arguing with herself. (Each leaves her art—fiction, acting—for a while, and then returns to triumph and gain wider acclaim by finding a new language and form.) Bogdan, the novel's intellectual, is another alter ego, and his diary entries are full of observations and assertions about the differences between America and Europe that seem to reflect Sontag's own views. Ryszard is its writer, and his reflections on his art also echo Sontag's comments on her own.

In America's story, inspired by that of the Polish actress Helena Modrzejewska, tells of the decision of a group of ten well-to-do Poles, led by Sontag's Maryna, who decide to emigrate with their children to California in 1876 to establish a utopian community. Each of the émigrés is seeking his or her own kind of new life and trying to leave aspects of an old one behind, and each sees America as the place where that dream can be realized. Maryna's plan is to leave the stage for a new pastoral life, but within a year the community has fallen apart and she finds herself heading for San Francisco where she hopes to begin her conquest of the American theater. She succeeds, becoming a media darling, a national celebrity, and the head of a traveling company that barnstorms throughout the United States on a private train. Bogdan, Ryszard, and the others who accompanied her from Poland have their own American adventures.

As she did in *The Volcano Lover*, Sontag captures the sights, sounds, and tenor of the era. The novel is packed with details of the period—with extended descriptions of the ocean voyage to America as it was experienced in both steerage and the upper decks; with a guided tour of the Centennial Exposition in Philadelphia; with brilliant set pieces describing the transformation of the isolated Polish mountain village of Zakopane into a tourist resort, the early years of Central Park, the feel of the streets of polyglot New York City a century after the Declaration of Independence, Chinese theater in San Francisco, and new inventions such as the telephone and the elevator; with an elaborate chronicle of the most popular plays and players of the day, the daily life of the theater, the profession of acting, and the age's version of our cult of celebrity.

As in *The Volcano Lover*, the novel is full of talk. And, as in the earlier novel, most of the time the main characters all sound the same. Once her American career begins and Maryna travels around the country, however, she meets a handful of deftly drawn characters who are as vivid and as individual as Emma's mother Mrs. Cadogan became at the end of *The Volcano Lover*. Characters such as the Polish con man Bruno Halek, the photographer Eliza Withington, the speech coach and companion Mildred Collinsridge, the theater producer Angus Barton, the personal manager Harry H. Warnock, the saloon-keeper Minnie Rance, the religious visionary Mrs. Winton, and the actor Edwin Booth, who are each more engaging and more memorable than most of the members of Maryna's émigré band.

The novel's prologue, one twenty-seven-page paragraph titled "Zero" that conveys the author's excitement at the prospect of beginning, is an absolutely breathtaking *tour de force*. In the first sentence, a narrator much like Susan Sontag crashes a party. In the second, through a single word of descriptive detail—"women in gowns and men in *frock* coats" (my italics)—she walks into the nineteenth century. Within the first ten lines she has transported us to Poland. And by the end of the first page we have been drawn into the novelist's imagination as she thinks herself into her story and plot. The prologue becomes a demonstration of how such an imagination works, as words and phrases like "I supposed," "But maybe," "because, say," "she would be," "It seemed to me," "if," "I guessed," "He would be, let me see," allow us to share in the process of invention. Without fanfare or pyrotechnical experimentalism, in an extraordinarily natural voice, Sontag becomes a time traveller and invisible woman, observing but unobserved, bringing the perspective of the present into a party in a hotel set in the past. And we travel with her.

"I thought if I listened and watched and ruminated, taking as much time as I needed," she writes, "I could understand the people in this room, that theirs would be a story that would speak to me. . . . even a long journey must begin somewhere, say, in a room. . . . They were ready to leave now. With a shiver of anticipation, I decided to follow them out into the world." Follow them she does and, with Sontag as a guide, readers will want to slip in behind her and join the parade.

The Tortoise and the Hares
Cynthia Ozick

Like runners, most writers have preferred distances. Cynthia Ozick is most at home in mid-length forms. Her most memorable fiction has been in *Bloodshed and Three Novellas* (1976), *The Shawl* (1989), and in the short novels *The Cannibal Galaxy* (1983) and *The Messiah of Stockholm* (1987). With few exceptions, the most impressive pieces in her first two collections of essays have been the ten- to twenty-page ones: extended examinations of Edith Wharton, Virginia and Leonard Woolf, Bernard Malamud, Harold Bloom, and "a new Yiddish" in *Art & Ardor* (1983); and of Cyril Connolly, Primo Levi, Theodore Dreiser, Sholem Aleichem, S.Y. Agnon and the Book of Ruth in *Metaphor & Memory* (1989).

In her foreword to *Art & Ardor*, Ozick acknowledged that most of the reviews, essays, articles, talks and journalism collected in that book were "instigated or invited," the products of stimuli that were "inevitably external." In most cases, in other words, she chose neither their subjects nor their length. The work in *Metaphor & Memory* was similar: mainly short pieces, written at the request of others. Since Ozick is a thoughtful, often surprising writer and a sensitive, book-obsessed reader, she is almost totally incapable of being uninteresting, regardless of length. But beginning with its first essay—a forty-seven page meditation on "T.S. Eliot at 101" which deservedly attracted a good deal of attention when it first appeared in *The New Yorker*—it is obvious that *Fame & Folly* (1996) contains essays that are fundamentally different from those in her earlier collections. These essays grow out of her own interests rather than assignments, and their lengths have been determined by her rather than by editorial constraints. The effect has been liberating, so that in *Fame & Folly* her particular passions and persistent concerns are placed in bold relief.

Cynthia Ozick is a self-consciously Jewish American writer, of course. She is also a connoisseur of failure and disappointment, whose every essay is an exercise in disguised or undisguised autobiography. The ones that stand out in *Fame & Folly* all seem inspired by a peculiar, occasionally discomfiting, combination of envy and sympathy. The careers of other writers—their ascents and declines, fame and infamy, wisdom and folly, success and neglect—obviously fascinate her. In part, it seems, because she cannot help but compare them to her own.

Her memoir "Alfred Chester's Wig" and her essay on Eliot are the most obvious examples of this autobiographical slant. In the memoir she spends nearly as many pages as she devotes to her essay on the most influential poet of the first half of our century dissecting her rivalry with a minor American writer who is now almost totally forgotten. She and Chester started out together at New York University in 1946 as precocious and ambitious readers and writers. In the Fifties and Sixties—while Ozick was struggling with a three hundred thousand word first novel that she ultimately abandoned—Chester quickly gained publication, reputation, literary friendships and a small portion of cultural power. His work appeared in *Commentary*, *Partisan Review* and *Paris Review*; he was an editor of the avant-garde little magazine *Botteghe Oscure*; he was included in one of *Esquire*'s annual reports on the "Red Hot Center" of American writing; he traveled abroad, living for several years first in Paris and then in Morocco. By the early 1970's—as Ozick was just beginning to gain recognition—he self-destructed, dying at forty-two of drink, drugs and dissipation.

Why, she asks, did he fall apart? She doesn't seem to ask because she is searching for an answer but because she is already sure she knows it. Based on the several years that they spent together in their youths, Ozick is convinced that it was because of the insecurities and crises of identity created by the childhood illness that left him bald and led him to wear terribly obvious, sadly comic, wigs as a young man; because he was rejected by women he loved and turned to homosexuality in response; and because he turned from the friends like her who might have supported and sustained him to friends who helped him to destroy himself. Her confidence that she understands Chester's psychology and sexuality better than he did is startling and more than a little presumptuous—especially since she demonstrates so little knowledge of or empathy for homosexuality.

Finally, this memoir is as much about Ozick as Chester, an effort to disentangle and differentiate her fate and career from his. In her mind, they were rivals. "He was better than I was!" she thinks at one point, but "I was stronger." She portrays herself as the tortoise to his hare. He speeds ahead into Bohemia, only to lose control of his literary style and his life; she plods along among the middle class, quietly laboring to perfect her craft at the little Sears Roebuck desk that she has used since high school, eventually establishing her reputation and surviving into her sixties.

Yet she also sees that they shared a common fate. In literary history, Ozick observes early in her memoir, there is no middle class. "The heights belong, at most, to four or five writers, a princely crew; the remainder are invisible, or else have the partial, now-and-then visibility that attaches to minor status. Every young writer imagines only the heights; no one aspires to be minor or invisible, and when, finally, the recognition of where one stands arrives, as it must, in maturity, one either accepts the limitations of fate or talent, or surrenders to sour cynicism." Like Chester, most of the writers "who on occasion reminisce about Chester have by now lived long enough to confirm their own minor status," she writes at the end. Clearly she includes herself among their number.

For most of this century, T.S. Eliot has been at the head of the "princely crew." Perhaps the most fascinating aspect of Ozick's treatment of Eliot, however, is that she reads him in much the same way she reads Chester, linking his writing and his biography in an essay that focuses on his meteoric rise to prominence and the decline of his literary and personal fortunes. Like her essays on Henry James, her examination of Eliot is most appealing in its ability to make us see the young man just starting out: Henry James before he became "Henry James," the Master; Tom Eliot before he became "T.S. Eliot," poetry incarnate.

She again begins with the decline, again goes back to recall and try to understand his rise, and again connects his fall, like Chester's, to flaws in his character. Along the way, she draws on and brilliantly synthesizes the findings of the several volumes that have helped readers to penetrate the facade of impersonality that Eliot so assiduously cultivated in his prime—Lyndall Gordon's *Eliot's Early Years* (1977) and *Eliot's New Life* (1988), Peter Ackroyd's *T.S. Eliot: A Life* (1984), and Valerie Eliot's edition of *The Letters of T.S. Eliot, Vol. I: 1898-1922* (1988).

Exaggerating more than a little, Ozick claims that Eliot's fall is evident in the fact that only "The Love Song of J. Alfred Prufrock" continues to be taught in the college and university English departments he and the New Criticism once dominated. In part, she suggests, this is because of anti-Semitic passages in his poetry and prose that readers are no longer willing to ignore or excuse; in part, it is because the poetic principles that he espoused so vehemently—"the objective correlative," "the impersonality of poetry"—have been rejected by his poetic successors and exposed as absurdly irrelevant to his own work by the recent biographies.

"The prodigy of Eliot's rocketlike climb from termite to superman" by the age of thirty intrigues her even more than Chester's smaller success did. "What was it," she asks, "that singled Eliot out to put him in the lead so astoundingly early? That he ferociously willed it means nothing. Nearly all beginning writers have a will for extreme fame; will, no matter how resilient, is usually no more efficacious in the marketplace than daydream." To Ozick, the size of his *oeuvre*—fifty-four poems—would seem to doom him to minor status. Yet he became "a god"—creator not only of poetic works but of a method for reading them. What singled him out, she proposes, was what singled out the young James: early "sovereignty," a voice that conveyed an erudition that awed and cowed.

In *Art & Ardor*, Ozick wrote of how Leonard Woolf's long-suffering and selfless nursing made Virginia Woolf's art possible. In *Fame & Folly*, Eliot becomes Leonard's funhouse mirror image. His first wife Vivien's mental illness was the "seizure that animated the poetry"; his failure to save or stand by her was the moral nightmare that both prompted and haunted his greatest work and led to the weaknesses she finds in his later poems and plays.

The same focus on the rise and fall of literary reputations is evident in the other major essays in the collection. Trollope captures her attention and earns her sympathy and defense because he, too, is an underrated minor writer whose works have fallen out of fashion. The "nervous breakdown" that Henry James suffered following the public humiliation accompanying the performance of his play *Guy Domville* captures her, becoming an explanation for the mystery at the center of his later, "modern" style. Isaac Babel's personal and literary impersonations capture her, because they challenge her to understand how continuing to write in the language he loved could lead a Jewish writer to complicity in pogroms conducted by the same anti-Semitic state that would eventually execute him. Mark Twain, in the *fin-de-siecle* Europe of Karl Lueger's Vienna and France's Dreyfus Affair, captures her attention because of the way his "The Man Who Corrupted Hadleyburg" could offer a clear-eyed commentary on that anti-Semitic culture while his essay "Concerning the Jews"—written at the same time—could demonstrate how he himself was blinded by stereotypes about the Jews. Salman Rushdie gains her sympathy once the Ayatollah's *fatwa* transforms him for her from a fashionable, highly successful, rigidly Third World figure who refused to sign a protest against Middle Eastern terrorism at a PEN conference in New York in 1986, into "a little Israel"—a writer hunted, isolated, yet unbowed, who deserves her support and that of anyone who cares about freedom of expression.

Two other pieces in this collection deserve special mention. "The Break" is a moving fictionalized confession in which Ozick's obsession with literary reputations and with the status of her own achievement in relation to that of other writers is painfully raw and undisguised. In it, a "terrifying operation" divides the "I" into two imaginary alter-egos: a still ambitious younger self who imagines that her career lies ahead, full of possibility, and a depressed and defeated older self who acknowledges that "She is little known or known not at all, relegated to marginality, absent from the authoritative anthologies. . . . She knows that she does not matter. . . she has been in rooms with the famous, and felt the humiliation of her lessness, her invisibility, her lack of writerly weight or topical cachet. . . she has not written enough. She is certainly not read."

"Saul Bellow's Broadway" is a reading of *Seize the Day* which makes the extraordinarily wrong-headed assertion that "*The Adventures of Augie March* struck out on a course so independent from the tide of American fiction that no literary lessons could flow from it: it left no wake, and cut a channel so entirely idiosyncratic as to be uncopyable." It is hard to imagine how she means this statement to be taken, since an entire generation of Jewish-American novelists who began writing in the 1950's and early 1960's, inspired by Bellow's yoking of the street and the library, attest to the absurdity of the claim. (For a more accurate assessment of the influence of Bellow's style, see Philip Roth's essay "Imagining Jews" in his *Reading Myself and Others*; for an eloquent and much more perceptive treatment of Bellow's style and concerns, see Ozick's 1984 review of *Him with His Foot in His Mouth*, collected in *Metaphor & Memory*.)

"What we think we are surely going to do, we don't do," Ozick wrote in her foreword to *Art & Ardor*; "and what we never intended to do, we may one day notice that we have done, and done, and done." To readers, what truly matters is that what Cynthia Ozick has done—both in fiction and in the essay—bears the unmistakable stamp of her particular, combative, and provocative intelligence. Like her earlier collections of essays, *Fame & Folly* is an important part of her continuing claim to our attention.

A First Life

William Styron

James L. W. West III, a professor of English at Pennsylvania State University, brings twenty-five years of acquaintance and conversation with the author, complete access to his papers, manuscripts, and letters, extensive access to many of his friends and family, and the broad perspective gained from three previous books on Styron to the task of writing *William Styron: A Life* (1998), the first biography of one of contemporary American literature's most controversial and prominent figures. The result is a solid beginning upon which every subsequent biographer will inevitably build.

To many, writing the biography of a living contemporary author is a dubious enterprise at best. Not only is it difficult to gain critical and historical perspective, but the temptation to gloss over unpleasant facts out of consideration for the author and his loved ones or gratitude for the cooperation he has provided is often both overwhelming and debilitating. Meeting these challenges requires judgment and tact, a sense of balance and proportion as well as knowledge and mastery of the facts. Like all biographers, the biographer of a contemporary must also avoid the poles of pathography and hagiography—of reducing his subject to nothing but flaws or becoming so blinded by familiarity that he sees no flaws at all. Ideally, the literary biographer will also remember that his subject is of interest to readers because of the work that his life has produced and recognize that the first purpose of recounting any author's life is to provide a fuller understanding of that work. West meets most of these challenges admirably.

He also understands that the primary justification for a contemporary biography is the biographer's ability to speak directly to the subject and those who have known him, and that its most important service is to use those conversations to lay out the basic facts that others will someday elaborate or place in larger contexts.

West writes appreciatively and perceptively about William Styron's experiments with narrative voice in his novels—experiments in which Styron artfully blends the perspectives of his narrators with those of other central characters. *William Styron: A Life* is marked by a similar technique: the life story that Professor West tells often seems not just *about* but *by* William Styron. Large sections of the book read like a form of third-person autobiography, as memories, analyses, interpretations and views that are obviously Styron's—of his feelings and thoughts about his childhood and early career, his goals and struggles as a writer, his sense of his family life, his relations with other writers—are recounted as facts in West's voice.

The story begins in Newport News and the Tidewater region of Virginia and follows Styron from college (Davidson and Duke) and Marine training in the Carolinas, through the composition of his first novel in Manhattan and the Hudson Valley of New York, to a year in Europe that included his helping to found the *Paris Review* and his marriage to Rose Burgunder in Rome in 1953, to their returning to establish the homes in Connecticut and Martha's Vineyard where he has lived and worked ever since.

West captures the character and spirit of each of these places and marshals the facts of William Styron's life with thoroughness and care. He describes Styron's ancestors, speculates about the impact of the loss of his mother when he was fourteen years old, reports his uninspired academic record at prep school and college, acknowledges the importance of his father's support and encouragement to his early career, summarizes his two stints in the Marines during World War II and the Korean War, describes his writing routine and family life, traces the composition, publication and reception of each of his books through *Darkness Visible* (1990), and suggests the range of his literary friendships and political engagements.

In the process, he seems to have kept in mind Styron's observation in a review of Andrew Turnbull's biography of one of his first literary heroes, Thomas Wolfe. "Too many biographies—especially of literary figures—tend to be overly fleshed out and are cursed with logorrhea," Styron wrote, "so that the illustrious subject himself becomes obliterated behind a shower of menus, train tickets, opera programs, itineraries and dull mash notes from lovelorn girls." *William Styron: A Life* is both well-written and well-focused. West does not tell his readers more than they want or need to know about such details. Instead, he keeps his focus on what is important to begin to understand the man, the writer, and the work.

With the publication of his highly-praised first novel, *Lie Down In Darkness* (1951), William Styron's life as a writer began. Ever since, he has been mentioned in any discussion of important contemporary American writers and has had a place at the center of the nation's literary culture. While contemporaries such as Mailer, Bellow, Roth or Updike have written shelves of novels over the past forty years, Styron has published comparatively little: three more novels, two books of shorter fiction—*The Long March* (1953) and *A Tidewater Morning* (1993), a collection of essays and reviews titled *This Quiet Dust* (1982), and his "memoir of madness" *Darkness Visible*. Yet, like Ralph Ellison or Thomas Pynchon, what he has written has been important enough to keep him at the forefront of American fiction.

One reason for this is certainly the extent of his artistic ambition and his willingness to grapple with difficult and controversial subjects. *Lie Down in Darkness* was a stunning debut, filled with echoes of Robert Penn Warren and Faulkner which led to Styron's being designated the heir apparent of Southern fiction. His response to that designation was to turn his back on his critics' expectations by setting most of his second novel among the expatriate community in Europe. *Set This House on Fire* (1960), published at the end of the 1950s, was a scathing critique of the values of postwar American culture and was noteworthy for the power of its existentialist vision. In *The Confessions of Nat Turner* (1967), Styron sought to confront the legacy of slavery and the racial conflict of the 1960s through a daring "meditation" on Nat Turner's rebellion. As if his subject were not controversial enough, he also chose to tell the story by inventing Nat Turner's voice and vision—a controversial choice, especially in the context of the racial cultural politics of the period, that resulted in his being viciously attacked by writers and critics of the Black Arts movement. With *Sophie's Choice* (1979) he opened himself up to charges of another kind of sacrilege by combining a comic *Bildungsroman* about a young Southern writer's sexual coming-of-age with a story of the Holocaust—and a Holocaust story that focused on a non-Jewish victim besides.

Although the critical reception of each of these novels was mixed, each was also anxiously awaited, heavily promoted, seriously discussed, and widely translated. *The Confessions of Nat Turner*, *Sophie's Choice*, and *Darkness Visible* were all national bestsellers; and the several million paperback copies of *Sophie's Choice* that were sold, together with the highly successful film version of the book, brought Styron to the attention of an even broader national audience.

Styron's role as a literary and public figure has also helped to establish his place as an elder statesman of American culture. He has regularly published in popular magazines such as *Esquire* and *Vanity Fair*, has contributed opinion pieces to the *New York Times* and the *New York Review of Books*, has signed various manifestoes and public letters, and has written and spoken out on issues such as Vietnam and capital punishment. President Kennedy invited him to the White House, took him sailing, and talked with him about his research on Nat Turner; at the family's request, he served as an honorable pallbearer at Robert F. Kennedy's funeral; he supported Eugene McCarthy and went to the Chicago convention in 1968 in an effort to be seated as a McCarthy delegate; Francois Mitterand was an admirer, like many French intellectuals, and West recounts his recommending *The Confessions of Nat Turner* to President Bush; President Clinton dined with the Styrons on Martha's Vineyard and invited them to the White House. Styron has been active in American PEN, as has his wife Rose, who has also been a leader of the American branch of Amnesty International. His literary friends have crossed generations: from elders such as Irwin Shaw, Lillian Hellman and Arthur Miller, to contemporaries such as James Jones, James Baldwin, Philip Roth, Peter Mathiessen, and dozens of others.

West does not fully explore most of Styron's relationships with other writers or the extent to which these relationships have contributed to his continuing reputation and stature. (The space he devotes to a feud between Mailer and Styron, on the other hand, seems much ado about nothing, much less important and interesting to readers than it appears to be to West, Styron, and Mailer.) West also tends to ignore an alcohol problem that appears to have been another central aspect of Styron's life. In *Darkness Visible*, Styron is a bit more candid: he admits that he abused alcohol until he was sixty, and then makes the familiar statement that it enhanced his creativity without undermining his family life or work habits. It will be left to subsequent biographers to determine if that is true.

While West is reticent about these and a few other personal matters, he is especially good at tracing the many experiences from Styron's life that appear, transformed, in his works. His biography makes the autobiographical sources of much of Styron's fiction clear. While Styron has not written *romans a clefs*, West's research reveals just how many of the characters and incidents in his fiction are based on people and episodes from his life. An encounter with John Huston and the cast of *Beat the Devil* on a visit to Ravello, for example, becomes a part of the fabric of *Set This House on Fire*. The wildly black comic episode at the beginning of that novel, which involves an accident with a motorcyclist on an Italian back road, turns out to have been the product of life not an absurdist imagination.

Another example of the relation between Styron's life and work is both more ambiguous and more profound. In the fall of 1960, Robert Silvers (later editor of the *New York Review of Books*), told the Styrons that James Baldwin needed a place to stay while he worked on his new novel, *Another Country*. The Styrons invited him to use the writing studio on their property in Connecticut, and during his stay from February to July 1961, Baldwin and Styron got together to talk nearly every day. Styron was the grandson of a slave owner, Baldwin the grandson of a slave. Baldwin had written a novel (*Giovanni's Room*) in which his first-person narrator was a white man; Styron was considering writing a novel (*The Confessions of Nat Turner*) in which his first-person narrator would be a black man. Their frank discussions about race, about stereotypes, and about artistic freedom, together with Baldwin's own voice and views, helped to encourage Styron in his narrative strategy and to shape both the language and themes of Styron's novel.

William Styron: A Life is full of such references and connections and these, together with its clear presentation of both the arc and the details of Styron's life and career, will make it essential reading for students of the author's work for years to come.

Paradise Lost

Jamaica Kincaid

When her first book *At the Bottom of the River* appeared in 1983, critics and fellow writers praised the originality of Jamaica Kincaid's voice and vision. Susan Sontag hailed an "unaffectedly sumptuous, irresistible writer" of "splendid stories about personal and cosmic desire." Derek Walcott promised that the book would "burn" on its readers' shelves, "too choked with love to invite envy, too humble for admiration, and too startling to escape astonishment." In her first novel, *Annie John* (1985), Kincaid more than justifies that early praise in a beautifully crafted and subtly modulated work, the story of a sensitive young girl's coming-of-age in the West Indies.

In a sense, *Annie John* elaborates the persona, emotions, and experience of the finest stories in *At the Bottom of the River,* reweaving those threads into a stunning tapestry of ecstasy and loss. Like the self-conscious young girl in "Holidays," Annie is "filled with sensations." "I feel," the girl in the story says, "oh, how I feel. I feel, I feel, I feel." Like the narrator in "Wingless," what Annie feels most are the disappointments of growing up. "Tears, big, have run down my cheeks in uneven lines," that narrator explains. She identifies the cause of those tears as her "disappointments": "My disappointments stand up and grow ever taller. They will not be lost to me. There they are. Let me pin tags on them. Let me have them registered, like newly domesticated animals. Let me cherish my disappointments, fold them up, tuck them away, close to my breast, because they are so important to me."

Like the girl in "My Mother," Annie is shaped by both the tremendous love and the importance she feels growing up as an only child at her mother's side and by the confusion and isolation she feels when that relationship begins to change during her adolescence. "Though glowing red with anger," the girl in the story returns to her mother's side and remains there. Yet once their relationship has begun to change, it is as if "my mother and I built houses on opposite banks of the dead pond. The dead pond lay between us; in it, only small invertebrates with poisonous lances lived." Finally, like the narrator of "At the Bottom of the River," Annie is forced to confront the power of death and its subversion of her own sense of her privileged existence. Instead of what she once thought life would be—"glorious moment upon glorious moment of contentment and joy and love running into each other and forming an extraordinary chain"—the story's narrator comes to recognize with intense regret that "in the face of death and all that is and all that it shall be I stand powerless, that in the face of my death my will, to which everything I have ever known bends, stands as if it were nothing more than a string caught in the early-morning wind."

Annie John begins with Annie's first encounters with death and ends with her departure from the island of her birth. Midway through it, a teacher orders Annie to copy the first two books of *Paradise Lost* as punishment for defacing a picture of Columbus, discoverer of the island. In between, Kincaid details the joys and disappointments of growing up in lyric, often exquisite, always compelling prose. Love and loss, security and insecurity, inclusion and expulsion—these are the emotional poles of Annie John's experience. Pervading that experience is the sense that growing up consists of a series of paradises found and lost, a series of expulsions from one garden after another—and that, as often as not, the serpent in the garden is the self.

The first-person narrator of the story of Annie John's growing is Annie John, grown. "For a short while during the year I was ten," she begins, "I thought only people I did not know died." In this first paradise, where death does not exist, Annie's innocence is complete. Like everyone around her, she fears the dead—"because we never could tell when they might show up again . . . standing under a tree just as you were passing by" – but she does not fear death, which is as yet unreal. As the first chapter "Figures in the Distance" proceeds, death swiftly comes closer to her and she approaches closer and closer to it, at first repelled and then intrigued. The daughter of one of her mother's friends dies in Annie's mother's arms. Annie's father makes the girl's coffin; her mother prepares the girl for burial. "For a while, though not for very long, I could not bear to have my mother caress me or touch my food or help me with my bath. I especially couldn't bear the sight of her hands lying still in her lap." She feels a similar revulsion when the mother of her first friend, Sonia, dies in childbirth. She "couldn't ever again bring herself to speak to her . . . . She seemed such a shameful thing, a girl whose mother had died and left her alone in the world."

Soon Annie begins to be intrigued by the mystery of death. At first, she lingers outside the local funeral home; next, she begins to sneak in to view the remains of people she has never met. Finally, when a humpbacked girl whom she once stood behind in the library dies, she finds that "someone I knew was dead." Instead of picking up fish for the family's dinner as she is supposed to, she attends the girl's wake and sees her body. When she returns home, she lies to her mother about the fish, is found out, and is punished. "As a punishment," the first chapter ends, "I ate my supper outside, alone, under the breadfruit tree, and my mother said that she would not be kissing me good night later, but when I climbed into bed she came and kissed me anyway."

With Annie's first taste of knowledge comes her first loss of innocence, her first fall from grace, her first lie, her first expulsion, and her first alienation from her mother. As the novel progresses, as this pattern in the distance emerges more clearly, Annie will experience it repeatedly. Gradually, reconciliation will not come so easily; inevitably, safety and security in the face of knowledge will become harder to recover; ultimately, Annie John will find herself alone.

In the novel's second chapter "The Circling Hand," this movement is presented with immense tenderness and nostalgia for what must be lost. It begins with an extraordinary paean to an all-encompassing mother love, "the circling hand" which makes Annie John feel that she is the center of the universe for a while. "How important I felt to be with my mother," Annie recalls. She and her mother bathe together. They shop together, her mother explaining why she buys each thing. She follows her mother around the house, "observing the way she did everything." They cook together, do the wash together, clean the house together. As they go through their days, Annie's mother tells her tales of her own youth and of Annie's. When they air out the trunk which holds mementos of Annie's life, "as she held each thing in her hand she would tell me a story about myself . . . . No small part of my life was so unimportant that she hadn't made a note of it and now she would tell it to me over and over again." Annie thinks "how terrible it must be for all the people who had no one to love them so and no one whom they loved so." Picking herbs together in the yard, "she might stoop down and kiss me on my lips and then on my neck. It was in such a paradise that I lived."

The trajectory of her experience, however, is such that this paradise, like the others she will find, must eventually be lost. The loss begins when she is twelve and her mother suggests for the first time that she should choose different material for a dress. "You just cannot go around the rest of your life looking like a little me," she says. Shortly afterward, she informs Annie that she "was on the verge of becoming a young lady, so there were quite a few things [she] would have to do differently." Since Annie knows that this loss of her previous relationship with her mother is linked to her growing up, she thinks of asking her father to build clamps so that she can stop growing. For "instead of days spent in perfect harmony with my mother, I trailing in her footsteps, she showering down on me her kisses and affection and attention, I was now sent off to learn one thing and another."

When Annie, expelled from paradise, fails to show an interest in piano lessons and manners, "my mother's back turned on me in disgust." Before this "young-lady business I could sit and think of my mother, see her doing one thing or another, and always her face bore a smile for me. Now I often saw her with the corners of her mouth turned down in disapproval." This movement away from her mother reaches a crisis when Annie rushes home with a certificate she has won in school and discovers her parents in bed together. When her mother speaks sharply to her later, she replies in kind and sees something in her mother fold up and become suddenly small. "She carried her hands limp at her sides. I was sure I could never let those hands touch me again; I was sure I could never let her kiss me again. All that was finished."

Annie turns her interest and affection to school. She does well and quickly falls in love with another girl, Gwen. One paradise lost, another comes into view. She meets another girl, "the Red Girl," whose wildness, strength, and adventurousness attract her. She then starts a "new series of betrayals." She lies to Gwen and her mother to hide her meetings with the Red Girl. She begins to steal small change from her parents to buy the Red Girl gifts. She steals books from the library and hides them under the house. She begins to get in trouble in school.

At fifteen, she is "more unhappy than I had ever imagined anyone could be." The conflict with her mother has escalated to the point where both have two faces: one for her father and the rest of the world, one for each other when they are alone. Annie begins to dream that "my mother would kill me if she got the chance. I would kill my mother if I had the courage." She turns away from Gwen, becomes more solitary, looks into a shop window and sees herself as Lucifer. This progression culminates when she suddenly becomes seriously ill and spends months delirious, tended by her parents and her grandmother Ma Chess, a believer in obeah cures and spells. At seventeen, she leaves for England. On the way to the jetty where she will board a boat, she passes one by one all the places that have been the center of her life and is again overwhelmed by her sense of loss.

Annie John's conflicts are not unusual. In fact, it is precisely their universality that draws readers into Kincaid's world and engages them. But her world is unique. It is a world where the dead walk; where spurned lovers have the power to disrupt the objects in someone's house; where angry spirits hang in the air like black wings; where a grandmother appears and disappears magically when she is needed; and where an illness that is more sickness of the soul than of the body resolves the plot's conflicts. It is a world where the common becomes uncommonly moving and the uncommon is accepted as part of the way things are. Finally, it is a world rendered so thoroughly, in such extraordinarily simple yet resonant prose, that to encounter it is to remember it vividly, long after the story is told and the book is placed, still "burning," on the shelf.

Strenuous Exercise

John Ashbery

At seventeen, John Ashbery wanted to be a painter; at eighteen, he wanted to be a musician; at nineteen, he wrote an honors essay at Harvard on W.H. Auden and entered graduate school in New York, where he would soon write an M.A. thesis on the fiction of the British experimental novelist Henry Green.

When he began to write poetry himself in the early 1950's—his first book was published in a limited edition by a New York art gallery—these early interests set him apart and helped to define the character of his work. At the start, he was more influenced by what was going on in music and art than by what was going on in poetry. "American painting seemed the most exciting around," he has said, while "American poetry was very traditional at that time and there was no modern poetry in the sense that there was modern painting. So one got one's inspiration from watching experiments in other arts."

Together with Kenneth Koch, James Schuyler, and Frank O'Hara, the unofficial leader of the group, Ashbery came to be known as a part of the New York School of poetry. What the poetry of each of these writers shared was a desire to translate abstract expressionism and the non-serial music of composers such as John Cage into poetic terms. And in the thirty years separating his first collection and *A Wave* (1984), his tenth, this has been Ashbery's special achievement. Abstract expressionism, "action painting," did not attempt to imitate reality; instead, the artist's canvas became a "field of action" on which the painter could express himself. In Ashbery's poems, this idea came to mean that a poem should be "the chronicle of the creative act which produced it."

The result is a poetry of surrealistic juxtapositions, convoluted syntax, associations and progressions that defy simple logic. Poems, in other words, that are both controversial and, for many, incomprehensible. Yet poems that display an extraordinary feeling for language, for tone and rhythm, and an apparently limitless capacity for astonishing and fresh verbal combinations. Ashbery has developed his own forms and voices, has established his own poetic terrain, has gradually taught his audience how to read him. In the process, he has become one of America's most important poets—a judgment that was underlined when one of his best books, *Self-Portrait in a Convex Mirror* (1975) won the National Book Award, the National Book Critics Circle Award, and the Pulitzer Prize for Poetry.

In *A Wave*, as in all of Ashbery's mature work, style and theme, form and content, are so intimately intertwined that to begin talking about one inevitably leads to discussion of the other. By suggesting *what* he writes about we find ourselves almost immediately talking about *how* he writes about it. Since Ashbery is a lyric poet, and since, in a sense, his subject matter is limitless, one must be aware of oversimplifying. But it seems clear to many who have read him closely that four themes or concerns have dominated his work to date and are reflected in his style.

First, Ashbery is preoccupied by the nature of consciousness, and with self-consciousness. His most fundamental concern is with the ways that the mind *perceives* experience, the relationship between experience and imagination. "It is the personal,/ Interior life that gives us something to think about," he writes in "But What Is the Reader to Make of This?," one of the poems in *A Wave*. "Your opinion/ Of you shaped in the vacuum-form of suppositions,/ Correct or false, of others," he writes in another, "Cups with Broken Handles," "and how we can never be ourselves/ While so much of us is going on in the minds of other people."

As Ashbery sees it, our minds work by often uncontrollable association. Ideas and things, art and breakfast, memories and immediate emotions cannot be separated if we are to remain true to experience. So to begin talking about one inevitably leads to talk of the other. "I think any one of my poems might be considered a snapshot of whatever is going on in my mind at the time of its composition," Ashbery once told an interviewer. And "it seems to me that my poetry proceeds as though an argument were suddenly derailed and something that started out clearly suddenly becomes opaque."

This means that his poetry is marked by quick changes in tone and attention, by titles that often seem totally unrelated to the poems to which they are attached, by the awkward comedy of unrelated thoughts and things pressing in at every moment on what we say and do. And what is "opaque" about this poetry is not its individual lines, phrases, or images—which are incredibly clear and vivid—but the fact that the *relationship between* those lines, phrases, and images is often obscure. What starts out as a logical progression veers off into a passing thought because, as he wrote in the title poem of *Houseboat Days* (1977), "The mind/ Is so hospitable, taking in everything/ Like boarders."

Ashbery recognizes the difficulties that this causes his readers, and often incorporates comments about those difficulties in the poems themselves, but he insists that to ignore the stream of consciousness is to betray reality. So he tries to put it all in, even though he knows that is ultimately impossible.

Second, since Ashbery sees experience as a flow he rejects generalizations for particulars. He refuses the role of prophet or great thinker, does not provide the lofty statements that so many seek in poetry. And when he occasionally does seem to be making such statements, more often than not he cancels them out in his next lines. "Any reckoning of the sum total of the things we are is of course doomed to failure," he says in *Three Poems* (1972), and this theme appears again and again as a baseline for his poetic improvisations. "The great ideas?" he writes in *A Wave*'s "The Ongoing Story." "What good are they if they're misplaced,/ In the wrong order, if you can't remember one/ At the moment you're so to speak mounting the guillotine/ Like Sydney Carton, if you can't think of anything to say?"

Stylistically, this emphasis on the particulars of experience means that the long poems that are the highlights of each of his books are rather unique in their form. He once described his friend Frank O'Hara's style as "a bag into which anything is dumped and ends up belonging there." His long poems are much the same. One critic has described them as being like "letters to a friend or lover, permitting the usual mixture of news and inconsequence, relying on the friend's good will, knowing that, within reason, anything goes." To put it another way, Ashbery's long poems do not tell stories; they are spaces for his mind to move around in. "The talk leads nowhere," he writes in the collection *As We Know* (1979), "but is/ Inside its space."

The particulars of experience as they come to him, then, are what get into these long poems. The voice, the talk, invites us to observe those particulars and defends itself against any charges of incoherence as it goes along:

> You have all lived through lots of
> these things before
> And know that life is like an ocean:
> Sometimes the tide is out

> And sometimes it's in, but it's always
> the same body of water
> Even though it looks different, and
> It makes things on the shore look
> different.

Third, because Ashbery is preoccupied with consciousness, because he rejects the general for the particular, another of his themes is the various divisions which disrupt and distort experience for each of us. In an effort to explore these divisions, Ashbery has developed a style marked by the play of contrasting voices. Sometimes he sounds like an art critic, sometimes like a street peddler; sometimes like a sociologist, sometimes like a hallucinating kid on speed. He can begin a poem like *The Double Dream of Spring* 's "Soonest Mended" with talk of *Orlando Furioso* and Fra Angelica's painting, and then start talking about Happy Hooligan. Or title a poem in *Houseboat Days* "Daffy Duck in Hollywood," mix references to La Celestina, *Amadigi di Gaula*, and the Princess de Cleves with cartoon characters like Speedy Gonzales, the Fudds, and Skeezix, and turn it all into a profound examination on the American character.

The most striking of his stylistic efforts to emphasize how complicated our experience is, perhaps, his use of personal and impersonal pronouns. Ashbery's poems are dotted with *I*'s and *you*'s, *he*'s and *she*'s, *someone*'s, *somewhere*'s, and *it*'s—but their referents are seldom clear, always shifting. At first the "you" may seem a lover, then another self, then nature, then death, then memory. Because these referents are unclear, his meanings are multiple and layered.

Finally, Ashbery is, like most of us, haunted by the past. If the old values and meanings are gone, his poetry says both implicitly and explicitly, then we must acknowledge that fact. Even if that does not diminish our *longing* for the old truths and the answers that they provided. This longing for a past that is, in fact, *past* and irretrievable appears in Ashbery's poetry in a variety of ways. Sometimes, as in *Three Poems*, it is itself the subject from which the poet's meditations begin. At other times, as in "The Skaters," the past intrudes upon the speaker's consciousness unbidden, shifting the scene and mood, putting what appeared to be the subject into a new context. And sometimes the past appears as allusions—musical, artistic, literary, from both high and popular culture—as in the "The Songs We Know Best," a poem in *A Wave* which combines the language of popular song with lines like "The others come and go . . ." and "I wish to come to know you/ get to know you all" that ironically echo the rhythm and language of Eliot's "The Love Song of J. Alfred Prufrock."

These four themes and this brief description of Ashbery's style hardly exhaust the important points to be made about him, or about *A Wave*, a collection that includes some of his finest poems. Reading Ashbery we often feel shipwrecked, adrift at night in a vast ocean, short of breath and struggling just to keep our heads above water. And then, just as it seems inevitable that we will sink, finally, into meaninglessness, a spar of insight, a piece of startling thought drifts past and we cling to it for dear life. This is more strenuous exercise than many poetry readers want, but it is undeniably as rewarding as it is exhausting.

As Common as Rain
John Irving

Before 1978, John Irving was the largely unknown author of the three critically praised but largely ignored novels *Setting Free the Bears* (1968), *The Water-Method Man* (1972), and *The 158-Pound Marriage* (1974). Since 1978, he has been famous as the author of one of the most phenomenally popular novels of the 1970's. The history of *The World According to Garp*'s success is pretty well-known: twenty-five weeks on *The New York Times* bestseller list; more than 100,000 hardcover copies sold; paperback rights auctioned for over a million dollars; and then, in 1979, one of the biggest promotional campaigns ever undertaken for the paperback edition of a literary novel. The book was published with six different covers portraying six different aspects of the story and delivered to bookstores in ready-made racks. There were Garp t-shirts, Garp bumper stickers, Garp posters plastered on buses and subway trains, Garp golf caps, wristbands, and headbands—all bearing the slogan "I Believe in Garp." This "Garp fever" sold over three million copies of the paperback *before* the movie version, starring Robin Williams, opened in the winter of 1981.

At the end of *Garp*, T.H. Garp, the novel's writer-hero is murdered. At the time of his death he is working on a new novel, titled *My Father's Illusions*. "My father wanted us all to have a better life," the novel began, "but better than *what*—he was not sure. I do not think that he knew what life was; only that he wanted it better." As he had in his earlier fiction,

Garp made up a family in *My Father's Illusions*, "he gave himself brothers and sisters . . . A plot, to his delight, thickened."

T.S. Garp's *My Father's Illusions* became John Irving's fifth novel, *The Hotel New Hampshire* (1981), a family chronicle about a father named Win Berry, one of whose illusions is that running a first-class hotel will provide him and his family with that better life. Like Garp's fictional family, the Berrys are a family of eccentrics. Mom and Dad "met cute," brought together while they were working at a Maine hotel one summer by a bear on a motorcycle and the bear's trainer, a Viennese Jew everyone called Freud. Eventually, they have five children: Frank, a homosexual who becomes a literary agent; Franny, the family star, who eventually marries a black pro football player; John, the book's narrator, described by the family as a "weight-lifting maiden aunt"; Lilly, a dwarf who becomes a bestselling novelist by recounting the family's story; and Egg, a cuddly little brother who says "What?" a lot and dresses up in unusual costumes. Together with Win's father, Iowa Bob, who coaches football at a second-rate New Hampshire prep school, and a big black dog named Sorrow, these characters are the center of Irving's fast-paced plot.

The family moves from the first Hotel New Hampshire in Derry, to the second Hotel New Hampshire in Vienna, to the last Hotel New Hampshire in Maine. Led by their dreamer father (Irving compares him to Fitzgerald's Gatsby) and their saintly mother, they encounter the worst the world has to offer, as well as the best. By the book's end, only three of the Berry children remain to tell the tale. "We are all terminal cases," Garp wrote.

The Berry family, one of the best things in the book, suggests one of the reasons for Irving's broad appeal. Few of our novelists treat the everyday realities of family life anymore. But Irving, like John Updike or Anne Tyler, writes novels in which those realities—the tensions and the joys, the intimacies and the silences, the fears and the hopes—count. True, the Berrys are not your average American family, but, as Franny says, "we *aren't* eccentric, we're not bizarre. To each other, we're as common as rain." And, thinks John, "she was right: to each other we were as normal and nice as the smell of bread, we were just a family." One of Irving's achievements in *The Hotel New Hampshire* is to succeed in making us come to see these people as they see themselves, to see them as people, not just eccentrics.

But if domestic life is the center of *The Hotel New Hampshire*, as it was in *The World According to Garp*, in the later novel as in the earlier that domestic life is juxtaposed with a wider world of violence and aberration which constantly closes in. Suicide, rape, incest, mutilations, maulings, plane crashes, terrorism, racism, prostitution, and a host of other such elements abound in the world of the novel. And, while they certainly manage to keep the plot thickening, their harshness would not seem likely to make Irving's novels appeal to a broad audience. And yet they do, because there is something about Irving's *treatment* of violence that does not alienate his many admiring readers.

"Everything is a fairy tale," Lilly observes, and in Irving's fiction this is true in an important sense. As Bruno Bettelheim explained in *The Uses of Enchantment*, one of the functions of fairy tales is to help children domesticate and cope with the anxieties of their existence. In fairy tales there are cruelties, grotesque characters and events, deaths—but no inconsolable grief, no unhappy endings. The spirit behind these tales is not malice or sadism, although malicious and sadistic acts may occur; the spirit is one of consolation, of hope.

Irving's fictions function in much the same way for the many readers who love them. Like fairy tales or films such as *Star Wars* or *Raiders of the Lost Ark*, they are non-stop circuses of characters, images, and events that entertain in spite of the violence and death that punctuate almost every major movement of the plot. But where popular films tend to go no further—they entertain and claim to do no more—Irving's fiction, like fairy tales, aims to help his readers deal with our anxieties by showing us that, while violence and cruelty may be all around us, we can survive them and still maintain our humanity. As in fairy tales, the violence in *The World According to Garp* or *The Hotel New Hampshire* happens and then is past; and what remains is a sense of the indomitability of the human spirit in the face of the fact that we *are* all terminal cases.

Two other elements define Irving's fictional world and contribute to his popularity. One is a sense of being in familiar territory that puts us at ease and makes us feel at home in his novels. Like Faulkner, Irving has created his own imaginative region, his own fictional world. But Irving's region is not, like Faulkner's Yoknapatawpha County, a geographically rooted one. Although New England, Vienna, and a few other places recur in his work, Irving's territory is primarily imagistic and metaphoric. The world according to Irving is full of recurring bears, hotels, motorcycles, prep schools, loveable eccentrics, writers, parents, wrestlers, and weightlifters. And that world is his alone—every bit as distinctive and personal as Faulkner's Yoknapatawpha or the particular universe of Kurt Vonnegut's fiction.

Mention of Vonnegut leads to another important element in Irving's appeal: his style. Again, it is distinctive and personal; again, it also seems connected to that of several other writers. Since *Garp* appeared, Irving has taken to writing occasional essays and book reviews, and the comments he has made in several of those pieces suggest some of his stylistic allegiances. His affection for Dickens' sentimentality, melodramatic plotting, and quirky characters, for example, is evident in his own work. His admiration for John Hawkes' peculiar vision is underlined by his own use of nightmare and dream imagery. His precocious, foul-mouthed, loveable adolescents and prep school settings inevitably remind us of J.D. Salinger. But it is to Vonnegut that his style seems most indebted. The surface simplicity of his language, the accessibility of his prose, his use of repeated tag lines like "Sorrow floats" or "Don't pass any open windows"—all make him enjoyable to read in a way that Vonnegut is and many critically admired novelists are not.

This style opens Irving up to the charge of shallowness that has often been leveled against Vonnegut. But in an essay defending Vonnegut, Irving defended himself as well, asserting that too many critics and readers make the mistake of thinking that what is easy to read was easy to write. It is not, and anyone who has tried to write knows that. *The Hotel New Hampshire* is vintage John Irving. And that means that it is one of the most inventive, original, imaginative, entertaining, and engaging American novels of the 1980's.

The Greenhouse and the Briar Patch

Toni Morrison

The setting of Toni Morrison's *Tar Baby* (1981) is an imaginary, legend-surrounded Carribean island where Valerian Street, a retired candy manufacturer from Philadelphia, has withdrawn with his wife Margaret and his faithful old black retainers, Sidney and Ondine Childs. As his name suggests, Valerian is accustomed to ruling over his domain and its subjects with the absolute power and occasional largesse of a Roman emperor.

As the novel begins, we meet Valerian where he spends most of his time: in an hermetically-sealed greenhouse, among his orchids and hydrangeas. This greenhouse is the novel's emblem of his desire for total control of his world, a control that is always threatened by natural forces beyond its walls. Like life in the greenhouse, life in Valerian's island mansion is a series of routine, patterned, and carefully calibrated relationships to which each of the four members of the household has become accustomed. There's a strain of tension and hostility between Valerian and Margaret whenever the subject of their absent son comes up, but for the most part it's kept out of sight and under control by his solicitousness toward her and her deference toward him. Sidney and Ondine may find their employers a bit odd, but after many years they have adjusted, have come to feel at home with the Streets, and have even come to feel some affection for and loyalty toward Valerian.

That loyalty has been reinforced by Valerian and Margaret's generosity to their niece Jadine. Valerian has paid for her education in Europe and America, has helped to clothe and support her throughout most of her life, and has come to view her as a kind of daughter. (She sleeps in the house while Sidney and Ondine sleep behind the kitchen in the servants' quarters.) Just before Christmas, when the novel begins, Jadine is on the island too, in retreat from the confusions and tensions of her life in Paris. Light-skinned, well-educated, very beautiful, she's made the cover of *Elle*, received her degree in art from the Sorbonne, and been proposed to by a rich white man—all in a single week. Unsure of what to do next, she has fled Paris to the island for security while she tries to make up her mind.

The peaceful life in the Street household is upset when Margaret begins to plan for the Streets' son to visit at Christmas. We learn that this has been an annual ritual for years, and that although she makes such plans every year, the son never shows up. Instead of their son, a few days before the holiday another young man appears—an escaped black man who has jumped ship just off the island and is found hiding in Margaret's closet. Sidney pulls a gun on him; Valerian invites him to dinner.

And from that moment until the Christmas dinner which ends the novel's second act, all of the highly patterned and stable relationships that Valerian has worked to build around him as a shield against the outside world begin to crumble. The young man they call Son smells of the swamp. He's lowdown and dirty and embodies everything that Sidney and Ondine are ashamed of in their race, that Margaret fears, and that Jadine has been trying to run away from all of her life.

At that Christmas dinner, long-hidden secrets and deep-seated grudges explode in a torrent of words, acts, and refusals to act that have the force of the reversals of a Greek tragedy. Son, whose origins are totally unknown to the Street household, brings emotional agony to it—but he also brings revelations and a catharsis that Morrison wishes us to see as a kind of redemption and promise of a new life for Valerian, Margaret, Jadine, Sidney and Ondine. After that dinner, they are all expelled from the idyllic garden of the greenhouse and thrown back into the briar patch of reality where, Morrison seems to say, they should have been all along.

The final act of the novel is a love story about Jadine and Son that follows them on a spiritual and geographical odyssey from the Caribbean island, to the island of Manhattan, to an all-black town in Florida, and then back to the island.

As this summary suggests, in *Tar Baby* Toni Morrison is not trying to present realistic portraits. She is a fable writer intrigued by stereotypes and cliches—by the rich white liberals with a violent guilty secret; by the Uncle Tom; by the contrast between the house and the field Negro; by the "high yaller gal" who's lost touch with her blackness but doesn't really fit in anywhere else. And the way that Morrison writes about all of this is closer in style to the Latin American magic realists than to most of her American contemporaries.

The hallmark of that style in Morrison's fiction, aside from its fabulous quality, is her love of language and the audacity of her metaphors and imagery. "Yardman's face was nothing to enjoy, but his teeth were a treat" she writes in describing the gardener. Margaret has her mind in "automatic park." Son has "wild, aggressive, vicious hair that needed to be put in jail. Uncivilized, reform-school hair. Mau-Mau, Attica, chain gang hair."

Morrison paints pictures with words, and in *Tar Baby* many of the most impressive of those pictures are of a natural world that is as alive as—more alive than—the people who are surrounded by it. This seems especially appropriate in a novel whose conflicts are between the greenhouse and the briar patch, order and disorder, restraint and impulse, simple stereotypes and complex reality. Everything on the island vibrates in Morrison's prose, and the effect is absolutely stunning. Consider the opening paragraph of the first chapter:

> When laborers imported from Haiti came to clear the land, clouds and fish were convinced the world was over, that the sea-green green of the sea and the sky-blue sky of the sky were no longer permanent. Wild parrots that had escaped the stones of hungry children . . . agreed and raised havoc as they flew away to look for another refuge. Only the champion daisy trees were serene. After all, they were part of a rain forest already two thousand years old and scheduled for eternity, so they ignored the men and continued to rock the diamondbacks that slept in their arms. It took the river to persuade them that the world was indeed altered. That never again would the rain be equal, and by the time they realized it and had run their roots deeper, clutching the earth like lost boys found, it was too late. The men had already folded the earth where there had been no fold and hollowed her where there had been no hollow, which explains what happened to the river. It crested, then lost its course, and finally its head. Evicted from the place where it had lived, and forced into unknown turf, it could not form its pools or waterfalls, and ran every which way. The clouds gathered, stood still and watched the river scuttle around the forest floor, crash headlong into the haunches of the hills with no notion of where it was going, until exhausted, ill and grieving, it slowed to a stop . . . The clouds looked at each other, then broke apart in confusion.

Or the beginning of the third chapter:

> Fog came to that place in wisps sometimes, like the hair of maiden aunts. Hair so thin and pale it went unnoticed until masses of it gathered around the house and threw back one's reflection from the

windows. The sixty-four bulbs in the dining-room chandelier were no more than a rhinestone clip in the hair of the maiden aunts . . . Jadine and Margaret touched their cheeks and their temples to dry the places the maiden aunts were kissing.

Passages like these appear everywhere in *Tar Baby*, until personification seems much too weak a term to describe their effect. It is overpowering, enchanting, genuinely enthralling.

I have said little so far about Morrison's themes, but that should not suggest that her beautifully told tale doesn't have them. On one level, Toni Morrison seems to be writing a parable about black-white relations—in the 1960's and earlier. On another, she is treating the tension she sees within black characters raised close to nature and suddenly thrust into the housing blocks of the city. On another, she is treating the perennial subject of civilization's tenuousness in the face of the overpowering forces of nature. On still another, she is writing of relations between black men and women, of the identities they have been given and those they struggle to make for themselves. And, on still another, she is writing her own variations on Zora Neale Hurston's *Their Eyes Were Watching God*, Nella Larsen's *Quicksand*, Eugene O'Neill's *All God's Chillun Got Wings*, Beckett's *Waiting for Godot* and *Endgame*, Harold Pinter's *The Caretaker*, and Edward Albee's *Who's Afraid of Virginia Woolf?*

In other words, this is an incredibly ambitious novel—at least as ambitious as her previous, breakthrough novel, *The Song of Solomon* (1977). It's also more than a little confusing. The title image of the Tar Baby, for example, has so many implications and applications that it is hard to know just what we are meant to make of it. Is the truth behind the absence of Valerian and Margaret's son a tar baby? Is Son a tar baby to the Streets and the Childses, since after contact with him they will never be the same? Is Jadine a tar baby to Son, because acting out the consequences of his obsession with her leads to his being thrown back into a state of nature? Is Son a tar baby to Jadine, since once she's met him and been forced to confront him and his blackness her life changes in ways that she could not have planned or predicted? And there are at least a half dozen more possible meanings of the title.

But if some of its ambitions are not fully realized or wholly clear, so many of them are that *Tar Baby* is sure to be viewed both as one of the most important American fictions of the decade and as further evidence of the power of Toni Morrison's unique voice and vision.

Stark-Naked Truth

Erica Jong

John Barth's essay "The Literature of Exhaustion," first published in 1967, has since become famous—not only as a source of understanding of his own career, but also as a key to understanding the impulses behind some of the works of his contemporaries. Barth suggested that if, as many were suggesting at the time, the novel was either dead or dying— due to competition from other media or to the sense that its subjects had become stale or used up—perhaps writers might be able to revitalize it by going back to the roots of narrative for their characters and forms. For Barth himself, this led to using Greek mythological characters in his collections *Chimera* and *Lost in the Funhouse*; trying to create his own mythology in *Giles Goat-Boy*; and using characters from his previous books in his epistolary novel *LETTERS*. It also led to his writing what is probably his best book, *The Sot-Weed Factor*, in the language and form of an eighteenth-century English novel.

In *Fanny* (1980), subtitled "the True History of the Adventures of Fanny Hackabout-Jones," Erica Jong tries her hand at creating a contemporary novel in the style and language of the eighteenth century. Like Barth's *The Sot-Weed Factor*, like John Fowles's *The French Lieutenant's Woman*, Jong's *Fanny* is a sparkling *tour de force* that combines an older literary style with a thoroughly modern sensibility to produce something genuinely original and wonderfully entertaining.

One of the essential elements for making this sort of thing work is having such a thorough grasp of the language and style of the time in which the book is supposedly written that the writing does not seem strained and the reader is not brought up short by (unintended) anachronisms. Before becoming a poet and novelist, before becoming famous as the author of *Fear of Flying* (1973), Erica Jong studied and taught eighteenth-century literature, and her extensive knowledge of the period and its characters lends an air of veracity and authenticity to her book. As a student of the period, she is naturally an admirer of the its masterpieces—of Defoe's *Moll Flanders*, Fielding's *Tom Jones* and *Joseph Andrews*, of Richardson's *Pamela* and *Clarissa*. And, of course—after all, she *is* the author of *Fear of Flying*—John Cleland's *Fanny Hill: The Memoirs of a Woman of Pleasure*. Echoes of all these books can be heard in *Fanny*.

In fact, the book, which is supposedly written by Fanny in 1750 as a gift to her daughter Belinda, is, we are told, prompted by Cleland's pornographic novel. Fanny claims to be the original of Cleland's character and intends her book to be a corrective to his since, as a man, he distorted her experience for profit. Like the other eighteenth-century heroes and heroines, Fanny is an orphan who is taken advantage of by a lascivious master and forced to go out into the wicked world where she encounters a multitude of adventures, many of them sexual. Like the other eighteenth-century narrators, Fanny insists on the truth of her story. "If these Pages oft' tell of Debauchery and Vice," she tells us at the outset, "'tis not in any wise because their Author wishes to condone Wickedness, but rather because Truth, Stark-Naked Truth, demands that she write with all possible Candor, so that the Inheritor of this Testament shall learn how to avoid Wickedness or indeed transform it into Goodness." "The World is so taken up of late with Histories and Romances in which Vice fore'er perishes and Virtue triumphs," she continues, "that the intended Reader may wonder why Vice is not always punish'd and Virtue not always rewarded in these Pages as in the Histories of Mr. Fielding and Mr. Richardson; to which our Humble Author can only reply that 'tis Truth we serve here, not Morality, and with howe'er much Regret we affirm it, ne'ertheless we must affirm that Truth and Morality do not always, Alas, sleep in the same bed."

In the interests of Education and Truth, then, we are treated to the adventures of Fanny Hackabout-Jones, who summarizes them as "Orphan, Whore, Adventuress, Kept Woman, Slaver, Amanuensis, Witch . . . Pyrate." And along the way we are introduced to the gallery of characters we expect of any self-respecting eighteenth-century novel. They include Fanny's artistic clients at Mrs. Coxart's brothel: Jonathan Swift, the playwright Colley Cibber's oldest son, John Cleland himself, and William Hogarth, the painter (each, of course, has his own peculiar sexual preferences which are fully detailed)—as well as the poet of the age, Alexander Pope, whose personal appearance and sexual technique, Fanny learns to her dismay, do not match his poetic prowess. Outside of the brothel, they include Lancelot Andrews—"Robin Hood reborn"—and his Merry Men, whose band she joins, first as a robber and later as a pirate; Anne Bonny, the famous woman pirate; and Horatio, as escaped slave and member of the Merry Men who is fond of quoting the Latin poets, in Latin.

But just as the eighteenth-century novels of Defoe, Fielding, and Richardson were more than just picaresque adventures, Jong's novel develops several underlying ideas. Most are suggested by the chapter titles that, in the eighteenth-century way, give us an extensive, often comic, idea of what we're about to read before we read it. Chapter XII, for example, is described as "Containing some Essential Information regarding the Nature of Esbats, Sabbats, Flying thro' the Air upon Broomstaffs, and other Matters with which the enlight'nd Young Woman of Parts should be acquainted; together with a most dreadful scene upon Stonehenge Down, which few Readers should venture upon in Ev'ning, especially when alone." Another chapter concerns ". . . some Philosophical Meditations upon the Phases of Childbirth, after which the Author enters into the Controversy (which raged thro'out the age) betwixt Midwifes and *Accoucheurs*, and thereafter ends the Chapter."

What these chapter titles suggest is that Erica Jong's rewriting of the eighteenth-century novel may seem to have the same kind of heroine as its predecessors, but she is a heroine created by a woman—with a woman's point of view and a late twentieth-century woman's raised consciousness. The novel's observations on relations between the sexes, on marriage, on childbirth and children, are all grounded in a feminist perspective. So is Jong's treatment of witches as the descendants of earlier "Wise Women," as liberated women who were persecuted and reviled because they refused to accept either male domination or a male God, and as midwives who competed with the dominant medical profession and were ultimately suppressed by it.

Fanny is guaranteed to amuse any reader who enjoys eighteenth-century novels, or feminist novels, or comic novels, or Erica Jong. It's also a wonderful recovery from *How to Save Your Own Life* (1977), Jong's previous novel and the much anticipated successor to *Fear of Flying*, which was generally viewed as self-indulgent and embarrassingly autobiographical. *Fanny* is neither. It's a charming, funny, and carefully-wrought novel in which Jong has expanded her horizons with remarkable results.

III

The Witness of Poetry

Czeslaw Milosz

Reality isn't just stranger than fiction; occasionally it's more artful. The plot that unfolded in Poland in 1980-81, for example, was marked by dozens of characters, images, and incidents whose symmetry and symbolism even the most inventive novelist must have looked on with envy. One such incident, largely unreported in the United States, took place on June 11, 1981. It wasn't the kind of confrontation that many of us anxiously watched and read about during that extraordinary time but, rather, a symbolic gathering of the various forces that made such confrontations not only possible but inevitable.

It happened in the city of Lublin. To the Polish people, as inveterately steeped in traditions and memories of the past as we Americans are in novelty and visions of the future, Lublin is far more than just another dot on the national map where more than 300,000 people live and work. Its name conjures up historical episodes that evoke wildly contradictory feelings.

Lublin reminds them of the glory days of the fifteenth and sixteenth centuries, when it was a provincial capital of the Jagiellonian dynasty and the site of the signing of the Act of Union between Poland and Lithuania, which created an empire that stretched as far as the environs of Moscow. But it also reminds them of the darkest days of World War II, when its outskirts housed Majdanek, one of the Nazi concentration camps. They connect it with the events of July 1944, when a Soviet-backed group called the Lublin Committee declared itself the legitimate government of postwar Poland. But it is also now remembered for the events of July 1980, when a transportation strike there against food price increases touched off a series of labor actions throughout Poland that culminated in the Gdansk strike, the fall of the Gierek government, and the birth of Solidarity. Finally, it is the home of the Catholic University of Lublin—a source of great pride, not only because it was the first Polish university to open its doors after the devastation and intellectual repression of the war years, but because it remained until 1989 the only private university functioning in the Soviet bloc.

On June 11, 1981, this university, which epitomized the independence and indomitability of the Polish spirit and is located in a city whose experience reflects all of the contradictions of Polish history, conferred its honorary doctorate on a writer who had officially been an "unperson" for thirty years in the land whose literature he has chronicled and enriched. A writer whose own independence and indomitability had made him Poland's unofficial poet laureate through all the years that his name could not be mentioned in print and his writing had to be passed from hand to hand in underground editions and tape recordings.

A year earlier, before the emergence of Solidarity, when the Catholic University had invited him to accept its doctorate, he could not get a visa to return to Poland to receive it. But in 1981, at the height of Solidarity's power, he was officially welcomed at the airport by ministers of the Communist government that had banned all but two of his many books for decades; was wined and dined by those same party functionaries; was interviewed and widely quoted on the state-controlled nightly newscasts; found his novel, *The Issa Valley*, being serialized on state-run radio; saw a commemorative stamp issued in his honor; and was treated to the spectacle of the first officially sanctioned edition of his collected poetry published in Poland selling out its initial press-run of 20,000 copies *in a single day*. (Within a month, 200,000 copies—of a book of *poetry*—would be sold.)

And while Czeslaw Milosz, the exiled poet laureate, was being openly honored by the Catholic University of Lublin, Lech Walesa, the voice of social change, was speaking just a half a mile away. Before the day was out, they met—Walesa quoted Milosz's poetry to its author—and, in that meeting, we are presented with a vivid image that sums up the elements in the Polish character and tradition that spawned what the Poles called their "renewal." That character and that tradition are what Milosz's writing has both reflected and helped to shape.

Czeslaw Milosz was born on June 30, 1911, in a small village near Wilno (now Vilnius) in Lithuania to Polish-speaking descendants of Lithuanian gentry. In his autobiography, *Native Realm: A Search for Self-Definition* (1958), Milosz reports that his first memories are of exile.

Like thousands of other refugees, his family fled Lithuania for Russia when the Germans invaded at the beginning of World War I. After the war, Milosz's family returned to a rural Lithuania that he describes as steeped in religion, superstition, and nature in his lyrical second novel *The Issa Valley* (1955).

He attended Zygmunt August High School and King Stefan Batory University in Wilno—a city he often recalls in his poetry—and was a founding member of the poetry group Zagary and its literary magazine. In 1931, he traveled to Paris, where he met the French poet Oscar de L. Milosz, a distant relative whose work and mystical temperament were a major influence on the younger Milosz's intellectual development. In 1933, he published his first book, *A Poem on Frozen Time*. In 1934 he earned a law degree, won an award from the Polish Writers' Union, and received a fellowship that allowed him to spend another year in Paris.

When Milosz returned to Wilno, he worked at its Polish radio station and published his second book of poems, *Three Winters* (1936). In 1937, he moved to Warsaw, where he joined a group of poets known as the Catastrophists because of their apocalyptic view of the future of Europe and Western civilization. In 1939, the Catastrophists' worst nightmares were realized when Germany again invaded Poland and the Nazis quickly occupied Warsaw. During the occupation, Milosz was an active member of the Polish resistance and a major contributor to the city's elaborate underground culture. He edited *Invincible Song*, a mimeographed anthology of resistance poetry; translated Jacques Maritain's *A travers le desastre*, an attack against French collaboration with the Germans; and wrote poems such as "The World: A Naive Poem" and "The Voices of Poor People," which were published by the underground presses and passed from hand to hand in the desolated city. When the Communists took power in postwar Poland, a volume of his collected poems, *Rescue* (1945), was one of the first books published by the new government.

As a prominent anti-Nazi, resistance figure, and poet, Milosz's support was eagerly sought by the new regime. At first, he gave it: between 1946 and 1950 he served as a Polish cultural attaché to Washington and Paris. But in 1951 he broke with the government and became an exile in Paris. At a time when most French intellectuals were still enamored of Stalin and the Soviet Union, Milosz courageously spoke the unwelcome truth about intellectual life in the East in the essays published as *The Captive Mind* (1953)—a book that the critic Irving Howe described as "a central text in the modern effort to understand totalitarianism." In the same year, his first novel was published in French as *The Seizure of Power* (1953) and awarded the prestigious Prix Litteraire Europeen.

In 1960, he accepted a position as a professor of Slavic languages at the University of California at Berkeley and moved to America—his final exile—where he has lived and worked ever since. Since 1960, his books in English have included an anthology of *Postwar Polish Poetry* (1965) and *The History of Polish Literature* (1969); ten books of poetry in Polish, selections of which were published in English in *Selected Poems* (1973); eight other books of poetry, *Bells in Winter* (1978), *The Separate Notebooks* (1984), *Unattainable Earth* (1986), *Collected Poems* (1988), *Provinces* (1991), *Facing the River* (1995), *Road-Side Dog* (1998), and *A Treatise on Poetry* (2001); four collections of essays, *Emperor of the Earth* (1977), *Visions from San Francisco Bay* (1982), *The Land of Ulro* (1984), and *Beginning with My Streets* (1992); the *Nobel Lecture* (1981) and *The Witness of Poetry* (1983), a series of lectures originally presented at Harvard; *The Year of the Hunter* (1994), a journal, and *Milosz's ABC's* (2001). In 1978, Milosz was awarded the Neustadt International Prize for Literature by the University of Oklahoma. In 1980, he was awarded the Nobel Prize for Literature by the Swedish Academy.

In the West, Milosz observes in *The Witness of Poetry*, "the separation of art and the public has been an accomplished fact" since the time of Baudelaire. "In various schools and manifestoes of the twentieth century there was a division into two camps: on one side those who earn and spend, with their cult of work, their religion, and their patriotism, and, on the other, the bohemians, whose religion is art and whose morality is the negation of all values recognized by the other camp."

"In Central and Eastern Europe," he wrote thirty years earlier in *The Captive Mind*, "a poet does not merely arrange words in beautiful order. Tradition demands that he be a 'bard,' that his songs linger on many lips, that he speak in his poems of subjects of interest to all the citizens." Czeslaw Milosz has himself been such a bard.

What these two statements by Milosz suggest is that to approach his poetry is to confront an aesthetic that many of us cannot help but find unfamiliar, even uncongenial. Children of modernism, with its emphases on the tradition of the new, the avant-garde role of the artist, the alienation of the poet from his audience, and the value of difficulty, we find ourselves challenged to understand a view of poetry as witness, of the poet as the voice *of* the people, speaking *to* the people, rather than an individual voice speaking to a select few poetry readers. His Polish readers, of course, do not have this problem. So when a monument was erected in 1981 to the memory of the Polish workers slain in the Gdansk food strikes of 1970, the words the workers chose to put on its base were taken from one of his poems: "You who harmed a simple man,/ Don't feel secure/ Because a poet remembers./ You can kill him/ but another will appear./ The words are written down, the deed, the date."

"A poet remembers . . . " To Milosz and his Polish readers, this is more than just a warning or a promise. It's a definition of vocation. For what Milosz has done in all the books he has written over more than half a century is, above all, to remember: to keep his and his era's past alive in the present through the power of his words. Those words have mostly been written in Polish, even though Milosz has lived in the United States since 1960. So the man whom Joseph Brodsky, the Russian émigré poet and another Nobel Prize winner, has described as "perhaps the greatest poet of our time" can only be read here in translation. And, in the case of poetry, even the best translation can be little more than an approximation in which much of the flavor and allusiveness of the original are inevitably lost.

Czeslaw Milosz, a translator himself, has always understood this predicament. "The abyss for me was exile," he wrote in *The Captive Mind* shortly after emigrating to the West. "My mother tongue, work in my mother tongue, is for me the most important thing in life... I did not want to become an émigré and so give up all chance of taking a hand in all that was going on in my country." And it was his sense of bring condemned to lose the only audience that could read him in the original that caused him to stay in Poland and cope with the demands of socialist realism and the cultural commissars during the first part of the Stalinist era. When he finally broke with his country, he says in *The Captive Mind*, he fully expected the consequences to be not just exile but "sterility and inaction."

"Wrong Honorable Professor Milosz," he writes sardonically of himself in the poem "A Magic Mountain," "Who wrote poems in some unheard-of tongue./ Who will count them anyway." In one section of the cycle "From the Rising of the Sun," he sums up his situation with even greater irony and wit. "Oh yes," he writes, "not all of me shall die, there will remain/ An item in the fourteenth volume of an encyclopedia/ Next to a hundred Millers and Mickey Mouse." Nevertheless, Milosz has remained faithful to both his native language and his Eastern European sense of the poet's vocation.

Memory, he declares in the early poem "Magpiety," has always been his Muse. In his *Nobel Lecture*, he explains why. "Perhaps our most precious acquisition is ... respect and gratitude for certain things which protect people from internal disintegration and from yielding to tyranny," he writes. Paramount among those things is memory. But, he goes on to say, "our planet that gets smaller every year, with its fantastic proliferation of mass media, is witnessing a process that escapes definition, characterized by a refusal to remember." This process, he insists, makes H.G. Wells's vision in *The Time Machine*—of an "Earth inhabited by a tribe of children of the day, carefree, deprived of memory, and, by the same token, of history, without defense when confronted with dwellers of subterranean caves, cannibalistic children of the night"—more credible than we would like to acknowledge. "During the thirty years I have spent abroad," he admits, "I have felt I was more privileged than my Western colleagues, whether writers or teachers of literature, for events, both recent and long past, took in my mind a sharply delineated and precise form."

In *Native Realm*, he speaks of a new organ: "the telescopic eye, that perceives simultaneously not only different points on the globe but also different moments in time . . . . New images cancelled out none of the old . . . . I do not see them in chronological order as in a strip of film, but in parallel, colliding with one another, overlapping." Memory "is our force," he explains in the *Nobel Lecture*, "it protects us against speech entwining upon itself like ivy when it does not find support on a tree or a wall." The poet's role must be *to see* and *to describe*. But "'To see' means not only to have before one's eyes. It may also mean to preserve in memory. 'To see and to describe' may also mean to reconstruct in imagination."

The reader of Milosz's poetry is immediately struck by this effort "to reconstruct in imagination," to make memories live again through description. Poem after poem is built of powerful and recurrent images of his Lithuanian boyhood, his World War II youth, and his California émigré adulthood. The poems vary in tone, of course—many of the more recent ones, for example, strive to make affirmations in the face of the historical tragedies he has seen in his long life. Many of his strongest and most memorable poems are those in which he recalls the war years and their aftermath with a survivor's painful guilt.

The poems written during and just after the occupation and destruction of Warsaw are given the general title "What Did He Learn" in his *Selected Poems*. The first is "Dedication," a homage to those who died from one who survived. In it, Milosz acknowledges the difficulty of speaking about the unspeakable, reveals his guilt at having lived to tell the story of those years, and dedicates himself to writing poetry that will grapple with history and memory.

"Dedication" begins by directly addressing those to whom it is dedicated—"You whom I could not save/ Listen to me"—as if the poet sees them before him, and must speak to give their spirits rest. He then confesses his own lack of skill and expresses his decision to abandon the aesthetic of complexity that characterized his pre-war writing: "Try to understand this simple speech as I would be ashamed of another./ I swear there is in me no wizardry of words." In the second stanza, he tries to understand why he survived and fails. All he can say is that, somehow, "What strengthened me, for you was lethal." He then recalls the excitement of the pre-war years, when the Catastrophists and other talented young people, now dead, faced anxiety with energy and art. "You mixed up farewell to an epoch with the beginning of a new one./ Inspiration of hatred with lyrical beauty,/ Blind force with accomplished shape."

The third stanza links the dead with the destroyed city, nearly burned to the ground by the Germans while the Soviet Army watched from the opposite bank of the Vistula River. "Here is the valley of shallow Polish rivers. And an immense bridge/ Going into white fog. Here is a broken city." The white fog literally describes the smoldering city; but it also suggests that what lay on the far side of the bridge—the Soviet Army, doing nothing to help—was shrouded in silence in Communist Poland, where official dogma whitewashed the Soviets into the city's saviors.

In the fourth stanza, the elegiac tone of the first three stanzas is replaced by an angrier, tougher voice. A voice that seems to rebuke the poet himself, while insisting that after this destruction poetry can never be the same. "What is poetry which does not save/ Nations or people?" the poet asks. And then he quickly and absolutely answers his own question: "A connivance with official lies,/ A song of drunkards whose throats will be cut in a moment,/ Readings for sophomore girls." The poet clearly speaks from bitter experience. Only now does he see what poetry must be and do. And, while he does not totally condemn his own earlier efforts in a different poetic vein, he strongly feels the need to move beyond them. "That I wanted good poetry without knowing it,/ That I discovered, late, its salutary aim,/ In this and only this I find salvation," he says. That "late" is a profound self-indictment which echoes throughout the remainder of Milosz's career—an indictment to which he pleads guilty and of which he will never quite exonerate himself.

In the final, haunting stanza, the young poet who wanted to escape the provinces for the cosmopolitan worlds of Paris and Warsaw (see his poem "Bypassing Rue Descartes") finds himself returning to his roots, as he compares the book he is dedicating with the village ceremonies of his childhood in Lithuania. "They used to pour millet on graves or poppy seeds," he recalls. "To feed the dead who would come disguised as birds./ I put this book here for you, who once lived/ So that you should visit us no more." This proves to be a vain hope. For in the other poems in his first postwar book, and in many of the poems that will follow, Milosz is drawn back, again and again, to these same memories of the war and its dead.

In the *Selected Poems*, the poet's education continues—from "Song of a Citizen" ("I, poor man, see a multitude of white-bellied nations/ without freedom . . ."); to "A Poor Christian Looks at the Ghetto" ("Phosphorescent fire from yellow walls/ Engulfs animal and human hair . . ./ Now there is only earth, sandy, trodden down,/ with one leafless tree"); to "The Poor Poet" ("Since I opened my eyes I have seen only the glow of fires,/ massacres/ Only injustice, humiliation, and the laughable shame of braggarts./ To me is given the hope of revenge on others and on myself/ For I was he who knew/ And took from it no profit for myself."). And then to the terrifying "Child of Europe," which begins "We, whose lungs fill the sweetness of day,/ Who in May admire trees flowering,/ Are better than those who perished"; moves on to a set of rules for survivors, "Love no country: countries soon disappear./ Love no cities: cities are soon rubble./ . . . Do not love people: people soon perish./ Or they are wronged and call for your help./ Do not gaze into the pools of the past./ Their corroded surface will mirror/ A face different from the one you expected"; and then concludes with a cynical realization, "He who invokes history is always secure./ The dead will not rise to witness against him./ You can accuse them of any deeds you like./ Their reply will always be silence."

But when Milosz himself gazes into "the pools of the past" he finds that, millet or no, the dead visit again and again. This has not been easy for him to live with or accept. "In Milan," written in France in 1955, expresses the conflict that he has faced throughout his career. As "Dedication" shows, he feels compelled to use his art to bear witness to his time. Yet he has always felt an equally strong attraction to embracing the beauty of existence and the pleasures of the senses, to transcending his experience of history through mysticism, nature, and art. These two impulses are apparent in the mix of poems he has chosen to include in each of his collections; and occasionally, as in "In Milan," they become the subject of the poems themselves.

The poem begins with two brief stanzas. The first recalls a time, years ago, when the impulse to celebrate the beauty of life led the poet to write poems on Italy. The second recounts a charge made by a friend as they walked at night through a piazza: that Milosz's art was "too politicized." The third, longest stanza records Milosz's reply—a response that is both deeply felt and tinged with regret. He would love to write poems about the beauty of the world, Milosz says: "I am for the moon amid the vineyards. I am for the cypresses at dawn." He could "compose, right now, a song/ On the taste of peaches, on September in Europe." In fact, "I would like to gobble up/ All existing flowers, to eat all the colors./ I have been devouring this world in vain/ For forty years, a thousand would not be enough." He would desperately like to be "a poet of the five senses"— because those senses are so powerful, because it would be easy to lose oneself in their pleasures—but "That's why I don't allow myself to become one." *Because* "thought has less weight than the word *lemon*," it needs a poet to express it, to defend it, to insist on its importance.

In this poem, Milosz manages to have it both ways. In a poem of ideas which regretfully insists on his commitment to ideas in poetry, he creates an occasion which allows him to write exactly the kind of poem he claims he must not allow himself: a poem full of beauty, emotion, and sensuous imagery.

More often, he accepts his role—a heartrending one—as the spokesman of those who are gone to those would just as soon forget. As he writes in "The Unveiling," part of a long poem in *Bells in Winter*, "Whatever I hold in my hand, a stylus, reed, quill or a ballpoint,/Wherever I may be . . ./ I attend to matters I have been charged with in the provinces." In a prose part of the same poem, "Over Cities," he thinks that "I became a teacher in a city by the sea . . . . A multitude of their faces before me, these boys and girls, born when I was composing the first stanza of a threnody to be read at a memorial service, grew up before I managed to finish the poem." "Have I fulfilled anything, have I been of use to anyone?" Milosz asks in "From the Rising of the Sun."

The self-doubt seems genuine, and is still evident in an extraordinary later poem such as "Far Away," published when he was eighty. But while Milosz may still be asking himself these questions, even after his Nobel Prize and his triumphant return to his native land in 1981, we need not. For to the rest of us, and to the Polish people who have honored him, the answers to his questions are clear. Czeslaw Milosz has created a body of poetry and prose that serves as an eloquent testament to the human spirit struggling with the extremes of twentieth-century experience. And in that—in his poetic witness—he has, indeed, been "of use" to us all.

Laughable Loves

Milan Kundera

Milan Kundera grew up in the provincial capital of Brno and then went to Prague to attend Charles University and the Film Faculty of the Academy of Music and Dramatic Arts. In 1947, he joined the Communist Party. Like the majority of his countrymen, he initially celebrated the Communists' rise to power after the war as a victory of the future over the past; and, like the majority of his countrymen, he soon regretted this decision and found himself at odds with the Party. In 1950, he was expelled for "ideological differences" and left Prague to work as a laborer and jazz pianist in the provinces. In 1956 he was reinstated in the Party; two years later he became an assistant professor at the Institute for Advanced Cinematographic Studies of the Academy of Music and Dramatic Arts.

In 1963, Kundera became a member of the Central Committee of the Czechoslovak Writers Union, and between 1963 and 1968 he emerged as one of the most important literary figures in Prague. His three collections of short stories, published under the general title "Laughable Loves," were immensely popular and awarded the Czechoslovak Writers' Publishing House Prize. His first novel *The Joke*—finally published, unchanged, in 1968 after a two-year battle with the censors—quickly went through three editions and received the Czechoslovak Writers' Union Prize. With other prominent writers such as Ludvik Vaculik and Ivan Klima, Kundera used his stature in the Writers Union to press for "socialism with a human face" and thereby helped to usher in the Prague

Spring. So when the Soviet tanks rolled into Czechoslovakia and crushed this reform movement, Kundera and these other writers were immediately classified as enemies of the state.

His books were removed from libraries and bookstores, his plays were banned, he was fired from his teaching position and denied the right to publish in his own country. (Since 1970, the first editions of his books have all been published in French.) Between 1970 and 1975, he was both forbidden to work in Czechoslovakia and prevented from traveling abroad. To support himself at one point he wrote several thousand horoscopes for Prague clients and published a monthly astrology column under a pseudonym.

At the same moment that Kundera was cut off from publishing in his own country, an international readership began to discover him. *The Joke* was quickly translated into a dozen languages. His second novel *Life Is Elsewhere* (1973) was awarded the French Prix Medicis; his third, *The Farewell Party* (1976), received the Italian Premio Mondello. And in 1974 Philip Roth enthusiastically introduced his works to American readers by selecting *Laughable Loves* as one of the first volumes in the Writers from the Other Europe series that he edited for Penguin Books.

In 1975, the Czech authorities finally permitted Kundera and his wife to leave the country so that he could accept a visiting professorship in comparative literature at the University of Rennes. He arrived in France, at age forty-five, with two suitcases, a few books and some records. *The Book of Laughter and Forgetting* (1979), the first book he published after his emigration, both solidified his place in contemporary world literature and led to the revocation of his Czech citizenship. In 1980, he moved to Paris to become a professor at the Ecole des Hautes Etudes en Sciences Sociales, and in 1981 President Francois Mitterand made him a French citizen. The novels *The Unbearable Lightness of Being* (1984), *Immortality* (1990), *Slowness* (1995), and *Identity* (1997), the play *Jacques and His Master* (1981), and two collections of essays on literature and the history and fate of Central Europe, *The Art of the Novel* (1986) and *Testaments Betrayed* (1993) followed—along with the Commonwealth Award (1981), the Prix Europa (1982), and the Jerusalem Prize for Literature on the Freedom of Man in Society (1985).

"I tried a lot of things" before turning to fiction, Kundera has said: "cinema, painting, music, poetry, criticism, theory, aesthetics. But none of it was serious; I think of all that now as a kind of prehistory." Intellectually and artistically, he has repeatedly emphasized, "I am attached to nothing apart from the European novel, that unrecognized inheritance that comes to us from Cervantes."

As Kundera sees it, that inheritance is a record of both an extraordinary sequence of discoveries and a series of roads not taken. With Samuel

Richardson, he argues, the novel discovered psychological realism and, ever since, most novels have followed the nearly inviolable standards of that tradition. In the second half of the twentieth century, Kundera notes, it has often been argued that the novel is dead. He disagrees, insisting instead that since Richardson the novel has ignored many of its possibilities. One of the most important of those unexplored possibilities, he argues, is the one suggested by Laurence Sterne's *Tristram Shandy* and Denis Diderot's *Jacques le Fataliste*: the idea of the novel as a field of play rather than a representation of reality.

After Sterne and Diderot, Kundera owes his aesthetic of the novel to the examples of Central European novelists and artists of the past century—especially to Hermann Broch and the Czech composer Leos Janacek. He shares Hermann Broch's view that every serious novel must discover something that the novel—and no other form—can discover. And he has also experimented with several of the formal ideas contained in his favorite Broch novel, *The Sleepwalkers*: that the novel's traditional unity of *action* can be replaced by a unity of *theme*; that the musical technique known as polyphony—the simultaneous presentation of two or more voices or melodic lines that are both bound together and independent—can be adapted to enrich the form of the novel; and that such novelistic polyphony can allow the author to combine radically different non-novelistic genres within his text. From Janacek, his favorite composer, Kundera learned to upset technical conventions through ellipsis: to replace traditional transitions with harsh, abrupt juxtapositions, to replace repetition with variations, to eliminate the superfluous.

For Kundera, then, "a novel is a long piece of synthetic prose based on play with invented characters. These are the only limits." By *synthetic*, he told Philip Roth, he means "the novelist's desire to grasp his subject from all sides and in the fullest possible completeness. Ironic essay, novelistic narrative, autobiographical fragment, historic fact, flight of fantasy: The synthetic power of the novel is capable of combining everything into a unified whole like the voices of polyphonic music. The unity of the book need not stem from the plot, but can be provided by the theme."

A novel, he believes, should search and pose questions. The questions his own works pose are existential: "Who am I? What is a self? To what extent do I define my self, and to what extent is it defined by others? Do my choices define me, or does chance? What does life, living, being a human being, really *mean*?" The fact that Kundera can explore such weighty questions in novels that are also witty and entertaining is an essential aspect of his art and his appeal.

In each of his novels from *The Joke* to *Identity* his exploration of these existential questions is structured around a series of key words (or themes) that appear and reappear from book to book. *Immortality*, he says in that novel, would have been called *The Unbearable Lightness of Being* if he had not already used the title. All of his novels, he told an interviewer, might have been called *The Joke* or *Laughable Loves*. And each is a book of laughter and forgetting.

The book he actually assigned that title to, like all of Kundera's novels except *The Farewell Party*, is divided into seven parts. Several of the parts have the same titles—two are titled "Lost Letters," two are titled "Angels"—to underline the idea that *The Book of Laughter and Forgetting* is a series of variations on a set of themes. Two parts focus on a young woman named Tamina, but each of the other five focuses on unrelated characters who appear only in that part. Each of the seven parts combines several genres, such as traditional novelistic narrative, autobiography, philosophical essay, dream, political commentary, linguistic analysis, realistic description, and fantasy. The parts are not linked by a single plot, but by their direct or indirect relationship to Kundera's exploration of the meanings he attaches to words such as *laughter, forgetting, angels*, the *circle, litost*, and *border*, by his reflections on Czech history; and by Kundera's voice and presence as the authorial "I."

They are also connected—to one another, and to all of Kundera's other fiction—by their exploration of the interrelationship of public and private life. In Kundera's work, the threat that the border between public and private life will disappear—the fear that it already has—is the nightmare that lies behind all of the verbal and sexual hijinks. Most often, this threat is expressed as an invasion of private life by public life, seen as a distortion of the sexual by the political. In Kundera, sexual relations are an arena where the politically powerless exercise power, where the oppressed oppress, where public tragedy begets private comedy and tragicomedy. But they are also the sphere where character reveals itself most fully. And one of the paradoxes at the heart of his novels is that in their most intimate moments his characters are both most themselves and most the product of the external forces acting upon them.

The first part of *The Book of Laughter and Forgetting* perfectly demonstrates Kundera's novelistic method. Each of its sections presents private and public variations on the theme of forgetting. The love story of Mirek and Zdena is intimately connected to both their individual political histories and the history of their country. Mirek's desire to forget his former love Zdena, to "airbrush" her out of the picture of his past and his life, is a private reflection of the public effort of the Czech people to erase the past deed that *they* would like to forget—their support of the Communists in 1947-48. The Party is also engaged in an effort to forget when it seeks to eliminate *its* own past mistakes by airbrushing Clementis from the photograph described on the novel's first page. The bare space on the wall where Clementis once stood in the photograph is tied to the bare space in his history where Mirek's memories of Zdena should be. Zdena's passionate love of Mirek is presented as both a product of and the impulse behind the passionate single-mindedness that also made her a loyal Party member; Mirek's decision to become a political dissident is connected to his desire to forget the embarrassment of his youthful relationship with Zdena. And the hat on Gottwald's head is an emblem of all the personal and public pasts that cannot be erased.

Similar variations on the theme of forgetting continue throughout the novel, joined by new themes that are introduced with their own variations in each of the succeeding parts. The novel, Kundera writes is "about Tamina . . . She is its main character and main audience, and all the other stories are variations on her story and come together in her life as in a mirror." In other words, the parts devoted to Tamina—the fourth and sixth parts, which are the parts that repeat the titles of the earlier parts "Lost Letters" and "Angels"—are the heart of *The Book of Laughter and Forgetting*. There, the novel's themes echo and reverberate in a story that combines sex, love, exile, memory, forgetting, laughter, the circle, angels, politics, and borders in both startling and extremely subtle ways. And there they come together in a story that also introduces the thematic notes upon which Kundera's next novel would be composed.

To Tamina, the unbearable lightness of being represented by the island of memoryless children is the ultimate nightmare: a world in which meaning disappears and nothing matters. Like the later novel's Tereza (even their names echo one another), Tamina clings to meaning, to memory, to mortality—and to the existential burden of spiritual heaviness that comes with them—because, for her, that is what it means to be human. The alternative, Kundera seems to suggest in the novel's final section and coda, is a freedom without meaning and a life without purpose.

The Unbearable Lightness of Being is a novel that explores the nature of responsibility and identity through the story of two romantic triangles before, during, and after the Russian invasion of Czechoslovakia in 1968. In many ways, it is a more traditional novel than *The Book of Laughter and Forgetting*. It, too, mixes genres and is tied together by variations on a series of themes—*lightness* and *heaviness*, *body* and *soul*, *vertigo* and *eternal return*, *the Grand March*. But it also tells several clearly related stories about four fully-developed characters: the waitress/photographer Tereza, the doctor Tomas, the painter Sabina, and the professor Franz. While it does not follow the conventions of the realistic novel—the fact of the main characters' deaths is revealed long before it occurs, thereby undermining the plot's suspense; a major character is introduced toward the end of the novel and then disappears; a section is told from the point of view of Tereza and Tomas' dog—it does create and resolve a central conflict among these characters and occur within a recognizable social and historical context.

The main characters are carefully paired, both romantically and thematically. Tereza and Tomas, Tomas and Sabina, Sabina and Franz, are each involved in love affairs. Tereza and Franz are both associated with the theme of weight and heaviness; Tomas and Sabina, with the theme of lightness. Weight and heaviness are associated with the soul, commitment, seriousness, responsibility; lightness with the body, betrayal, infidelity, and selfishness. Through Tereza's influence, in the course of the novel Tomas makes the moral journey from lightness to heaviness. Sabina and Franz remain largely unchanged.

Tereza first comes to Prague from the country because of her love for Tomas, a man whose personal life is dominated by his numerous sexual conquests. When they and Sabina join the flood of émigrés after the Russian invasion and end up in Switzerland, Sabina finds Tereza's counterpart in Franz. When Tereza feels adrift in Zurich and returns to Czechoslovakia Tomas follows her, although he has lost his position at the hospital and is forced to become a window washer. Although his commitment to her is real, he continues to spend every free moment in dalliances with other women until his love for Tereza finally leads him to agree to leave the city and its temptations for a collective farm. There they eventually die together in a truck accident. Sabina rejects Franz's desire for commitment, and becomes a fashionable artist who travels throughout Europe and America. Franz joins a group of European Leftists who travel to Cambodia, drawn by the idea of "the Grand March" of international revolution, which he sees as somehow related to his love for Sabina. There he is fatally injured.

As Kundera tells the story, the personal and sexual lives of these four characters are intimately bound up with the social and political realities of Czechoslovakia before and after the Russian invasion. He presents vivid glimpses of the Prague Spring, of the Russian invasion, of post-1968 life in Prague, of the emigration of Czechs to the West, and of Western political attitudes toward émigrés and toward the idea of revolutionary change. And, in spite of his many comments about the unreality of fictional characters, in *The Unbearable Lightness of Being* he also creates four believable and interesting characters whose fates are made to matter to the reader. As a consequence, perhaps, this has so far been the most widely-read and highly-praised of his novels.

Milan Kundera has often objected to political readings of his fiction, emphasizing that his novels are about the existential dilemmas of his characters and complaining that Western readers are drawn to the work of writers from "the other Europe" for the wrong reasons. He has also spoken often of his ideas about the novel, the fate of Central Europe, and the role of Central Europe in the culture of the West. His interviews, essays, and comments are required reading for anyone who is interested in any of these matters. But, finally, Kundera will be remembered for the power and accomplishment of his novels themselves—works which, together with those of his contemporaries from Eastern, Central, and Western Europe, North, Central, and South America, amply demonstrate that the novel is anything but exhausted or dead in our time.

Life with a Star

Jiri Weil

Jiri Weil's *Life with a Star* (1948) has been described as the first important work of Czech fiction to come out of World War II. Its reception and its author's fate now seem all too familiar, indeed, exemplary. Weil's first novel *From Moscow to the Border* (1947), which described what he observed of the purge after Sergei Kirov's murder and the beginning of Stalin's Great Terror while he was working in Moscow in the International Department of the Comintern, earned him expulsion from the Communist Party and the Czech Writers Union, as well as a year in the labor camps of Central Asia. In 1948, Weil sought readmission to the Party and the Writers Union, submitting the required self-criticism of his former failure to become a "good Communist"; he was rejected by the Party but readmitted to the Writers Union and, therefore, allowed to publish once again.

In the early 1950's, Weil was expelled a second time as a result of *Life with a Star*, which was banned shortly after its publication as a "decadent" example of "pernicious existentialism" by the cultural apparatchiks whose dogma remained Socialist Realism. In 1957, during the cultural thaw following Nikita Khrushchev's secret speech attacking Stalin and his "cult of personality," Weil was once again admitted to the Writers Union, permitted to publish a collection of short stories, and named director of the Jewish State Museum in Prague. He remained a marginal man, however, and when he died of leukemia in 1959 all of his works were out of print in his own country. He left two completed novels that were published posthumously: *Mendelssohn Is on the Roof* (1960) and *The Wooden Spoon*, a sequel to *From Moscow to the Border* that was first published in Italian translation in 1970 in a volume that included both the earlier work and the sequel.

Life with a Star appeared in English thanks to Philip Roth who, in his role as editor of Penguin's Writers from the Other Europe series, also helped to introduce American readers to the work of Milan Kundera, Bohumil Hrabal, Tadeusz Borowski, Tadeusz Konwicki, Danilo Kis, Ivan Klima, Jerzy Andrzejewski and other Central and Eastern European writers. In 1960, as a young writer whose eyes were focused primarily on the near-at-hand, Roth delivered a speech that has since become famous titled "Writing American Fiction." The American writer, he said, "has his hands full in trying to understand, describe, and then make credible much of American reality. It stupefies, it sickens, it infuriates, and finally it is even a kind of embarrassment to one's own meager imagination. The actuality is continually outdoing our talents, and the culture tosses up figures almost daily that are the envy of any novelist."

By the early 1970s, Roth's horizons had expanded considerably, largely because of his fascination with Franz Kafka, and he began making annual visits to Prague and other cities in Eastern Europe. There he met writers whose history and everyday reality were challenging to the novelist in ways that his younger self had never imagined. He first heard of Weil in 1973 on one of his earliest visits to Prague. When he returned to New York, he met a translator who had completed English versions of two of Weil's short stories. Their publication in *American Poetry Review* in 1974, with an introduction by Roth, marked both Weil's first appearance in English and Roth's emerging interest in contemporary Eastern European writers.

Life with a Star, which appeared in English translation in 1989, is a novel stamped on every page by Weil's personal experience both before and during World War II. Like his hero Josef Roubicek, and tens of thousands of other Czechs, Weil wore a Jewish star during the Nazi occupation. Like Roubicek, he passed up a chance to emigrate to England early in the war. Like Roubicek, he watched the transports begin to leave for Terezin and points unknown in 1942, heard the rumors about their ultimate destinations, and grasped at the hope that the rumors were not true. And, like Roubicek, one day he received the summons to report to the Radio Mart for transportation. *Life with a Star* is a novel about a man trying to make up his mind. It ends when Roubicek decides to turn to the friends who have offered to hide him rather than to report as ordered. Roth tells the reader what happened next to Roubicek's creator after he made the same decision: Weil left a briefcase with his identification papers on a bridge over the Vltava River, faked suicide by jumping into the water below, and disappeared until the end of the war.

While clearly autobiographical, *Life with a Star* is also rich in literary antecedents and affinities. Roubicek is part of a long Central European line of oppressed "little men," a direct descendant of Jaroslav Hasek's Schweik and Kafka's Josef K. (It is hardly coincidental that Weil names him Josef.) Weil's consciously simple, spare and understated style—"It was good to sit quietly and listen. It was good not to think about the chapel, about the circus, or about the transports to the east; it was good not to think of bread spread with lean cheese or barley cooked in water; it was good not to know about the decrees and prohibitions, about being throw out of streetcars, or about processions and the sound of metal-tipped boots"—echoes the Hemingway who was admired by both existentialists and socialist realists in the late 1940's and early 1950's.

Life with a Star also invites comparison to some of the most powerful works of fiction to have emerged from the Holocaust. Like the concentration camp stories in Tadeusz Borwoski's *This Way for the Gas, Ladies and Gentlemen*, Weil's novel forces the reader to confront the ways in which human beings faced with imminent extermination became compliant cogs in the machinery of destruction; how the desire for self-preservation could lead one person to exult at being spared while he saw thousands of others condemned; how the struggle for a slice of bread or a cup of soup could become the whole world. Like Aharon Appelfeld's *Badenheim 1939*, *Life with a Star* is also a novel whose power grows out of its obliqueness. The camps are not shown in Weil's novel. Instead, he depicts the bureaucracy that helped to fill them, the signposts that pointed to them, and the complex emotions that the vague prospect of them engendered. His story is filled with the petty restrictions that eventually became a prison of separation and isolation, with the trickle of rumors that became a torrent, with the growing doubts that were quieted by ever-greater self-deceptions, with the declining hopes that were kept alive by faith and pure will, with the ultimate despair that finally sapped the spirit when will could no longer deny reality.

It is not hard to understand the reaction of the Party hacks who condemned Weil's novel. At a time when workers' solidarity was expected, Weil focused his attention on the thoughts and feelings of a radically isolated man. At a time when the prescribed tone was optimism, his novel was wracked with despair. At a time when both Czechs and Communists were trying to forget their complicity in the extermination of the Jews, Weil presented unforgettable reminders of that complicity. In 1948 Josef Roubicek's destruction of almost all of his possessions may have been susceptible to interpretation as a rejection of bourgeois materialism consistent with the sacrifices required in the name of the radiant future; his portrait of the Nazis may have accorded with the approved postwar demonology; his portrait of the worker Materna and the socialist workers' cell he led may have presented an appropriately positive image of the enlightened proletariat; and Josef's increasing understanding of the importance of political change and united effort may have fallen within acceptable bounds for portraying the necessary struggle to overcome prerevolutionary false consciousness. But even the official protectors of Socialist Realism were sensitive enough to know that *Life with a Star* had more in common with the work of Dostoevsky, Kafka and Camus than with the literary nonentities they praised and published.

Like Dostoevsky's Underground Man, Kafka's Josef K. and Camus' Meursault, Weil's Roubicek is caught in a web of consciousness and choice. When we first meet him, he has been stripped—or has stripped himself—of almost everything except his own consciousness and his ability to choose. The necessity of choice is Weil's essential theme. The emptiness and horror of existence in a world devoid of such choice is the nightmare he portrays in most of *Life with a Star*. The liberation that comes with making one's own choices is his faint vision of hope; the overwhelming odds against exercising such self-assertion in a totalitarian society shape his conflict.

"It was too much of a burden to be a different Josef Roubicek, to be a rebel who had a price on his head, who would go into hiding and have to prowl at night," his hero thinks, even on the last page of the novel. "Perhaps it would be better to become a number, a leaf carried by the wind until it falls to the ground and is trampled into the mud." But then Roubicek reconsiders: "I must come to a decision. It would have been easier to leave the decision to others, but there were no others. There was only myself between the cold, bare walls . . . There was no one to ask for advice and there was no one to pray to, because now I had to cross the line."

The triumph of *Life with a Star* is that, in spite of the powers marshaled against him, Roubicek finally chooses life over death, rebellion over conformity, continuing to struggle over giving up and giving in. The triumph of Jiri Weil was that seeing what he had seen, living through what he had lived through before, during and after the war, he could still imagine that human beings in a society such as his had such a choice. Roubicek's and Weil's hard-won triumphs reverberated in late 1989 as, just months after the English translation of *Life with a Star* appeared, millions of Czechs turned Weil's imagination of the possibility of choice into the reality of "the Velvet Revolution."

Into the Realm of Nightmare

Aharon Appelfeld

It is easy to sympathize with George Steiner's insistence that "in the presence of certain realities art is trivial and impertinent." But serious writers have always been allergic to No Trespassing signs; and if the struggle to comprehend the twentieth century's enduring nightmare has defeated more than one fine writer, it has also produced some of the most powerful fiction of the postwar era. We would all be significantly poorer in our understanding of both ourselves and twentieth century history without the testaments of Holocaust survivors like Tadeusz Borowski's *This Way for the Gas, Ladies and Gentlemen*, Andre Schwartz-Bart's *The Last of the Just*, Jerzy Kosinski's *The Painted Bird*, and Elie Wiesel's *Night*; poorer, too, without American novels like Edward Lewis Wallant's *The Pawnbroker*, Isaac Bashevis Singer's *Enemies: A Love Story*, Saul Bellow's *Mr. Sammler's Planet*, William Styron's *Sophie's Choice*, or Susan Fromberg Shaeffer's *Anya*; and poorer without the haunting fictions of Israeli novelist Aharon Appelfeld.

His *Badenheim 1939* (1980) is an elliptical marvel, a Kafkaesque fable that takes us to the edge of the abyss and leaves us there staring in stunned silence. In deceptively simple and laconic prose, it introduces us to a cross-section of German-speaking Jews visiting a resort spa, and then traces the emotional roller coaster of fears, self-deceptions, and avoidance reactions that they experience as they are gradually cut off from the outside world and tightly sealed into a gilded ghetto. We know from the first, as they do not, that history will ultimately allow them no escape. And by treating their inevitable fate obliquely—the novel ends as its characters are herded into cattle cars headed for Poland, with their leader, still blind and still hopeful, announcing "If the coaches are so dirty it must mean we have not far to go"—Appelfeld manages both to skirt the temptation to melodrama and to create a powerfully ironic fiction.

The Age of Wonders (1981), the second of Appelfeld's novels to be translated into English, is a companion piece to *Badenheim 1939*. Divided into two parts, its perspective belongs to one Bruno A., like Appelfeld a survivor now living in Jerusalem. In the first part he recalls the gradual disintegration of his family's comfortably middle-class way of life during a year that ends with their deportation to the camps. In the second, he describes his return, many years after the war, to the Austrian town that had once been their home. The first section is dominated by train journeys that end at deserted platforms with shuttered kiosks, foreshadowing, in their futility, his family's efforts to escape their final journey; the second section is dominated by images of shadows, the ghosts of an innocent youth and a world destroyed.

Bruno A. recalls the events of 1938-39 as part of a life lived "under a bell jar" where everyone seemed somehow "lost or misdirected." The most lost, the most misdirected, was Bruno's famous father. A friend of Max Brod and Stefan Zweig, an admirer and imitator of Kafka, a writer whose works, written in German, introduced him into intellectual society in Vienna and Prague, he is the center of the first part of *The Age of Wonders* and the novel's unsettling triumph. At the beginning, he is so caught up in his literary success that he has effectively cut himself off from his wife and son, and from his Jewish identity. As his newly-won success begins to disintegrate under the growing barrage of anti-Semitic attacks against his "Jewish decadence" and "Jewish sentimentality," he turns increasingly to self-hatred as a last-ditch defense. "I deny the Judaism others attribute to me," he thunders. When a servant girl tells him of a deceitful Jewish lover, he is indignant. "What can you expect from those Jews," he tells her, "They should be rooted out."

His anger here, and his most vehement attacks throughout the first part of the novel, is reserved for the wandering *Ostjuden*, vivid symbols and reminders of the heritage he is desperately—and unsuccessfully—trying to deny through assimilation. For in the end, he and his family, like all of the other Jews in the town—the old and the young, the Eastern and Western, the orthodox and the assimilated, the observant and the secular—are ordered to report to the local synagogue, where they are imprisoned overnight before being placed aboard a train bound for the camps. And there in the synagogue the first part ends, with a startling and overwhelmingly powerful expression of the violent self-hatred that Bruno's father has embodied.

After this scene, the second part of the novel seems overlong, repetitive, uninspired, and anticlimactic. But the first part of *The Age of Wonders* is, in its own painful way, a masterpiece. A reminder of how self-preservation can become suicidal, of how assimilation can become disintegration, and of how dark and morally ambiguous human motives can be. Dark and ambiguous—but not unfathomable. Not as long as there are writers like Aharon Appelfeld who have the courage to plumb their depths and honestly report what they've found.

Imaginary Homelands

Salman Rushdie

Salman Rushdie was born in Bombay on June 19, 1947, two months before India gained its independence from the British, but the place and date that will forever be attached to his name are Tehran, Iran and February 14, 1989. On that Valentine's Day, a writer whose persistent literary themes have been metamorphosis and exile found himself transformed overnight into a target and underground man by Iran's Ayotollah Ruhollah Khomeini, who issued a *fatwa* sentencing him to death and encouraging all Muslim believers to hunt him down and kill him.

Like Saleem Sinai, the hero of *Midnight's Children* (1981), Rushdie grew up in an upper-middle-class Muslim family in Bombay—in fact, Salman and his three sisters grew up in the home described in *Midnight's Children*—and Sinai attended the same British-style school that Rushdie did. At fourteen, Rushdie was sent to England to continue his education at Rugby. Like Saladin Chamcha in *The Satanic Verses* (1988), he was made to feel like an outsider throughout his time at the school and learned to adopt the accent and manners of his peers as a protective mask. In 1964, he enrolled in King's College at Cambridge, where he studied history, read Eastern and Western literature, was involved in the college's theater productions, and earned his M.A., with honors, in 1968.

While Rushdie was in England, his family had emigrated to Pakistan. After graduating from Cambridge, he purchased a one-way ticket to Karachi and joined his family in their new home, fully expecting to make his life there. But he immediately found himself in conflict with the Islamic authorities when a production of Edward Albee's *The Zoo Story* that he put together for the government television station was censored because the play contained the word "pork." An article that he wrote for a magazine on his first impressions of Pakistan met the same fate. Within the year he went back to England to live and work. At first, he worked as an actor in London; during the 1970's he earned his living as an advertising copywriter and wrote fiction at night. In 1973, he completed his first novel *Grimus* (1975), which was variously described as a science fiction tale, a fable, a fantasy, and a political satire.

Rushdie first gained international attention with the publication of his second novel, *Midnight's Children*, which won the prestigious Booker Prize and an award from the English-Speaking Union in 1981 and the James Tait Black Memorial Prize in 1982. The book's success allowed him to quit advertising and devote himself to fiction full-time. His next novel, *Shame* (1983) was also highly praised. Using a technique similar to that of Milan Kundera's novels, *Shame* mixes genres—memoir, political essay, history, autobiography, myth, and fiction—to present a multigenerational saga of modern Pakistan. The book was nominated for the Booker Prize and awarded the French Prix du Meilleur Livre Etranger.

While working on his fourth novel, Rushdie wrote *The Jaguar's Smile: A Nicaraguan Journey* (1987) and many of the essays and reviews for British and American periodicals that he would eventually collect in *Imaginary Homelands* (1991). *The Satanic Verses*, published in Britain in the fall of 1988, was also nominated for the Booker Prize and received the other major British publishing award, the Whitbread Prize. Almost immediately, however, the novel turned into an international incident. Because of episodes treating fictional versions of the prophet Muhammad and his wives in a way that many Muslims considered blasphemous, India and most Muslim countries banned *The Satanic Verses*. Riots broke out in Great Britain, India, and Pakistan, leaving dozens dead and injured; in Bradford, England, Muslims burned the novel and hung its author in effigy. Rushdie was forced to go into hiding, guarded at an undisclosed location by the Special Branch of Scotland Yard.

After the *fatwa*, the novel and its author became the central figures in a worldwide debate about censorship and freedom of expression. Rushdie issued a statement of regret from his place of hiding in an effort to pacify the Iranian mullahs; his statement was rejected and, instead, a bounty of $5.2 million for anyone who would carry out the *fatwa*'s death sentence was soon placed on his head. Bookstores and the offices of Rushdie's publisher's in England and America were threatened, several were bombed, and this led the major bookstore chains to announce that they would no longer display or sell the novel. (Later, when the immediate crisis was past, most put it back on their shelves.) Eventually, many writers spoke in Rushdie's defense, pledging their solidarity and support, but in the first days after the *fatwa* the silence of most of Rushdie's fellow writers was deafening.

Rushdie continued to write essays and reviews and defended himself in three major essays published in 1990: "Is Nothing Sacred," "In Good Faith," and "In God We Trust." His fable *Haroun and the Sea of Stories* also appeared in 1990. Both an extraordinary children's story and a pointed allegory of his own situation, the book demonstrated that its author's imagination and courage had not been destroyed by his isolation. In December 1990, still in hiding, Rushdie again attempted to make peace with those who had sentenced him to death. After his Japanese translator was assassinated and an attempt was made on the life of his Italian translator, he issued a statement embracing Islam and announcing that he had agreed to prohibit new translations or an English-language paperback edition of *The Satanic Verses*. Once again, his effort at reconciliation was rejected and the Iranian government renewed its calls for his death.

A year later Rushdie made a dramatic, unscheduled, and heavily guarded appearance at Columbia University in New York City. He withdrew his earlier decision and asked that an English-language paperback edition be published as soon as possible, so that the novel would be freely available and affordable. If the book is not read and studied, he argued, his years of forced isolation will have no meaning. In February 1992, three years after the *fatwa*, a consortium of publishers announced that they would issue a paperback edition of the book. At the time, no publisher was willing to risk publishing the paperback on its own.

II

"Putting down roots in memory," Rushdie wrote in *Grimus*, "is the natural condition of exile." To the exile, he argues, reality is suspect: "Having experienced several ways of being, he understands their illusory nature. To see things plainly, you have to cross a frontier." Since *Midnight's Children*, Salman Rushdie has become one of the most prominent voices of those who have crossed that frontier—of all the migrants such as himself who have been torn from their language, place, and social norms, and been forced to reshape themselves in a strange new world.

One of the ways that he suggests the instability of their identities is by giving his major characters more than one name and, often, uncertain parentage; a physical fall—from the sky in *Grimus* and *The Satanic Verses*, from a bicycle in *Midnight's Children*—is his recurring symbol of their loss of the firm footing of home and self. Since the self is, above all, a narrative, a construction of memory, each of his novels is built of stories that characters tell to define themselves and their worlds. Yet like most products of memory, the stories that fill his novels are flawed, unreliable, skewed by the obsessions and blind spots of their tellers. In such stories there can be no externally verifiable reality, so Rushdie's novels cannot be contained by the conventions of the realistic novel.

Instead, his books are a unique and fascinating blend of literary genres, religious and cultural traditions. To be true to his own sense of reality, his own layered consciousness, he has had to develop a novelistic form that allows him to bring together the widely disparate parts of his own experience—East and West; secular humanism and religious fundamentalism; sacred and profane; Hindu, Muslim, and Christian history and myths; First, Second, and Third Worlds; Bombay cinema, British television, and American rock and roll; India, Pakistan, and Britain. "We are here," Rushdie has said, "and we've never left anyplace that we've been." He once described the perspective that is required to capture this plural experience as "stereoscopic vision," a vision that allows him to look simultaneously at two societies from both the inside and the outside."

In Rushdie's work, this stereoscopic vision is supported by a spendthrift imagination and an esthetic of excess that have reinvigorated both the language and the form of the novel. His writing overflows—with a melange of voices, images, and inventions; with episode piled on episode, character on character, plot on plot, pun on pun, comic name on comic name, digression on digression; with disquisitions and anecdotes, mundane details and philosophical meditations; with jingles, song lyrics, catchphrases, brand names, and ideas that only he could have brought together. Drawn from both the world he left behind and the world into which he has been thrust, it expands our sense of what is while enriching our appreciation of what the novel can be and do. Mixing the narrative energy of *The Arabian Nights*, the playfulness of *Tristram Shandy*, and the political and psychological ambition of *The Tin Drum*, this aesthetic has provided Rushdie with the formal space he needs to treat the multitude of subjects that press themselves upon him.

The central conceit of *Midnight's Children* is that 1,001 children were born during the midnight hour of India's independence on August 15, 1947, that all of them were born with magical powers, and that the extent of the powers they were given decreased as the hour progressed. Two boys were born at the exact stroke of midnight, and they had the greatest powers of all. One of them, Saleem Sinai, is the novel's narrator; the other, Shiva, is his alter ego and nemesis. In reality, Saleem is the illegitimate child of a poor family and Shiva is the legitimate son of the wealthy Sinais. But because they were secretly switched at birth by a nursemaid in love with a man who opposed the caste system, they unknowingly grow up with each other's names, living each other's lives.

"I had been mysteriously handcuffed to history, my destinies indissolubly chained to those of my country," Saleem says at the beginning of his tale. A self-consciously postmodern Scheherazade, Saleem relates the story of his ancestors and his life to his housekeeper Patma over thirty-one Indian nights. In the process, he shares his version of the saga of sixty-four years of Indian history—of the years under the British, Mahatma Gandhi's assassination, the religious and language riots following Partition, the conflict between secular nationalism and religious fundamentalism and faction, the wars between India and Pakistan, the birth of Bangladesh, Indira Gandhi's "Emergency," and the rise and fall of her son Sanjay. His version of all of these events and more tumbles onto the page from his faulty memory, with dates jumbled and facts twisted into falsehoods.

Like Tristram Shandy, Saleem Sinai is not born until midway through the novel in which he tells his story. His most important feature is his nose, he discovers, when at age nine he realizes that it functions like a radio antenna. Through it, he has the power to hear the voices and thoughts of others—including all of the other children of midnight—and the power to transmit the thoughts of each to all the others. How he suddenly learns that he has this power and how he loses it are two of the novel's most hilarious and inventive scenes.

Rushdie's treatment of Saleem's nose is a perfect example of his literary method and "stereoscopic vision" at work. It is, first of all, outrageously comic and bawdy—as is so much in his fiction. In the Western literary tradition, it connects Saleem to Pinocchio (thereby undermining his veracity), to Nikolai Gogol (highlighting his monomania and calling his sanity into question), and to Cyrano de Bergerac (forecasting his fate in love). Yet it also links him to the elephant-headed god Ganesh in the Hindu literary and religious tradition. Ganesh is a comic figure, the patron deity of literature, and is supposed to have sat at the feet of the poet Valmiki to copy down the *Ramayana*. In the myths, Ganesh is both the child of the gods Shiva and Pavrati—names Rushdie assigns to other major characters in Saleem's story—and of uncertain parentage like Saleem. In other words, like so much else in Rushdie's fiction Saleem's nose functions on several levels at once—as comic device, as plot element, as a clue to character, as a signal of how to read his tale, and as literary and religious allusion to the several traditions that Rushdie sets out to blend in his work.

The Satanic Verses begins with its two heroes falling to earth on New Year's Day after terrorists blow up the plane in which they were traveling to London. Is it any surprise that what follows is one of the most extraordinary novels ever written? Although it can be compared to the works of Jorge Luis Borges, Italo Calvino, Gunter Grass, Gabriel Garcia Marquez, and Vladimir Nabokov, it is uniquely Rushdie's own and it stands as a compendium of all of the themes and techniques of his career.

When they miraculously land on the British coast alive, Gibreel Farishta and Saladin Chamcha find that they have been reborn and transformed. Gibreel, an amoral movie star who has nevertheless been known to play as many as fifty gods in a single week in the Bombay cinema's "theologicals," has lost his faith and had a breakdown before leaving India. He lands with what appears to be a halo around his head. Saladin, an actor who has rejected his Indian roots to become as British as possible and has achieved great success in London because of his chameleon-like power to create exactly the right voice to advertise every product, lands and immediately begins to turn into a cloven-hoofed devil.

The novel that tells their story moves from London to India and the Middle East, from the time of Muhammad to the era of Margaret Thatcher and the Ayatollah Khomeini, from the farthest reaches of fantasy to the day's headlines. Saladin becomes an outcast, rejected by his wife and friends, protected by the very immigrants whom he had earlier despised, transformed into their hope for revenge on the racism of the British, before he returns home to India, reconciliation with his father, and a happy ending. Gibreel goes mad, imagines himself as both the Angel Gibreel and the Prophet Muhammed's scribe, rewrites the story of Muhammad—whom he calls by the derogatory medieval name Mahound—and imagines another prophet, the young girl Ayeesha, whom he leads to destruction. Along the way, both have love affairs, fantasies, memories, and adventures that keep the novel whirling like a dervish from one plot to another. As one critic observed, *The Satanic Verses* is several of the best novels Salman Rushdie has written.

Islam prohibits images of Muhammad and holds the words of the Koran to be sacred. Early commentators on the prophet and the Koran described an episode, which they called "The Satanic Verses," in which Muhammad was tempted to accept three local deities as subsidiary gods to Allah in order to win over the people to his new religion, then renounced the verses as dictated by Satan rather than the Angel Gibreel. Modern Islam rejects the entire episode as apocryphal and blasphemous. By depicting his prophet as subject to human frailties and giving him an offensive name, by inventing a character who changes the words that the prophet dictates, thereby suggesting that the holy book may not be entirely the sacred word of God, and by inventing an episode in which a group of prostitutes assume the names of Muhammad's wives in order to improve their business, Rushdie committed unforgivable acts of blasphemy in the eyes of true believers. His explanations that his book was a work of *fiction*, that all of the offending passages were the dreams and delusions of a god-obsessed madman, that he was not a believer and therefore could not be a traitor to Islam, all fell on deaf ears. The fact that Rushdie had also viciously satirized an exiled imam much like the Ayotollah Khomeini, who returns in triumph to his country to stop time and tyrannize his people, probably didn't help his case.

Yet the novel deserves to be read as what it was intended to be: an exploration of the deepest religious and personal conflicts within its author and many others, an attempt to capture the sense of rootlessness and alienation that comes with displacement and migration, and an effort to encompass the extremes of contemporary experience in a form that would allow the freest possible range to its author's talent and imagination.

"Once upon a time—it was and it was not so, as the old stories used to say, it happened and it never did—maybe, then, or maybe not"—with these words from *The Satanic Verses* Rushdie has suggested what connects the ancient storytellers of the East with the contemporary magic realists of the West. Drawing on both traditions, he has written novels that consciously blur the dividing lines between fairy tale and novel, myth and fiction. Born at a moment of tremendous change, he has sought to capture and reflect the turmoil and dislocation of his times in his work, only to find himself their victim. His voice and vision are unique, and his novels are important contributions to understanding the conflicts that permeate contemporary culture.

III

Throughout the 1980's, Rushdie wrote essays and reviews, eloquently and often: about the politics of religion and race in Margaret Thatcher's Britain, Indira Gandhi's India, and Mohammad Zia-ul-Haq's Pakistan; about writers and books from India and Pakistan, Africa, Britain, continental Europe, South America, and the United States; about the vocation of the writer and the powers of literature, the potential of the imagination and the dangers of censorship; and—repeatedly—about migration as the archetypal experience of the twentieth century. *Imaginary Homelands* brings most of these essays together with the several major statements he wrote in the wake of *The Satanic Verses* controversy to form what amounts to a fascinating intellectual autobiography.

Although his parents were members of the Muslim minority in India, neither they nor he were religious. At fifteen, he reports in "In God We Trust," he lost his faith and found himself "drawn toward the great traditions of secular radicalism—in politics, socialism; in the arts, modernism and its offspring." At Rugby he experienced British racism at first hand; at Cambridge he discovered the writers who shaped his aspirations.

Gradually, the experience that he would make his own—the experience that made *him*—pressed itself upon him as his inevitable subject. Migration—losing one's country, language, and culture and finding oneself forced to come to terms with another place, another way of speaking and thinking, another view of reality—became his great theme and metamorphosis became its metaphor. Reflections on migration and metamorphosis permeate his essays as thoroughly as embodiments of them populate his novels.

"Writers in my position, exiles or emigrants or expatriates, are haunted by some sense of loss, some urge to reclaim, to look back, even at the risk of being mutated into pillars of salt," he writes in the collection's title essay. Such a writer comes to understand, however, that "we will not be capable of reclaiming precisely the thing that was lost; that we will, in short, create fictions, not actual cities or villages, but invisible one, imaginary homelands, Indias of the mind." In his own fictions, Rushdie has created just such imaginary homelands: an India of the mind in *Midnight's Children*, a Pakistan of the mind in *Shame*, a Bombay and London of the mind in *The Satanic Verses*. While they are not precisely real, these imaginary homelands capture the essence of reality as seen through the eyes of characters who, like their creator, face the challenge of straddling two cultures.

The word "translation," he points out, comes from the Latin for "bearing across," and "having been borne across the world, we are translated men. It is normally supposed that something also gets lost in the translation; I cling, obstinately, to the notion that something can also be gained." As he writes in an essay on John Berger, "the migrant is not simply transformed by his act; he also transforms his new world." As Rushdie has amply demonstrated in his own writing, the gains from this transformation are real and many.

"Description is itself a political act," he writes, "redescribing the world is the necessary first step towards changing it." This suggests another contribution that the migrant can make to world culture. By describing the world as he does in his fiction and nonfiction, Rushdie can try to help change those aspects of society that he so often laments and protests against in these essays. Like the institutional racism and nostalgia for past glories of Margaret Thatcher's Britain, where immigrants are daily victims of discrimination and a stubborn adherence to a self-image drawn from the nineteenth century ignores the millions of people whose arrival in Britain has changed it from an island of homogeneity to a polyglot crossroads of cultures. Like the religious sectarianism that has led to the assassination of three Gandhis and threatens to tear the very idea of a united India apart at the seams. Like the politicization of Islam into a nationalistic "revolt against history" by leaders such as General Zia or the Ayotollah Khomeini.

Another contribution that the migrant can make, Rushdie argues in a landmark 1984 essay on one of his intellectual heroes, Gunter Grass, is a commitment to tolerance. "To experience any form of migration is to get a lesson in the importance of tolerating others' points of view. One might almost say that migration ought to be essential training for all would-be democrats." It is difficult to read such a statement without thinking of how much Salman Rushdie has suffered at the hands of people who have not learned this lesson. Although he has attempted to conduct his professional life as normally as possible since being forced underground in 1989, although he has avoided inserting his personal situation into most of his essays and reviews, many of the comments Rushdie makes in essays written both before and after his ordeal began cannot help but have a deeper and more immediate authority in the light of what has happened to him.

Rushdie's comments on the role of the writer in confronting the powers-that-be in "Outside the Whale," for example, now seem almost prophetic. Attacking George Orwell's 1940 essay "Inside the Whale" for counseling the writer to choose quietism rather than political activism, Rushdie insists "that works of art, even works of entertainment, do not come into being in a social and political vacuum; and that the way they operate in a society cannot be separated from politics, from history. For every text, a context . . ." Consequently, he argues, "there is no whale. We live in a world without hiding places." In "Imaginary Homelands," he argues that "the real risks of any artist are taken in the work, in pushing the work to the limits of what is possible, in the attempt to increase the sum of what it is possible to think." Unfortunately, his experience has demonstrated how true the former statement was, and how incomplete the latter—has shown just how dangerous it can be to increase the sum of what it is possible to think in a world where many wish to diminish freedom of thought and expression.

Occasionally, Rushdie does refer explicitly to his predicament in reviews written after 1989. Reading Philip Roth's description of the conflict that arose between him and some members of the Jewish community with the publication of *Goodbye, Columbus,* he cannot help but find Roth's responses to being vilified "very moving, even helpful, to this similarly beleaguered writer." Noting in his review of Gabriel Garcia Marquez's *Clandestine in Chile* that the book was impounded and burned by the Pinochet government, but that the book continues to exist while Pinochet is falling, he consoles himself with the thought that "to burn a book is not to destroy it." He praises Christopher Ransmayr's novel *The Last Word* as "a parable of the ability of art to survive the breaking of the artist," but he cannot help but qualify his praise for Ransmayr's vision of art conquering all. "Art can look after itself," he wryly observes. "Artists . . . can be crushed effortlessly by any tyrant's whim."

Rushdie also sometimes uses his situation for comic effect. He admits to envying Isaac Bashevis Singer's freedom to be irreverent about God and the Devil—"no fundamentalists are after *him*, no government has banned *his* book for blasphemy. Look at what the fellow gets away with!" His response to Thomas Pynchon's fabled desire for privacy is the funniest sentence to have appeared on the front page of the *New York Times Book Review* in memory. "So he wants a private life with no photographs and nobody to know his home address," Rushdie writes in the argot of one of Pynchon's zonked-out space cadets. "I can dig it, I can relate to that (but, like, he should try it when it's compulsory instead of a free-choice option)."

Imaginary Homelands is full of similarly witty and apt observations on other subjects as well. The message of Richard Attenborough's film *Gandhi*, Rushdie says, "is that the best way to gain your freedom is to line up, unarmed, and march towards your oppressor and permit them to club you to the ground; if you do this for long enough, you will embarrass them into going away." Edgar Allan Poe is one of the myriad references in Umberto Eco's *Foucault's Pendulum*, "but it doesn't help. This Pendulum is the pits." The collection is also full of careful, insightful, and provocative readings of several dozen writers, ranging from Saul Bellow and Italo Calvino to Julian Barnes and Kazuo Ishiguro. Nadine Gordimer, Rushdie writes in a typically sensitive and perfectly phrased observation, "has been radicalized by her time—or, rather, by her attempt to *write* her time—and it's fascinating to watch history happening to her prose." "The real plot of *Moby Dick* takes place inside of Ahab; the rest is a fishing trip," he states. "Magic realism," he observes in a comment on the fiction of Garcia Marquez that also explains much about his own work, "is a development out of Surrealism that expresses a genuinely Third World consciousness."

Gunter Grass's *The Tin Drum* was one of the primary inspirations of Rushdie's own desire to be a writer, and his summary of the lessons he learned from Grass is a fair description of the aesthetic that has made his own novels so extraordinary. "This is what Grass's great novel said to me in its drumbeats: Go for broke. Always try to do too much. Dispense with safety nets. Take a deep breath before you begin talking. Aim for the stars. Keep grinning. Be bloody-minded. Argue with the world." He has tried to remember and learn those lessons, he says. "And one more, which I got from that other, immense work, *Dog Years*: When you've done it once, start all over and do it again and do it better."

The last section of *Imaginary Homelands* reprints the three 1990 statements of self-defense, of himself and of art—worth the price of admission all by themselves—and concludes with the December 1990 statement "embracing Islam" that he later retracted. Within a year of that last statement, Salman Rushdie published two books, *Imaginary Homelands* and *Haroun and the Sea of Stories*, making it abundantly clear that he continued to remember all of Grass's lessons. And that he's learned a few from James Joyce, too.

"I will express myself in some mode of life or art as freely as I can and as wholly as I can," Stephen Dedalus declared, "using for my defence the only arms I allow myself to use—silence, exile, and cunning." Like Joyce's migrant artificer, Rushdie continues to find ways to express himself from his exile, steadfastly refusing to be turned into a silent pillar of salt.

IV

Images and Impulses
The Chicago Novel

Surveying the history of the Chicago novel in a few pages threatens to be as superficial as a conventioneer's three-day visit to the city. He arrives at O'Hare, hustles through the terminal, grabs his baggage, hails a cab, moves through a maze of ramps and underpasses, and—if it isn't rush hour—soon finds himself speeding along the Kennedy Expressway. In a few minutes, he sees three buildings rising to dominate the horizon in front of him. On the left, the cabbie tells him, is the John Hancock building; in the center, the Standard Oil headquarters; off to the right, the Sears Tower. Fifteen minutes later, they exit the expressway, fight their way east through traffic, and he's dropped off at his hotel. And for the rest of the time he's in the city, his forays beyond that hotel's meeting rooms, cocktail lounges and lobby are likely to take him to State Street, Michigan Avenue, Rush Street and back—with a twenty-minute side-trip to Marshall Field's to pick up something for the wife and kids.

When he gets home, he tells family and friends that he's just seen Chicago. Of course, he's done no such thing. At least he hasn't seen much of the Chicago that we who have lived there know and see. His Chicago, bounded by Michigan and State, Adams and Division, is just a part of our city. In fact, it sometimes seems as if most Chicagoans don't live in the visitor's city at all—as though the "Chicago" you find on the map is a political and geographical fiction. We live, instead, in places the conventioneer has often never heard of: in Lincoln Park and Marquette Park, Albany Park and Dearborn Park; in Mt. Greenwood and Cabrini-

Green, Bogan and Beverly and Bridgeport; in Englewood and Edgewater, Sheffield and Woodlawn, Old Town, New Town and Uptown. And we know that to really see Chicago you have to go beyond the skyscrapers and landmarks of the Loop and the Magnificent Mile; you have to explore the neighborhoods.

To survey the history of the Chicago novel and do it justice, we have to go beyond its skyscrapers, beyond the brief litany of immediately recognizable names like Farrell, Algren and Bellow. For though they are as important a part of the literary landscape as the Loop and the Gold Coast are of the physical terrain, they too are just a part of the landscape. Anyone who hasn't met Farrell's Studs Lonigan—a young man shaped by the Irish Catholic world around him, sentenced by his precisely described environment to be just what he becomes, twisted by the codes of the poolroom and speakeasy until he turns into the ultimate Chicago victim and victimizer—has not felt the punch the Chicago novel is capable of landing. Anyone who hasn't walked Nelson Algren's Division Street—a street peopled by failures and frauds who yearn, like you and me, for something a bit better than they have; a street that embodies Algren's lover's quarrel with the city that inspired his best work—has been shortchanged of the chance to see another layer of the place the Indians called "the Wild Onion." And anyone who hasn't spent some time with Saul Bellow's Chicago heroes—each a unique combination of street kid and philosopher, *schlemiel* and *mensch*, Humboldt Park and Hyde Park—has missed some of the finest, and funniest, American writing of the past fifty years.

But to read and talk about their work, and the work of the several others like Theodore Dreiser and Richard Wright whom everyone has heard about, isn't enough. We also have to explore the literary neighborhoods, to observe the images and impulses that have shaped the work of the diverse group of writers whom the best-known Chicago novelists overshadow; writers who are their predecessors, contemporaries and descendents. For together, these writers created "the Chicago novel."

The pattern of Chicago's literary history parallels that of American literary history as a whole: exploration and frontier narratives gave way to historical romances; romances were succeeded by humor, local color and regionalism; and regionalism shaded into realism and naturalism. But Chicago's romances—books inspired by the Fort Dearborn Massacre like Major John Richardson's *Hardscrabble; or the Fall of Chicago* (1850) or Juliette Kinzie's *Wau-bun, The Early Days of the Northwest* (1856)—are not in the same league as the romances of Irving or Cooper, much less Hawthorne or Melville. And fictionalized accounts of the Chicago Fire like E.P. Roe's *Barriers Burned Away* (1872), dime novels like Shang Andrews' *Chicago After Dark* (1876) or *Cranky Ann, the Street*

Walker: A Story of Chicago in Chunks (1886), aren't even up to the standards of Charles Brockden Brown. Hundreds of such books appeared between 1850 and 1890, but nearly all of them are now forgotten. They helped to claim Chicago as a literary subject, helped to establish Chicago publishers, helped to create an audience for the books that were to come—but their main interest today is historical not literary. It was only with the local color humor of George Ade, Eugene Field and Finley Peter Dunne, and its evolution into turn-of-the-century realism, that Chicago writers began to find their own special subjects and voices.

From its earliest incarnation in *Don Quixote*, the realistic novel has been built of disillusionment and description. The realist was fated from the start, it has often been said, to be a disenchanted idealist, a professional iconoclast committed, like Cervantes, to exposing the giants of illusion his age has constructed for the broken-down windmills they actually are. Since disillusionment has always been realism's impetus, stories of youths coming of age, of the inevitably painful passage from innocence to experience, of the clash between self and society in which the self usually ends a victim, have been its perennial subjects. Since the accurate description of things as they are—rather than things as they're supposed to be—has always been realism's touchstone, detailed descriptions of specific times, specific places, specific networks of social relationships, have always defined its style.

When we think of the masterpieces of 19th-century European realism, we recall novels in which these subjects and this style combine to create works that are both psychological maps and cultural guidebooks. These are works in which the characters all seem more real because of the vivid descriptions we are given of the worlds in which they move; and the reality of those characters, in turn, serves to make their time and place come alive for us. This realistic tradition, the English critic Raymond Williams has written, results in the kind of novel in which "every aspect of the personal life is radically affected by the quality of the general life, yet the general life is seen at its most important in completely personal terms."

II

When we speak of "the Chicago novel," we are talking about that part of the fiction written about Chicago that flows out of this realistic tradition—the part that, at its best, achieves this integration of personal fate and social fact. To read these Chicago novels is to be confronted with tale after tale of conflict, loss and disillusionment suffered in, and because of, a particular, carefully described, Chicago setting. And in them, as Bernard Duffey has observed, the persistent preoccupation has been with "the young man or woman at odds with a world he never made—one which threatens to undo him by forcing him into the power of hostile and foreign circumstances." Most often, those "hostile and foreign circumstances" have been the realities and commercial values of the city itself.

But why, we may ask, is this so? Why did the Chicago novel develop this way instead of another? Why did it develop so fully and rapidly at the turn of the century that it attracted national, and ultimately international, attention? And why only the Chicago novel—why wasn't there a St. Louis novel or a Minneapolis novel of comparably distinct character and importance?

The conflict between an individual and the urban experience that the Chicago novel documents was certainly not Chicago born and bred. It was Balzac's theme, and Dickens's; and it was available in every city of any size. But a subject, by itself, doesn't generate memorable fiction. There have to be sensibilities attuned to it and capable of giving it form and expression. While other Midwestern cities certainly had their share of such sensibilities when the Chicago novel began to emerge, geography, demography and economics combined to decree that Chicago would have more of them.

By the early 1890's, the city was already the Midwest's largest, most populous and most heterogeneous. A hub of commerce and industry, a railroad and shipping center, it was also a magnet, as Dreiser wrote in *Sister Carrie* (1900), "drawing to itself, from all quarters, the hopeful and the hopeless—those who had their fortunes yet to make and those whose fortunes and affairs had reached a disastrous climax elsewhere." By the turn of the century, Armour and Swift, Field and Wieboldt, Yerkes and Insull had made their reputations and fortunes. In the 1880's and 1890's they, their wives and others like them began to spend their wealth to bring cultural respectability to the city. An "upward movement" developed, dedicated to raising the level of Chicago culture and, in a brief time, the results were nothing short of spectacular. Its members supported the establishment of the Newberry, Crerar and Chicago Public Libraries, the Symphony and Art Institute, the Auditorium and Fine Arts buildings, the Armour Institute (later the Illinois Institute of Technology), and the University of Chicago. They built the "White City" for the 1893 Columbian Exposition and captured the attention of the nation and the world. They supported literary magazines like *America* and *The Dial*, created literary clubs like "The Little Room," and helped to support eight daily newspapers

The result was an atmosphere that attracted writers and aspiring writers from throughout the Midwest and West, and inspired the writers already in the city, at the same time that it attracted the hopeful entrepeneurs and the new immigrant workers who would be the Chicago novel's first subjects. If you were a Midwestern newspaperman, Chicago was soon viewed as the big time. If you were a small-town boy or girl with artistic aspirations, one who felt alienated and stifled, the literary lights which began to dot the Chicago skyline, the bohemian life your folks heard of and shook their heads about, gleamed and beckoned with the promise of acceptance, excitement and freedom. If you were an established writer intent on capturing the spirit of America in all its contradictions, turn-of-the-century Chicago was a made-to-order specimen under glass. And, finally, if you were already a Chicagoan, by accident or birth, you were surrounded from the start by an urban struggle, a babel of voices and chaos of conflicting values, that virtually demanded that you make sense of it to survive.

So they came—from Galena and Springfield, Davenport and Denver, Oak Park and West Lafayette; from Elyria and Moberly, St. Louis and Minneapolis. A literary snowball began to roll. And when it stopped it had formed the Chicago novel.

It's almost as difficult to reach consensus about the first Chicago novel as it is to pass a transportation package in the closing hours of an Illinois General Assembly session. Some argue for Richardson's *Hardscrabble*; others for Kinzie's *Wau-bun* or Roe's *Barriers Burned Away*; and some make a case for Martha J. Lamb's *Spicy: A Novel* (1873). But if by the first Chicago novel we mean the first of the kind that I've been describing here—not just the first fiction set in the city, or the first by a Chicago writer—the surest claim belongs to Henry Blake Fuller's *The Cliff-Dwellers* (1893).

In this book, and in its companion *With the Procession* (1895), Fuller defined the conflicts, the characters and the setting that would dominate the Chicago novel's first decade. The conflicts now appear classic: morality vs. money, idealism vs. materialism, inexperienced youth vs. the corrupt values of the time. So do the characters: the young person, often fresh from the country, trying to make it, to seize "the main chance" in Chicago's business and/or social worlds; the rich, powerful, amoral or immoral businessman, and his culturally and socially ambitious wife; the Chicago architect; members of the struggling middle class. (The immigrant workers who were to become the focus of later Chicago novels also appear in Fuller's novels, but only in cameo roles.) The setting of *The Cliff-Dwellers* is, generally, the Loop and the near North and West sides. Specifically—and this was a stroke of social and symbolic genius—it is the eighteen-story Clifton (the Monadnock Building), the city's first skyscraper and Fuller's perfectly apt symbol of the towering importance of money and commerce to the Chicago ethos of his day.

Dominating the downtown, inhabited from nine to five by the "cliff-dwellers" of the title, the Clifton is one of the most telling and memorable images in all of Chicago fiction. In seizing upon it, Fuller captured for all time the novelty of what would come to be the commonplace: the office building as self-enclosed universe, with restaurants, cigar store, bank; the hierarchy of height (his George Ogden begins his climb from the Underground National Bank located in the building's basement, like some clear-eyed, bright-cheeked American cousin of Dostoevsky's Underground Man). And in his name for the building's inhabitants he suggests his sense of the primitive and precarious nature of their existence in it. New men in the new world the Clifton epitomizes, they try to claw their way up the building to wealth and power. Some succeed for a while, only to lose their grip and tumble back to the bottom; others never really have a chance. But all, as Duffey has noted, are in some way corrupted by the city. Though Fuller's vocabulary was genteel and his characters were middle-class, *The Cliff-Dwellers* is not as far from *The Jungle* and *The Pit* as it may at first seem.

In *With the Procession*, Fuller treated the efforts of a young woman and her family to gain a foothold in Chicago society. Though Fuller was himself a major figure in the upward movement, in this novel he shows how the upper and middle classes' desire for culture was often a sham, tainted by dark motives, corrupted by false values. Jane Marshall and her family try to jump through all the right social hoops—the children must make their formal debuts; the family must build a new office tower and a Michigan Avenue mansion designed by the city's most fashionable architect; and they must make a gift to construct a building in the family's name at the new university. But, as Robert Bray has pointed out, to Fuller all of this was "dangerously wrongheaded" because wrongly motivated. Again, the novel's main characters fail. Jane Marshall and her family, like George Ogden before them, are defeated in their quest for social status and forced to let go of the city's illusory material values. Again, the characters are mainly victims. And, again, the novel's central symbol is one of its most powerful elements. Fuller begins almost cinematically, with a long shot of traffic crossing a bridge over the Chicago River, and then moves in for a close-up of one of the many vehicles in this Chicago procession—the Marshall family's "carry-all." Jostled and bumped, it is as hemmed in, as unable to control its direction and power, as the Marshall's will be by Chicago's social procession.

The critique of Chicago's businessman, of the city's social and commercial values, which Fuller was the first to articulate was soon elaborated by several of his contemporaries and was later developed by writers like Dreiser, Sinclair and Norris. In Will Payne's best novels, *Jerry, the Dreamer* (1896) and *The Money Captain* (1898), we are presented with opposite sides of the same Chicago coin. In the first, a young innocent nearly drowns in the tide of commercial corruption and political graft; in the second, another young man, secretary to the robber baron known as the "Duke of Gas," finally capitulates and learns to float along in that tide quite well. The former, of course, ends poor; the latter, rich. But if, like Fuller, Payne exposes the businessman's corruption, he also cannot help but be attracted—like Norris in *The Pit* (1903), Arthur J. Eddy in *Ganton and Company* (1905) or Dreiser in *The Titan* (1914)—by the businessman's energy and power. The Duke of Gas may bribe politicians, lie, cheat and steal, but he gets things done and so wins Payne's grudging admiration.

Robert Herrick had no such ambivalence about the city's moneymakers and their values. He came to the city from Harvard to join the faculty of the new University of Chicago in 1893, the year of both *The Cliff-Dwellers* and the Columbian Exposition, and this coincidence was appropriate. For, together with Fuller's, Herrick's work in the last decade of the old century and the first decade of the new helped to define the critical stance that would characterize the Chicago novel; and Herrick's disillusionment with the city mirrored the disillusionment many felt when the hopes for progress attached to the Exposition were not realized after it ended. The fair's "White City" rose at the same time as the "Grey City" of the university just across the Midway—but beyond them the "Black City" of injustice and poverty in the midst of plenty survived unchanged. This contradiction became Herrick's subject.

It didn't take him long to find out that the University of Chicago wasn't Harvard and Chicago wasn't Cambridge. Though he stayed for twenty years, he never quite got over the shock. And out of his alienation he produced four important Chicago novels. In them the attack on the corrupting influence of the city which Fuller began is yoked to an examination of the alternative ideals of professional men and artists which Ben Hecht and Floyd Dell would develop later. In the least significant of his novels, *The Gospel of Freedom* (1898), the contrast is schematic. A Chicago woman is torn between the contradictory values of two suitors—one a businessman, the other an artist—and ultimately rejects the extremity of the values of both.

In *The Web of Life* (1900) and *The Common Lot* (1903), Herrick's protagonists are a young doctor and a young architect. Each of these men begins as an adherent of Chicago's dominant values and ends as their opponent. The story of the young doctor, Howard Sommers, traces his moral development—a development which is contrasted to the dissolution of Chicago's social fabric in the period during and just after the Exposition. The poor "had come lean and hungry out of the terrible winter that followed the World's Fair," Herrick writes. "In that beautiful enterprise the prodigal city had put forth her utmost strength, and having shown the world the supreme flower of her energy, collapsed." The "White City" is Herrick's symbol of Chicago's democratic and cultural aspirations; and when it goes up in flames at the end of 1893, so does hope. In the course of the novel, Sommers resigns from a lucrative Loop practice to work in a poor neighborhood, leaves the comfort of convention and social acceptance for a common-law marriage and a bohemian existence, and then finds his new life a failure too.

The architect—caught between aesthetic and commercial values, challenged to join them—is a frequent character in many early Chicago novels. In *The Common Lot* he is the center of attention. Jackson Hart is a successful architect precisely because he's willing to cut corners and bribe inspectors, to build what his clients want rather than what he believes in. Like Sommers, he, too, undergoes a crisis which results in his moral development. When one of his buildings burns due to his cutting corners and he acknowledges the second-rate quality of the designs he's produced for a major commission, Hart rejects success at any price and returns, poorer but wiser, to a lower-paying but ethically and aesthetically more satisfying job in a firm he once disdained.

Perhaps the best-known of Herrick's novels, *The Memoirs of an American Citizen* (1905) follows a somewhat different pattern. Herrick casts it as a first-person autobiographical narrative by a self-made businessman, Edward Van Harrington. The object of earlier novels' attacks, the Chicago businessman here becomes the self-important, self-deluded subject of his own fond regard. Van Harrington recounts his rags to riches story with pride, but through him Herrick indicts the corruption of an entire culture. Van Harrington serves on the jury of the Haymarket anarchists— and gloats over his role in their conviction; he visits the Fair—and spouts all of the platitudes that Herrick had found to be hollow. And as a reward for his scheming, his total acceptance of Chicago's materialism, Van Harrington is ultimately sent to the Senate as the meatpackers' man in Washington. This is the Horatio Alger story seen through a funhouse mirror of irony, where nothing is as it seems, where to rise is to fall and to succeed is to fail. In no other major Chicago novels, except *The Titan* and *The Pit*, are we asked to share the businessman's view of himself so intimately. The result here is devastating.

III

The businessman of the earliest Chicago novels appears and reappears— sometimes in a different guise—as a pivotal figure in many of the novels which followed. In Saul Bellow's *The Adventures of Augie March* (1953), *Herzog* (1964) and *Humboldt's Gift* (1975), he has a law degree; in Eugene Kennedy's *Father's Day* (1981) and Andrew Greeley's

The Cardinal Sins (1981), he wears a Roman collar. But in the Chicago novels of the first decade of the twentieth century, as in most subsequent Chicago novels, the focus shifts elsewhere. The upper- and middle-class characters of Fuller, Payne and Herrick are shouldered aside by working class heroes. The struggle is no longer to succeed but to survive. The scene isn't the Loop but working class neighborhoods like the Back of the Yards and Pullman. The underlying faith is not in reforming capitalism but establishing socialism. The "White City" is supplanted by the "Black City," and Chicago is treated as an elemental force capable of butchering a great deal more than Sandburg's hogs. The mode is not just realism but naturalism—a treatment which sees human character and experience as biologically and environmentally determined, which views life as a Darwinian struggle in which only the "fittest" survive.

This naturalistic version of social experience is clearly expressed in a childhood memory recalled by Dreiser's "titan," Frank Cowperwood. In *The Financier* (1912), which traces Cowperwood's career before he arrives in Chicago, the ten year-old Cowperwood witnesses a struggle that shapes his philosophy of life and reflects Dreiser's. He sees a tank at a fish market, one where "odd specimens of sea-life" were kept. One day a lobster and a squid are put into the tank, and what follows is "a tragedy which stayed with him all his life and cleared things up considerably intellectually." He returns daily, fascinated by the piecemeal destruction of the squid by the lobster, until finally, one night, he finds the squid severed, destroyed by the fitter creature:

> "That's the way it has to be, I guess, " he commented to himself. "That squid wasn't quick enough. "
> The incident made a great impression on him. It answered in a rough way that riddle which had been annoying him so much in the past: "How is life organized?" Things lived on each other—that was it. Lobsters lived on squids and other things. What lived on lobsters? Men, of course. Sure, that was it! And what lived on men? he asked himself. Was it other men? . . . That was it! Sure, men lived on men.

This stark vision of existence as a life or death struggle is most completely expressed in Upton Sinclair's *The Jungle* (1906). The owners of Packingtown live off the lives of their workers, who are personified by the family of Jurgis Rudkus. They tear those workers apart, one by one, piece by piece, member by member—just as surely as the lobster destroyed the squid. The Rudkus family comes to America from Lithuania, as many before and after them came from around the world, to escape oppression and live in freedom. "America was a place of which lovers and young people dreamed. If one could only get the price of passage, he could count his troubles at an end." Like many others, Jurgis hears that the friend of a friend has written that the streets are paved with gold. And, since the friend of a friend had supposedly gotten rich in a place called Chicago, "Chicago" is the only English word Jurgis and his family know when they arrive on the boat—the word that embodies first their hopes and then their doom. The novel, like many Chicago novels after it, traces the Rudkus's ultimate destruction by the city in searing episodes of heartrending power.

That destruction is hinted at in the novel's opening, where Jurgis' old-country wedding feast in Packingtown is marred by guests who have already been corrupted by the new country's values. And Sinclair doesn't let up for three hundred and fifty pages. Children rummage through trash for scraps of food, fall into vats at the meatpacking plant and become part of the processed meat, are eaten by rats or drowned in fetid pools of water that accumulate in the streets and alleys; women are seduced and forced into prostitution; old people die of diseases left untreated for want of proper medical care; strong young men are broken and discarded like used machinery, only to be replaced by other strong young men who will suffer the same fate. Meanwhile, the packers grow rich and the politicians line their pockets with graft.

Jurgis finally sees the "world of civilization" as one in which "nothing counted but brutal might, an order devised by those who possessed it for the subjugation of those who did not. He was one of the latter; and all the outdoors, all life, was to him one colossal prison, which he paced like a pent-up tiger, trying one bar after another, and finding them all beyond his power. He had lost in the fierce battle of greed, and so was doomed to be exterminated; and all society was busied to see that he did not escape the sentence."

The impact of Sinclair's novel is well-known: within six months of its publication in February 1906 the Pure Food and Drug Act was passed to control the abuses in the meatpacking industry which the book had documented. Sinclair's reaction to this is also well-known: "I aimed at the public's heart," he lamented, "and by accident I hit it in the stomach." Less than a tenth of the novel had been devoted to his carefully researched description of the gruesome details of meat production; nine-tenths had been devoted to the human waste and destruction that supported and surrounded the packing industry. But the novel's notoriety caused change in the former while leaving the latter undisturbed. Today, *The Jungle* is often dismissed as a melodramatic propaganda piece. It is much more— an unforgettable portrait of Chicago as a modern Inferno, of the city as predator. It may be melodramatic, but it still has the power to shock and move us.

The Jungle's naturalistic vision of the urban struggle as a raging battle between the oppressed common man and a denatured environment dominated by the power of unchecked capitalism permeates a host of other Chicago novels, such as I. K. Friedman's *Poor People* (1900) and *The Radical* (1907), Clarence Darrow's *An Eye for an Eye* (1904), Meyer Levin's *The New Bridge* (1933), Albert Halper's *The Foundry* (1934) and *The Chute* (1937), Richard Wright's *Native Son* (1940), Willard Motley's *Knock on Any Door* (1947) and *Let No Man Write My Epitaph* (1958)—as well as all of Nelson Algren's fiction.

Dreiser's Chicago novels were neither as stark nor as clear-cut a statement of the struggle in the tank because Dreiser, like his Cowperwood, was at least as fascinated as he was appalled by it. Like Norris, Dreiser was an anomaly—both a romantic and a naturalist—and, for him, Chicago "seethed with a peculiarly human or realistic atmosphere. It is given to some cities, as to some lands," he wrote, "to suggest romance, and to me Chicago did that hourly. It sang, I thought, and I was singing with it."

Sometimes he sang off-key—as he did in *The Titan*, which contains at once some of Dreiser's very worst prose and some of the most vivid anecdotes of Chicago's social, political and business life yet recorded. Sometimes he had perfect pitch—as he did in *Sister Carrie*. Carrie Meeber, another small-town emigrant who clutches a scrap of paper with a Chicago address scrawled on it as she travels toward the city by train, is Frank Cowperwood's soul sister. Like him, she is a survivor. Dreiser puts it plainly on the novel's second page: "Self-interest with her was high but not strong. It was, nevertheless, her guiding characteristic." And we soon come to see that, while she may destroy others, she herself will not be destroyed. She is what the first chapter's title labels her—"A Waif Amid Forces"— but she's one tough little waif, with forces of her own. Before she's even off the train she's flirted with the traveling salesman, Drouet; and when sweatshop labor quickly loses its appeal, she turns to him with little hesitation. She has even fewer qualms about leaving him, in turn, for the richer and more attractive Hurstwood. And she eventually drops Hurstwood rather than sink with him.

Throughout the novel—and especially at the conclusion—Dreiser tries to mouth the appropriate sentiments of moral condemnation of Carrie's behavior; but they're really only sentiments—both to him and to her. (This was clear enough to delay the book's publication for several years on moral grounds.) He cannot find it in his heart or philosophy to condemn her, regardless of what the morality of his time requires. And few of *Sister Carrie's* readers will disagree with him. For Carrie Meeber is special. In the long history of the Chicago novel, there are few more vivid characters and even fewer who are, like her, more than passive victims of their fate. She is preceded by the heroine of Hamlin Garland's *Rose of Dutcher's Cooley* (1895), and succeeded by the heroines of Edna Ferber's *The Girls* (1921) and Willa Cather's *Lucy Gayheart* (1935), as well as by the heroines of society novelists such as Edith Wyatt, Isabella Holt and Janet Ayer Fairbank. But no other heroine, before or after her—and few heroes—comes close to being as fascinating, or to having as much significance to the record of the impact of the Chicago experience on the human spirit.

IV

The excitement of the Chicago literary scene in the 1920's has often been documented. By then, the turn-of-the-century's most influential literary critic, William Dean Howells, had expressed his admiration for the work of Ade, Fuller, Herrick and others for decades. And his successor as a literary arbiter, H. L. Mencken, lavished praise on Chicago with an enthusiasm that he usually reserved for his scorn of American culture. In 1917, he described Chicago as more "American" than Boston, New York or San Francisco, and went on to say that "all literary movements that have youth in them . . . and a fresh point of view, and the authentic bounce and verve of the country and the true character and philosophy of its people" were products of this, "the most civilized" city in America. "Find me a writer who is indubitably American and who has something new and interesting to say, and who says it with an air, and nine times out of ten . . . he has some sort of connection with the abattoir by the lake—that he was bred there or got his start there, or passed through there during the days when he was tender." In 1920 he repeated these sentiments, calling Chicago "The Literary Capital of the United States."

But the excitement Mencken heralded was not especially evident in the Chicago novel during the late teens and the 1920's. Sherwood Anderson lived here when he was writing *Winesburg, Ohio* (1919), but his Chicago novel, *Windy McPherson's Son* (1916), wasn't very effective. Sinclair Lewis spent some time here, and devoted the opening pages of his *Main Street* (1920) to Carol Kennicott's Chicago experiences, but *Main Street* is a Midwestern *Madame Bovary* not a Chicago novel. Both Fuller and Herrick continued to publish—Fuller's *On the Stairs* (1918) and Herrick's *Chimes* (1926) appeared during this period—but both had already done their best work. In retrospect, it now seems that only two Chicago novels of any lasting interest appeared in the 1920's.

Floyd Dell's *The Briary Bush* (1921) is the central novel in his autobiographical trilogy about a young writer named Felix Fay. Dell came to Chicago from Davenport, Iowa, in 1908 and left for New York in 1913. In the five years he was here, he became a major voice in support of the new Chicago writing (as an editor of the *Evening Post*'s weekly book section, *The Friday Literary Review*) and a major figure in the city's artistic and bohemian community. In the first novel of his trilogy, *Moon-*

Calf (1920), Felix Fay rebels against the Presbyterianism, the lack of culture, the sexual repression and political conservatism of the village of Port Royal, and "escapes," on the last page, to Chicago; in the last novel, *Souvenirs* (1923), Fay goes to Greenwich Village where he becomes an editor and active socialist.

In *The Briary Bush*, Dell presents a lyrical and affectionate portrait of the charmingly naive Chicago bohemians of his day. Felix, his girlfriend Rose-Ann and his friends see themselves as free spirits, as opponents of Chicago's and America's crass commercial and middle-class values, and as exponents of the new art and the new morality. But Dell portrays them as emotionally attached to the very same conventional middle-class aspirations their philosophy and rhetoric claim they abhor. Rose-Ann is more aggressively bohemian than Felix: she is the one who rejects the conventional apartment that he picks out for them and finds, instead, a 56th Street studio in one of the wooden buildings left over from the World's Fair. ("They were to remain free," Felix thinks. "For that was what living in a studio meant. They would not subordinate their lives to a domestic arrangement.") But in this novel, whose sections are named after Chicago neighborhoods that reflect its conflicting values—Canal Street, Woods Point, 57th Street, Garfield Boulevard, Wilson Avenue—Rose-Ann also turns out to be conventional enough to want to get married. Through the story of their relationship to one another and to their friends, in all their contradictions, Dell provides insight into the self-image and slightly hidden contradictions that characterized, and ultimately dispersed, Chicago's most famous bohemian group. (By the end of the novel, their liberation wearing thin, Felix and Rose-Ann are talking about building a house.) In the history of the Chicago novel's treatment of the artist, few books are as warmhearted or as appealingly self-deprecating as this one.

Ben Hecht is mainly remembered as a newspaperman and the co-author of *The Front Page*, rather than as a fiction writer. But before he left Chicago for New York and Hollywood, he published a number of short stories and novels. The most intriguing of the novels is *Erik Dorn* (1921). While it treats many of the same themes as *The Briary Bush*, Hecht's tone could not be more different. And the most striking thing about Hecht's novel is that tone—a kind of lyrical cynicism, a self-centered misanthropy, an insistently reiterated existential anguish.

"Life did not live in him," Hecht begins; so "to himself he seemed a perfect translation of his country and his day." The novel's plot concerns Dorn's love affair with a young woman; but the plot is really only a hook on which Hecht can hang a series of comments on society and existence. They range from clever turns of phrase, to hyperkinetic metaphors, to poetic evocations of the common life like the stunning opening of Part Two, "Dream":

In the evening the women stand washing dishes in the kitchens of the city, men light their tobacco and open newspapers. Later, the women gather up the crumpled sheets and read . . . The years hammer away—digesting paint from houses. The years grind away, yet life persists. Beneath the grinding of the years, life gropes, shrieks, sweats . . . The stone houses stand ticking away the years, and within them men and women tick. Doors open and shut, lights go on and off, day and night drop a tick-tock across the miles of roofs. And in the hour of the washing of dishes men kindle their tobacco and read the newspapers.

The words that tick-tock through the book itself are the ones that the existentialists would later make familiar: "nothing," "despair," "emptiness," "boredom," "insincerity." And although *Erik Dorn* is not nearly as effective as some of Hecht's Chicago stories—such as "Broken Necks," an account of a public hanging that was first published in Margaret Anderson's *Little Review*—these and similar elements lend it a mordant fascination. If Sinclair's Chicago recalls Dante's Inferno, Hecht's seems a spiritual first cousin of Baudelaire's Paris and—precisely because of its frequently labored and baroque excesses—his novel is a memorable minor episode in the history of literary decadence.

The naturalism and socialism of Upton Sinclair were reborn in the proletarian novels of the 1930's, when the Crash and the Depression produced a crisis of faith in capitalism deeper than anything that had come before and novelists applied a Marxist critique to their Chicago experiences. The novels that resulted varied widely in interest and quality, but work of two of those 1930's writers later came to epitomize the Chicago novel. In James T. Farrell's Studs Lonigan trilogy— *Young Lonigan* (1932), *The Young Manhood of Studs Lonigan* (1934), and *Judgment Day* (1935)—and in Richard Wright's *Native Son*, the proletarian novel crossed the border between ideology and art, and Chicago naturalism was given its ultimate expression.

In "How Bigger Was Born," Wright wrote that street-corner talk about going back to Africa "told me that the civilization which had given birth to Bigger contained no spiritual sustenance, had created no culture which could hold and claim his allegiance and faith, had sensitized him and had left him stranded, a free agent to roam the streets of our cities, a hot and whirling vortex of undisciplined and unchannelized impulses." The description fits Studs Lonigan as well as it does Bigger Thomas. And Farrell described his conception of Studs in similar terms. Studs was, Farrell wrote, "a normal American boy of Irish Catholic extraction. The social milieu in which he lived and was educated was one of spiritual poverty." The lack of "spiritual sustenance" in Bigger's world, Studs' society's "spiritual poverty," define their characters and determine their fates.

Farrell thought of naturalism as a style of writing which "chooses understanding rather than myth, truth rather than comfort." He began with a story written for a University of Chicago composition class and ended with a trilogy chronicling sixty-five days selected from fifteen years of Studs' life. Having set out to capture the "forces at work in a section of American life," he "began to see Studs as a character but also a social manifestation . . . I set as my aim the unfolding of the destiny of Studs Lonigan in his own words, his own actions, his own patterns of thought and feeling." Wright also felt that "the main burden of all serious fiction consists almost wholly of character-destiny and the items, social, political, and personal, of that character-destiny."

Both Bigger and Studs are destroyed by a culture that offers them nothing worthwhile to do with themselves. Studs' aspirations are distorted by his Chicago surroundings. Respect, he learns on the streets, is earned by force and violence; heroism is embodied in Al Capone; hooky is the accepted approach to education, and idleness leads him to boredom and crime; manhood is defined in terms of drinking and sex; love is to be ridiculed. Studs is changed by the experience of the city's values, and as he changes his fate is sealed. Bigger is poor and black in a city where being either is enough to virtually guarantee victimization. He suffers a fate similar to Studs' and for much the same reason: he has no alternatives. Bigger wakes to the sound of a rat scurrying through his apartment; in less than a hundred pages he will be a murderer, hunted like a rat himself; and in the novel's closing scene he will declare, "What I killed for I am."

Character becomes destiny. And for Bigger, as for Studs, the Chicago forces that shape character, and so destiny, are all negative. Two angry young men prowl the streets, twisted and finally killed by the city that molded them. Two characters saunter out of the pages of their books into today's city, staring at us from under hooded eyes, hurtling a question at us about whether things have really changed very much that we'd rather not be asked because we know the answer—and that answer frightens us.

V

After *Studs Lonigan* and *Native Son* there wasn't much left for the naturalistic novel to do. It continued in Willard Motley's *Knock on Any Door* and *Let No Man Write My Epitaph*, and still appears in books like Cyrus Colter's *The River of Eros* (1972), *The Hippodrome* (1973) and *Night Studies* (1979) or William Brashler's *City Dogs* (1976). But, with the exception of Nelson Algren—who managed through the strength of his style to resuscitate naturalism by making it something else, a prose poetry of carefully gauged moods and emotional impact—Chicago writers since the 1940's have largely abandoned naturalism as exhausted and turned in other directions.

The main direction—signaled by Saul Bellow's first novel—has been inward, not outward; toward the impact of social and political forces on the survival of the spirit rather than the flesh. This new direction is stated boldly in the opening of Bellow's *Dangling Man* (1944), and reappears in his subsequent work, as well as in Isaac Rosenfeld's *Passage from Home* (1946) and Sam Ross' *Someday, Boy* (1948) and *The Sidewalks Are Free* (1950).

Dangling Man is written in the form of a journal. Its first entry, dated December 15, 1942, introduces a wholly original Chicago voice:

> There was a time when people were in the habit of addressing themselves frequently and felt no shame at making a record of their inward transactions. But to keep a journal nowadays is considered a kind of self-indulgence, a weakness, and in poor taste. For this is an era of hardboiled-dom, Today, the code of the athlete, the tough boy ... is stronger than ever .... If you have difficulties, grapple with them silently, goes one of their commandments. To hell with that! I intend to talk about mine, and if I had as many mouths as Siva has arms and kept them going all the time, I still could not do myself justice .... I do not feel guilty of self-indulgence in the least. The hardboiled are compensated for their silence; they fly planes or fight bulls or catch tarpon, whereas I rarely leave my room.

This is a new note in the Chicago novel, a new note in the American novel—and a radical departure from the note established by Chicago naturalists since the turn-of-the-century. Bellow's later heroes will manage to get out of their rooms, will travel to Mexico, Europe, Africa and back and forth across the United States—"look at me, going everywhere," Augie March will proclaim. But wherever they are, the self will be their constant preoccupation, their perennial subject. Bellow's selves are educated, thoughtful men, so when they think of themselves they will also think of history, sociology, psychology, literature—but the self, not society, is the focus of *The Adventures of Augie March*, *Herzog* and *Humboldt's Gift*.

In Isaac Rosenfeld's *Passage from Home*, as in Dell's *The Briary Bush*, city geography reflects psychology; in Rosenfeld as in Hecht, existentialism's sense of radical alienation takes on a Chicago accent. A friend of Bellow's—the original of the intellectual Bellow portrays in his story "Zetland: By a Character Witness" (included in *Him with His Foot in His Mouth*) and, with Delmore Schwartz, one of the friends upon whom Bellow modeled his Humboldt—Rosenfeld wrote two novels before his early death in 1956. But *Passage from Home,* one of the most extraordinary of the many novels of coming-of-age in Chicago, is enough to secure his place in the city's literary history.

"I remember the year in which I first felt respect for human intelligence," he begins. "I was 14, a precocious child, as sensitive as a burn. Human intelligence meant my own. Without growing more than an inch, I had suddenly shot up—that is, in my own estimation—and it seemed to me that I towered over life. Life meant the family." And from this perfectly modulated beginning, Rosenfeld goes on to write not just a Chicago novel but one of the first to define the characters and conflicts that would shape the Jewish-American fiction that emerged in the following decades.

Young Bernard Miller is torn between two impulses, pulled toward the mutually exclusive poles of traditional Judaism and assimilation, and Chicago neighborhoods embody states of mind in his struggle to establish his own identity. Home—the Jewish West Side—is family warmth, religious tradition (fading fast, but still powerful), and fleeting moments of mystical vision (reflected in a group of Hassids); but it is also family squabbles, tension with his father and stepmother, and a set of values that seem to stunt and smother his development. The Near North Side, where his Aunt Minna and his cousin Willy live, separated from the family, is freedom, liberation, mysterious possibility; but it is also sorely lacking in the sustaining qualities of home. Between them lies Downtown, an undiscovered territory, a carnival of lights and sounds where anything can happen.

During the course of his "passage from home," Bernard runs away to live with his aunt and cousin for a few weeks and then returns. But in Rosenfeld's novel as in Bellow's, the emphasis is on what he experiences within himself—on Bernard's journey as an odyssey of the spirit, of consciousness, of self-discovery. Unable to accept either of the worlds he finds available to him for very long, attracted and repelled by both, he ends where he began: at home, but homeless. Having undertaken a quest for identity, he ends stranded with his own alienation. An archetypal Jewish-American hero, he is also one of a long list of Chicago voyagers. His voyage is one that too few Chicago readers have shared.

Superficially, Sam Ross' *The Sidewalks Are Free* is similar to *Passage from Home* in a number of ways. Again, the hero is an adolescent. Again, the neighborhood is the Jewish West Side. Again, religious tradition, the family, and the struggle both to become American and retain Jewish values are central elements in the drama. But *The Sidewalks Are Free* differs from *Passage from Home* in a crucial way: where Rosenfeld's Bernard is the center of the action, the character in conflict with and rebellion against the life around him, Ross' Hershey Melov is a sensitive observer of another's struggle.

The novel begins on a powerful wave of nostalgia, as it recounts the story of Hershey's parents' immigration to America from Russia and describes the warmth of the Jewish family life that sustains Hershey—a life Ross clearly cherishes. Hershey and his young friends are their parents' guides to the strange new world of America: he reads English, so he accompanies his mother to the movies to translate for her, and hears the murmurs of hundreds of other children doing the same thing. Like his friends, Hershey loves city life:

> He knew the street when it had ice on it and when asphalt got sticky from heat; he had jumped, walked, hopscotched, slid, coasted, fallen and played over every inch of it. He knew the curbs from sitting on them and leaping from them, from using them as bases on the corner when playing kick-the-can baseball, and from the angry, popping sounds they made when he and his gang roasted potatoes in a bonfire. He knew the sewers, especially how to stuff drains with leaves on a rainy day so that he could go wading and sail paper boats . . .

But the center of the novel, and one of the modern Chicago novel's most powerfully drawn characters, is Hershey's father David. A simple man, a carpenter, he wants nothing more than to have the freedom to live his life as a *mensch* and teach his son to do the same. When he inherits $10,000 from a brother killed in World War I, the America he loves becomes the scene of his heroic battle to retain the love and respect of his family while remaining faithful to his ideal of a decent life. In this story of a man fighting for what he believes in, Sam Ross creates a portrait of heroism in everyday life that is unforgettable.

"You can be a typical Parisian," Nelson Algren wrote in *Chicago: City on the Make* (1961), "you can be a typical New Yorker if that helps when the cocktail lounges close, But if you can find anything in pants, skirts or a Truman Capote opera cape passing itself off as a typical Chicagoan we'll personally pay his way back to *Flair*." To suggest as I have here that there are such things as typical Chicago novels—in fact, that there is something called the Chicago novel—is not to deny the individuality that Algren means to insist on. It's merely a way of saying that Chicago has inspired certain kinds of novels, certain kinds of characters, rather than others.

Obviously, I have not been able to discuss all of the novelists who are worthy of the attention of readers interested in Chicago's literary history. And readers interested in learning what the Chicago novel is like today will find a wealth of other writers to discover. Like Harry Mark Petrakis, whose works offer an epic of Greek immigrant life in Chicago, as well as an affirmation of the values of family and tradition that is as uncommon in the Chicago novel as it is in American fiction as a whole. Or Bette Howland, one of contemporary Chicago fiction's most intriguing voices, who has begun to create a body of work which joins the focus on the self of Bellow and the attraction to the underdog of Algren. Or Leon Forrest, whose extraordinary novels of black experience, *There Is a Tree More Ancient Than Eden* (1973), *The Bloodworth Orphans* (1977), and *Two Wings to Veil My Face* (1984) are parts of an ambitious cycle about African-American experience that will make readers recall Joyce, Faulkner, and Ellison. But any survey is bound to exclude writers who don't deserve to be excluded, and every year brings new writers worthy of attention.

On the basis of what I have said, though, there will probably be some who wonder why Chicagoans should *want* to remember a literature that seems so critical of their city and what it stands for. I think that question has several answers. For one thing, great writing—and more than a few of these Chicago novels are that—presents us with our own experience clarified and made more meaningful. For another, the Chicago novels I've talked about provide their readers with a vivid guided tour through the city and its history.

But the more fundamental reason for a confirmed Chicagoan's interest in the novels discussed here is one Nelson Algren expressed, in his characteristically hard-headed and cranky way, in *Chicago: City on the Make*. Chicago, he wrote, is an odd sort of place, but "once you've come to be a part of this particular patch, you'll never love another. Like loving a woman with a broken nose, you may well find lovelier lovelies. But never a lovely so real."

A Special Eloquence

Leon Forrest

Most of the several hundred novels published each year come wrapped in promises that they are "memorable" or "unforgettable," "unique" or "extraordinary." But anyone who reads much contemporary American fiction knows that it is a rare novel that leaves an impression that lasts even a few weeks. Novels that actually express a singular vision in a singular voice—that grab you by the collar and shake you with their fierce and uncompromising originality—are even more rare. During the 1970's and 1980's, Chicagoan Leon Forrest wrote not one but three such novels: *There Is a Tree More Ancient Than Eden* (1973), *The Bloodworth Orphans* (1976), and *Two Wings to Veil My Face* (1984).

To say that Forrest's fiction is unique is not to suggest that it is without influences. Far from it. Leon Forrest is as careful a reader as he is a writer, and his literary debts are clear. Like Joyce, Forrest's aim is to "forge the uncreated conscience of his race in the smithy of his soul" and art, to express the epic and heroic complexity of "common" lives. Like Faulkner's, his obsession is the presentness of the past, the contemporary consequences of the heritage of slavery, the secrets of yesterday that shape the lives of his characters today. And, like Faulkner, Forrest conceives of his novels as episodes in a continuing project—each internally coherent and yet each linked to the others. Forrest openly acknowledges this emulation of Faulkner by placing his novels in "Forrest County, Illinois"—and in Forrest County as in Faulkner's Yoknapatawpha, characters and events appear and reappear from book to book, move from the fringes of the action to the center and back again. Like Ellison's, Forrest's subject is what he has called the "Afro-American soul struggle" and his method insists on using the entire Western literary heritage as a touchstone. Like Joyce, like Faulkner, like Ellison, Forrest focuses on a particular people in a particular time and place, but in telling their stories he touches on universal experiences and themes that speak to us all.

What makes Forrest's fiction unique is the way that he combines these various influences with an imagination and verbal music that are his alone. Like the speeches of Great-Momma Sweetie Reed, the center of *Two Wings to Veil My Face*, Forrest's eloquence and power are "astonishing and terrible, wonderfully fashioned and forged with racial memory, history, personal witness and largeness of Biblical" reference. That special eloquence encompasses both the language of the untutored poet—"I looked down upon him as a lapsed life insurance policy that could not be revived"; "marrying didn't bring me no consolation inside the previous condition of my burning heart"; "I never weaved no spite-work up in my head for Jericho Witherspoon"—and a heightened rhetoric that has never been spoken anywhere *but* Forrest County. "I.V.Reed ," Great-Momma Sweetie says to her dying father, "if the backbone of my heritage is lined to the labyrinth of your vertebrae, then the matrix of my mix must look like a furious mesh of crossroads; ports pouring into ports. Crisscrossed to zigzagging . . ."

In *Two Wings to Veil My Face*, his most beautifully shaped novel, Forrest's language enriches and complicates a superficially simple plot. The time is 1958. The setting is Great-Momma Sweetie Reed's small Chicago apartment. On his twenty-first birthday, Nathaniel Witherspoon—the central observer in each of Forrest's novels—sits recording the memories of his bed-ridden ninety-one year-old grandmother on yellow legal pads. That is all that physically *happens*. But through Nathaniel's memories and Great-Momma Sweetie's tale the room soon fills up with other voices, other rooms, other places, other times.

Nathaniel is keeping an appointment that he made fourteen years earlier, when Great-Momma refused to attend the funeral services for her estranged 117 year-old husband, Judge Jericho Witherspoon. "When you reach your majority," she told him then, "you come on back to Great-Momma Sweetie Reed and she'll unfold it all to you, without leaving out a jot of the picture so you can look into the mirror for yourself and know the full of my hurts, my wrongs, my history, our history and what went wrong, from the beginning time."

Unfold it all she does: her youth in slavery; her and her mother's attempted escape during the Civil War; her being sold into marriage by her own father, when she was fifteen and Jericho was fifty-five; her interview with that dying father, I.V. Reed, fifty-one years before this interview with Nathaniel; and what made her separate from Jericho Witherspoon on June 5, 1905. As she tells her tale, Nathaniel is forced to redefine his own identity, to translate as well as transcribe the meaning of her memories. In the process, this story of a story filled with other stories moves us, directly and personally, from contemporary America to the plantation life of the Old South and back. In the end, the secrets Great-Momma Sweetie reveals to Nathaniel—like the secrets I.V.Reed once revealed to her—radically alter both their lives.

This is a novel full of parallels carefully wrought—of two visits in search of answers to dying relatives; of two stories told in detail and ending in shattering revelations; of two arguments between young and old, two separations of husband and wife; and of the many meanings of the spiritual that sings of "Two wings to veil my face. . . two wings to fly me away." It is also about how Aunt Foisty's Christian voodoo brought Master Rollins Reed back from the dead; how Reece Shank Haywood got caught trying to escape the Reed plantation; why I.V.Reed wore his master's shoes to the end of his days; how Mistress Silvia Reed committed suicide with a master key, and what she left behind; what the Reverend Pompey C.J.Brown had to say at Jericho Witherspoon's funeral; why Great-Momma Sweetie sneaked into Memphis Raven-Snow's funeral parlor and made sure that a lock of her mother's hair was buried with Jericho; and much, much more.

Some will find all of this complex and difficult—and it is. For Forrest refuses to compromise in his efforts to bend language in the service of his perception. Some will find the novel static—and, in a sense, that is true too. For Forrest's concern is not with the motion of the body, but with the movement of the heart, the journey of the soul. And some will challenge the book's realism—with cause. For Forrest is an inventor, not a secretary, and realism is just one of his tools.

Two Wings to Veil My Face, in other words, is not for everyone. Just for those who love the excitement of watching a truly unique writer practice his art; for those who can recognize the magic beneath the mundane, as Leon Forrest does; for those who are willing to accept the challenge of a novel that really is both extraordinary and unforgettable.

The Outsiders

Bette Howland

It would be hard to think of two contemporary American writers who seem more different in tone and temperament. Yet reading the stories in Bette Howland's *Things to Come and Go* (1983) I kept being reminded of a line from one of Donald Barthelme's: "Fragments are the only form I trust." The connection between them isn't really a matter of style. Although the stories in *Things to Come and Go* skip back and forth in time and perspective, unfold as a series of anecdotes and impressions, don't so much conclude as end, they aren't nearly as logically or graphically disjointed as Barthelme's stories typically are. It's a matter of vision. For both writers, fragmentation and isolation are the fundamental facts of our lives, and escaping those facts is always a struggle.

Howland is a poet of connections missed, words unspoken, feelings left unexpressed. And each of the stories in *Things to Come and Go*, like the best parts of *Blue in Chicago* (1978), is the chronicle of an outsider. The stories may be set in a meticulously observed Chicago or Indiana or Florida, but their common emotional terrain is a landscape of loneliness and loss. That landscape is suggested in the ending of the title story of *Blue in Chicago*, where we find Howland's autobiographical narrator "looking at the back of Rudy's neck; thick, remote. For he is remote—my uncle is a blunt and mysterious man to me. His life flows in another direction; I shall never understand it. And yet I felt closer to him that to anyone I had seen all day . . . Rudy and I are both outsiders, as far as the family is concerned. Out of the mainstream." And it's suggested again in

"To the Country," another of the stories from her first collection, when Howland confesses that "mine is a makeshift sort of life; I didn't plan it that way. I just don't have all the pieces."

The same sentiments shape the three stories in *Things to Come and Go*. Esti, the narrator of "Birds of a Feather," recalls her youth with wry confusion. She grew up surrounded by a family of "big, brassy yak-yakking Abarbanels . . . all talking at once, shouting over the rest, getting louder and louder, like people carrying on in a foreign language . . . all . . . cheek-clickers and cheek-pinchers." Like her old-country grandfather, she "wondered what [she] was doing in their midst."

Sydney, the young mother in "The Old Wheeze," thinks that "she had never picked a life for herself and so she thought that all were still available." But, waiting for her current boyfriend to come back from taking the babysitter home, she also thinks "about other people's lives and felt that her life was no life at all." Her old black babysitter, Mrs. Cheatham, is another lonely observer. She "went into people's houses, she knew what their lives were like." But she can't remember the last time that someone knew her well enough to call her by her first name. All of her old friends are dead and, because she sees the "sneak-thief, the mugger-in-the-hall, the knife-in-the-ribs" in every encounter, she's unable to let her guard down long enough for anyone new to get close to her. Instead, "She talked to herself. She had to talk to someone, didn't she? And someone had to talk to her."

Sally Horner, in "The Life You Gave Me," flies to Florida when her father is hospitalized with colon cancer. During the flight from Chicago and the days she spends in her parents' retirement village, she thinks back on her complex relationship with her father. "My father and I were not on the best of terms, not on the worst. No finalities, no formal estrangements. Words had been spoken—plenty of words; but not the most bitter. Not the last word. Nothing that couldn't be taken back. We hadn't shot all the arrows in our quivers." She recalls an earlier episode when her father was in the hospital after an accident, thinking that their brief conversation then was "an old story. I had come to ask, to seek to plead—and not to give." She, too, begins as an outsider. But, unlike the characters in the other two stories, she has the chance to change things and she does. Thinking back over her life with these old people who were once her young parents, she looks at the things that they have accumulated in their retirement and realizes that while "there is nothing here that I would ever choose," there is also "nothing I can ever part with."

"Birds of a Feather" is a family album, loosely connected to the perennial theme of a young person's movement from innocence to experience. Since the family is a boisterous and slightly eccentric one—Aunt Flor married a small-time racketeer and always wears all of the jewelry he gave her before being sent to prison, having "taken a vow to wear it next to her, day and night, until they let him out"; Uncle Reuben married a "hillbilly" named Luellen who buys two of everything for her twins and spends her days lying in bed reading confession magazines—their story is an entertaining one. "The Old Wheeze," though marred by a weak use of shifting points of view, allows Howland to treat the feelings and fears of an old woman—and few writers are better at describing what those feelings and fears are, as readers who remember the stories "Public Facilities," "Golden Age," and "How We Got the Old Woman to Go" from *Blue in Chicago,* already know.

But "The Life You Gave Me" is far and away the most powerful and most moving story in this collection. As Sally Horner comes to accept the mortality of her father, as she traces the history of their relationship and the inability to communicate that has always been central to it, as she tries to understand what her parents life has been and is, as she comes to realize how much they have meant and mean to her, we are inescapably drawn into the web of contradictory emotions that is the heart of every family's life, are compelled to face the fact of mortality and loss ourselves. It isn't an especially pleasant task. But, like Sally Horner, we cannot help but grow and be changed by the experience.

Lost Illusions

Morris Philipson

Morris Philipson is best known as the longtime director of the University of Chicago Press, but he is also, as *A Man in Charge* (1979) confirms, a talented novelist of manners whose fiction deserves to be more widely recognized than it is. His first novel, *Bourgeois Anonymous* (1964), is an often hilarious burlesque of intellectual and Beat anti-middle-class pretensions that has been justifiably compared with the social satires of Aldous Huxley and Evelyn Waugh. Written while Philipson was an editor at Vintage Books, the novel is set in Greenwich Village and takes its title from an imaginary secret society modeled on Alcoholics Anonymous. BA's mission, we learn, is to do for the chronically bourgeois what AA does for chronic drinkers: help them kick the habit. ("Remember," BA's leader says, "being bourgeois is not incurable . . . Adjusted of the world, *unite!*—you have nothing to lose but your adaptation!") Though its second half is perceptibly weaker than its first, *Bourgeois Anonymous* is still an engaging and entertaining intellectual romp that scores its satirical points in several unforgettable funny scenes.

In *The Wallpaper Fox* (1976), Philipson retains his satiric thrust but substitutes wit for the earlier novel's broad comedy. Like *A Man in Charge*, its companion piece, his second novel is reminiscent of the fiction of Louis Auchincloss in its focus on the complex moral dilemmas faced by a privileged, comfortable, self-possesed man of power and prestige. In *The Wallpaper Fox*, the man is Henry Warner, affluent owner of New Haven's largest and most successful department store. His fiftieth birthday begins with his savoring the successes and accomplishments of his personal and professional lives. By the end of that day, his marriage, his relationship with his children, his closest friendships, his social status, and his self-esteem are all threatened by a rapidly growing chain of small and large deceptions and dishonesties.

In the wake of that day, Henry Warner finds himself drifting farther and father out to sea, until he is finally forced to laboriously crawl his way back to self-respect and stability with the help of nothing but his defective moral compass. Philipson handles his themes and his characters, as well as the novel's tightening web of coincidences, with so much skill that he makes us care about Warner and his family, and about how—and if—Henry will manage to put his life back together again.

The action of *A Man in Charge* concludes on the summer day in 1974 when *The Wallpaper Fox* begins; its central characters, Conrad and Isabel Taylor, are important minor characters in the previous book, and Henry Warner reappears here. (The novels can be read separately, but readers must turn to *The Wallpaper Fox* to learn the identity of Isabel's lover in this book.) Like Warner, Taylor is intelligent, articulate, surrounded by the trappings of wealth; as executive vice president of Yale University, he, like Warner, appears to be "a man in charge."

But, as with Henry Warner, on the day we meet Conrad Taylor his carefully organized private and public worlds begin to crumble around him. He receives an unsigned note telling him that his wife is having an affair, discovers that a thief has burglarized his office, and learns that the provost, his immediate superior at the university, has suffered a heart attack. As we get to know him—as we watch him handle his job, remember how he pursued and married Isabel, jockey for appointment as provost, serve as a Washington consultant during Nixon's final days, groom a protégé, confront his emotionally estranged daughter, cope with his wife's infidelity—it soon becomes clear that appearances are, in many ways, deceiving. And that Philipson's interest is in exploring the reality behind the image of his title.

For what the novel shows, in every one of its episodes, is that Conrad's power to influence and shape events is far less than he imagines. Again and again, what is most carefully planned goes awry, what succeeds comes as an unexpected gift. The reversals of his (and our) expectations that result from this paradoxical fact provide subtly powerful emotional moments, true epiphanies, in several of the novel's best scenes.

A Man in Charge suffers from a few predictable turns of plot and some awkward language and unnecessary repetition, but these are more than made up for by its underlying intelligence and the quality of its perceptions. It is, finally, a novel of sensibility full of minor details that are just right and suggestive parallels with the political events of 1974.

Though it is a novel set in the university, it is not an "academic" novel. In part, because Philipson manages to make us feel the lesson Conrad learned as a graduate student reading La Rochefoucauld's *Maxims*. "He never lets us forget how little control we have of our lives," Conrad explains. What Conrad's story shows is that, for "a man in charge," as for the rest of us, one of the most important things in life is to be able to recover when La Rochefoucauld turns out to be right.

The Red Menace

Michael Anania

As a poet, a critic, an editor, a lecturer, a teacher, and a spokesman for the arts, Michael Anania has been at the center of the Chicago literary scene for decades. With his first full-length fiction, *The Red Menace* (1984), his multi-faceted career entered an exciting new phase.

Like Milan Kundera's *The Book of Laughter and Forgetting*, Anania's *The Red Menace* isn't an easy book to classify or describe. Part novel and part essay, part memoir and part tall tale, part meditation and part portrait of the artist, its unity grows out of its themes and its underlying sensibility, rather than out of a single plot line. More like a series of musical variations or the parts of a long poem than like the chapters of a typical novel, *The Red Menace*'s twelve sections come together as the quilts of the narrator's grandmother once did.

"Bits and pieces," he explains in one of the book's passages of lyrical memory. "My old flannel shirt, strips from a house dress she wore for cleaning, remnants of the curtain that had covered the door of the closet in my room in the housing project—she is gathering it all up, hooking and twisting, slowly spiraling it out across her knees . . . It is a shoal of pasts—hers, mine, the familiy's . . . all knotted in and turned. I would sit with my chin on the back of a chair and watch her work." Like those quilts, *The Red Menace* gathers up, hooks and twists strands of memory— of the common and uncommon, public and private, timeless and particular experiences of a man named Michael. A man who grew up poor in Omaha's Logan Fontenelle housing project in the 1940's and 1950's, and who remembers those experiences today with a mixture of wonder, nostalgia, humor, and rue.

The book begins by recounting one of those unforgettable moments in the collective memory, as a group of boys gather around a television set in one of the apartments in the project before school one morning to watch an atomic bomb test. The Bomb, like the specter of Communism—which is just one of *The Red Menace*'s meanings in the book—haunts the imaginations of the people in the book as it haunted the imagination of the era. *The Red Menace* also treats, often hilariously, many of the other common experiences of a 1950's adolescence: air raid drills, cars, sex, music, rebellion, the rituals of cool. Its uncommon, private memories are of a different order: of a father who died young, and his legacy to a son who hardly knew him; of a grandmother, forever wreathed in a scent of berries; of an old Communist's loyalty to his youthful dreams; of an Indian, Russell, nicknamed "The Red Menace," and the imaginative leap by which he once momentarily recovered power over America for himself and his people; and of Whiskey Nose Louie, "dishwasher and moralist," who is, like Russell and Michael's father, a character the reader won't soon forget.

Louie is so real you can smell him. Dressed in "garbage-stained chartreuse pants, their wide Palm Beach cuffs soaked with dishwater, [a] Ringling Brothers and Barnum and Bailey T-shirt, gray hair curling through the holes at the armpits, a wet, gray garbage ground under its faded lion and flaming hoop, yellow golf shoes turned up at the toes, no socks or shoelaces," and sporting a permanent three-day beard, Louie has "skin dinged and limp as an old rag, and his nose, his famous nose, looked as though it had been roughly shaped out of old hamburger." He could go on non-stop, we are told, eight hours at a stretch, "rasping out sexual advice, insult, salvation, and could curse longer without repeating himself than anyone I ever knew."

Since Whiskey Nose Louie's language matches the cleanliness of his clothes, it's difficult to convey just how incredibly funny he is. Yet the quality and range of voices in *The Red Menace* can't be captured without him. Listen, then, to a slightly expurgated version of Louie's thoughts on Communism:

> "A Communist'll talk at you like a preacher . . . cept Communists won't shut up till you agree with them. And you don't even get a bowl of soup."
> "Louie, you don't know nothin' bout Communists."
> "Don't know, don't know. Why I been shouted at by Communists from here to San Francisco and back again. No sooner they get out of Communist school than they look me up. Sometimes I go out the back door just to keep from steppin' on them."

"Bull."

"Comes with bein' a deegenerate. They hunt you down—preachers, social workers, democrats, missionaries, Communists—all of em. And outa the whole bunch, the worst is a Communist."

"You ever see the women that go around with Communists. Ugly and fat, every damned one of them, big fat arms, legs like pool tables. That's cause they hate good-lookin' women, just hate 'em."

"Louie, that doesn't make any sense."

"Course it don't. If they made any sense, they wouldn't be Communists . . . Never trust a man who's got a smart reason for having somethin' he don't want. . . I was in Portland one night, in a freightyard, not bothering nobody, drinkin' Seattle wine with this here gandy-dancer. And up come this Communist. Spends half-a-minute talkin about the weather, then gets goin' on the capitalists and how they put us all outa work, and I says to him, where's your fat girlfriend, and I tells him that . . . he's entitled to a fat girlfriend. Then me and the gandy-dancer bust a gut laughin'. And he asks what's so funny, and I says, They're s'posed to give you a fat girlfriend. It goes with bein a Communist. And he says he ain't no Communist, he's a socialist worker. And I says, long as you're gonna do somethin' dumb, might as well be a Communist, cause a fat, ugly woman is better than no woman at all."

Later, Whiskey Nose Louie explains his views on Stalin:

"Stalin ain't no Communist!"

"What?"

"Can't you hear either. How you get the idea Stalin's a Communist?"

"How'd I get the idea? Everybody knows he's a Communist, the head Communist."

"Woman, you're too dumb to be loose on the streets. Stalin ain't no Communist. Stalin's a tricker."

"A tricker?"

"That's right. He tricked Hitler and he tricked Roosevelt and he tricked Churchill and he tricked Harry Truman. One of the best trickers in the world, and a tricker ain't a Communist. Never was a Communist tricker and they ain't never gonna be one."

"Stalin is the head of Russia and Russia is a Communist country. Right?"

"Damn right, and that's one of the best tricks of all. You want to worry about somethin', old woman, you worry about when Stalin dies, cause soon as he does that whole country's gonna be run by Communists. Then we'll all be in trouble."

"Louie, Stalin's already dead. He died last year."

"Huh?"

"He died last year."

"Leo! Did Stalin die last year?" Leon nods. "Jesus! Stalin dead. Don't surprise me they tried to keep it a secret."

Whiskey Nose Louie shares much more of his inimitable wit and wisdom in *The Red Menace* and this reader, at least, found himself laughing so hard at Louie's comments that the tears in his eyes made it difficult to keep reading. Learning the rest of what Louie has to say is just one of the reasons for reading Michael Anania's *The Red Menace*—and for looking forward to his next work of fiction.

A Legend of the City

Nicholas von Hoffman

Organized Crimes (1984), columnist Nicholas von Hoffman's second novel, is a Chicago buff's delight, overflowing with people and places, voices and episodes that are the stuff of the city's legends. It begins one day in 1930 as a rich young man from Winnetka passes the newspaper stand in front of the Chicago Public Library at Michigan Avenue and Randolph Street, walks down the stairs into the tunnel leading to the Illinois Central railroad station on his way to a graduate class in sociology at the University of Chicago, and suddenly finds himself watching helplessly as Jake Lingle, a *Chicago Tribune* reporter, is gunned down by a mob hit man.

Before it ends, the fictional Allan Archibald will learn more than he ever expected about the intricate web of corruption connecting the worlds of politics, banking, business, and crime in Depression-era Chicago. And we will have been treated to a tale in which a rogues' gallery of such familiar figures as Big Bill Thompson, Ten Percent Tony Cermak, Bathhouse John Coughlin, Al Capone, Frank Nitti, Machine Gun Jack McGurn, and Samuel Insull wheel and deal, swagger and strut, brag and boast their way through the city noted for the nation's worst gangsters and best architecture.

They are joined by a cast of equally memorable fictional characters, including Fast Father Frank Rooney, the archdiocese's pipeline to the underworld; Mona Jupiter, McGurn's seductive wife; Irena Giron, Allan's Back of the Yards Polish American girlfriend and fellow sociologist;

William "Zep" Moneypenny, the biggest bookie in Chicago; and Elting Archibald, Allan's banker father, who becomes a pathetic pawn in the hands of Insull and the pols. All of these characters—real and fictional—provide Allan with the kind of education his professor pushes him toward when he tells him to get out of Harper Library and "start being with people instead of reading about them."

The frame for Von Hoffman's novel is both the oldest plot of all and the one the Chicago novel has traditionally depended on most, the loss of innocence through experience. As Allan gathers information for a thesis on organized crime, he is tested, tempted, and found wanting at the same time that he loses his illusions about himself and the world. But this plot line, and the love story that is a part of it, are not the main reason to read *Organized Crimes*. The novel's real pleasures are its characters, and the Chicago voices that Von Hoffman has captured so well.

Like the voice of the establishment reformer and businessman Elting Archibald, who responds to his son's description of Lingle's murder by saying that "We need a full-scale committee to stamp out crime. Something full-scale. Representing all segments: meat packing, steel, light manufacturing, something across the board. You might want to talk to the people on the Chicago Crime Commission. I'm on the board, Allan."

Or the voice of the University of Chicago graduate student Irena, who greets Allan's plans to study organized crime with enthusiasm. "You will be an urban Margaret Mead! Instead of sailing away 10,000 miles to live among primitives, you, Alan Archibald, will dwell among the criminal anthropothagi of Chicago and describe the daily life of savages who inhabit and area only seven miles away. Think of it!"

Or the voice of the first gangster Allan meets, Patsy O' Dea, "I'm Allan Archibald from the University of Chicago," he begins. "Die!" orders O' Dea. "What?" "Die. Stop living." To which Allan responds, "Mr. O' Dea, you don't have to cooperate with the University of Chicago if you don't want to, but you do have to be polite."

Or the voice of Al Capone himself, "the ugly man with the beautiful clothes" who has Allan prepare a Thanksgiving meal for the unemployed and appears, trailed by reporters, in a "soft yellow suit with faint raspberry stripes, cerise tie, buff shoes, a white hat [and] a white cashmere overcoat." "I'm feedin' the unemployed in this emergency," he explains. "This ain't no publicity stunt . . . Look at that stuff! We got piccalilli. They got that at the Volunters of America? We got olives and we got beets. They got that at Catholic Charities? We got mince pie. The Sallies got mince pie?"

Or, my favorite, the voice of legendary Chicago alderman Bathhouse John Coughlin, who proposes an ordinance to cope with both depression and *the* Depression. "I do believe that conditions are what they are on account of a poor mental attitude. Laughter and a light heart make prosperity," he explains. "I'm introducing an ordinance for 12-foot high stone walls to be put around all the cemeteries. This is no bosh. A graveyard has a deadening effect on a neighborhood and I want 'em covered up."

Then there is Ten Percent Tony Cermak, the recently elected mayor, who calls Frank Nitti to explain the new arrangements. "Ya know, Frank, I got elected on a reform ticket." "What does that mean?" Nitti asks. "It means the price is double," the new mayor of Chicago explains. The mob will cooperate, he says, or policemen will deliver beer from another bootlegger in City of Chicago Street Department trucks. "Oh, Jesus," Nitti says, "I used to think Big Bill Thompson was a crazy man."

Organized Crimes is hardly the Great American Novel, but it doesn't pretend to be. It is another chapter in the myth-making about Chicago in the era of Capone, an entertaining trip down a well-worn path. And, as that, it's a genuine success.

The Myth of Crows

Charles Dickinson

Charles Dickinson is a writer fascinated by our impulse to turn people and experiences into myths, by the gap between appearances and realities, between public perceptions and private facts, by the struggle of isolated individuals to come to terms with themselves so that they can come to terms with those they care about most.

Harry Waltz, the principled loan shark at the center of Dickinson's first novel *Waltz in Marathon* (1983), is the richest and tallest man in his small Michigan town. His house is Marathon's largest and highest, his twin daughters, Marathon's prettiest. His reputation reaches all the way to Flint, where his personal and business affairs are as avidly discussed as they are in the local Marathon barbershop (which keeps a pair of binoculars on hand for the curious to spy on Waltz's house on the hill). "He is a witness to legend," one of Harry's clients thinks during a transaction; "this is a Harry Waltz story unfolding."

In *Crows* (1985), the subjects of local legend are Ben Ladysmith—a popular biology professor at the college who drowns in a freak accident on Mozart, Wisconsin's Oblong Lake—Ben's family, and Robert Cigar, the twenty-seven year-old unemployed sportswriter who moves in with the Ladysmiths and becomes obsessed with understanding the truth about Ben's life and death.

"He was a mythical figure," Ethel Ladysmith says of her late husband. "Some of us harbored a faint hope he might return to claim his things," one of Ben's faculty colleagues tells Robert. For most of Mozart's residents Ben becomes "a cog in Oblong Lake folklore. Of 106 drownings in the lake in the eighty-four years that records had been kept, every body had been recovered except Ben's."

Ben's oldest son Buzz is the star pitcher for the Mozart High School baseball team. His daughter Olive is a record-breaking champion swimmer. Both have been subjects of articles in the local paper written by Robert Cigar. And Robert, who spends three summers diving in Oblong Lake in search of Ben's body, becomes something of a local legend too. Scattered throughout the book are the legends Ben himself created and embellished with each telling: enthralling, lyrical, hauntingly suggestive tales of the world of crows—tales of "grief orbits" and "forgetful sleep," of crow funerals and crow trials, of crow legends and crow rituals, of crow heroism and crow luck.

But just as the focus of *Waltz in Marathon* was on the life inside the legends, on Harry's efforts to understand and accept his children, his brother, the woman he loved, and himself, the focus in *Crows* is on what it really meant to be Ben Ladysmith, Ben's wife, Ben's mistress, Ben's child, Ben's admirer—and on what it means to be Robert Cigar.

In exploring these questions, *Crows* implicitly asks and answers others. Why is Robert obsessed with Ben's memory? Why does he leave one home (his parents'), where he *feels* as if he's an intruder, for another (the Ladysmiths), where he's *told* he's an intruder—and a "parasite," a "mooch," and a "quasi-leech"? Why does Ethel Ladysmith nonetheless let him stay—*for three years*? Why did Ben tell his crow tales to everyone but his family? What happened the night Ben died? And why does Robert both dive for Ben's body and avoid finding it?

It is, in other words, a novel full of the mysteries of character, by a writer whose greatest strength is characterization. The plot of *Crows*, like the plot of *Waltz in Marathon*, occasionally creaks with incredibility and inconsistency. Dickinson can write with wit and poetic beauty: witness the detailed and fabulous crow tales, or lines such as "Ben discouraged water sports by the fact of his absence" and "a puff of pocket lint lay across the air slot [of his whistle] like a tiny footbridge." But he can also slip into awkwardness, letting Ethel tell Robert that "you've moved out of the mainstream of human interaction" or letting Robert tell her that "my presence is a bargain and a godsend to your family."

When it comes to his characters, however, Dickinson, a Chicago newspaperman, seldom takes a false step. Like Kurt Vonnegut or John Irving, he is attracted to, and has a talent for creating, believable and charming eccentrics. Like them, he enjoys giving these characters whimsical names like Robert Cigar, Buzzard and Duke Ladysmith, Arabesque Mason. (The Mozart High School teams are called the Wolfgang.)

"You can't be satirical at the expense of fictional characters because they're your creatures," John Updike once said. "You must only love them." Dickinson seems to agree, and in *Crows* he treats each of his characters with both sympathy and affection. He cares about them all—not just about Ben, Robert, and the Ladysmiths, but about Robert's charming, perennially unsuccessful father Dave; about Joe Marsh, the faded ex-basketball star, and his shoplifting wife; about Arabesque, Ben's mistress; about Herm Branch, head of the Sportsheaven sporting goods chain where Robert gets a job; and about Stephen, Ethel's unsuccessful suitor. Because he cares enough to make every one of them engaging characters, we care too.

According to Updike, again, "the idea of the hero is aristocratic. You cared about Oedipus and Hamlet because they were noble and you were a groundling. Now, either nobody is a hero or everyone is. I vote for everyone." So does Charles Dickinson.

Everyday Heroes

Harry Mark Petrakis

For the writer, the only thing more frustrating than being unpublished is being out of print. Yet the economics of publishing virtually guarantee that a year or so after most books appear they have vanished from bookstore shelves. Horror stories abound: in 1946, just four years before he was awarded the Nobel Prize for Literature, all but one of William Faulkner's fifteen books were out of print; before Dell decided to reprint them in 1966, almost all of Kurt Vonnegut's novels were unavailable. In the 1970's, even so well-known a Chicago novel as Nelson Algren's *Man with a Golden Arm* could only be unearthed in used bookstores, and the reader whose appetite for Chicago's contemporary writers was whetted by Leon Forrest's *The Bloodworth Orphans*, Morris Philipson's *The Wallpaper Fox*, or Richard Stern's *Natural Shocks* found only frustration if he searched for their earlier works. With Doubleday's publication of *A Petrakis Reader* (1978), admirers of Harry Mark Petrakis' fiction had better luck.

A Petrakis Reader reprints all of the stories originally published in *Pericles on 31st Street* (1965) and *The Waves of Night* (1969) and, in the process, displays much of the range of Petrakis's considerable talents. All of these stories exhibit the careful craftsmanship, love of language, and strong moral sense for which he is noted. While most of them are firmly grounded in a particular time (the present), a specific place (Chicago), and a specific group of people (Greek Americans), out of these particulars Petrakis repeatedly weaves a universal tapestry of love and hate, youth and age, hope and disappointment, birth and death, comedy and tragedy.

"Journal of a Wife-Beater," "The Wooing of Ariadne," "Pa and the Sad Turkeys," "The Courtship of the Blue Widow," and "The Shearing of Samson" are uproariously funny first-person narratives reminiscent of Ring Lardner's "You Know Me, Al" in their use of naïve points of view for comic effect. Like his novels, "The Song of Rhodante," "Pericles on 31st Street," and "The Ballad of Daphne and Apollo" support and extend the impact of contemporary incidents by grounding them in Greek history and myth. In "Dark Eye" and "The Judgment," Petrakis sketches moving portraits of the destructive effects of American life on immigrants unable to escape the old country's ways and superstitions. And in "The Prison," "A Hand for Tomorrow," and "The Witness" he writes of old age with an understanding and power that few American writers can match. One of the best stories in the collection, "The Passing of the Ice," is a *tour de force* that combines all of these elements—humor, myth, nostalgia, and the experience of old age—in the story of the death of an iceman and the creation of a legend. At base, the story is about the myth-making process, about how the deeds of the past are passed down from generation to generation by word of mouth until they become more than just stories, become the stuff of men's dreams.

Petrakis's characters are always common men and women, but they are seldom the helpless victims or *schlemiels* we find in much contemporary American fiction. The difference is one of perspective. "Calamity is not the divine right of kings," one of his narrators observes, and Petrakis's fiction presents everyman and everywoman as capable of heroism and great tragedies, as well as occasional joys. His world is a world of coffeehouses and luncheonettes, of corner bars and corner groceries, of kitchens and bedrooms—a world populated by bartenders and bakers, priests and cynics, and, most of all, by husbands and wives, parents and children. It is a world where family and neighborhood dominate consciousness, where politics and social upheavals are felt only in domestic terms. A world where anguish is felt more often than ecstasy, but where people continue to struggle, doing the best they can.

We recognize that world and, again and again in these stories, it touches us. We meet a pregnant wife who, after learning of her husband's infidelity, sits at the kitchen table thinking "I don't know just how to go on or how to turn back." We hear an old priest insist that "we are saved by hope and not by memory" to an old rake who finds his sole respite from pain in the past. We recognize the son who ponders " the ways in which the past locked me into a shell I could not break." And we have met the aged grocer, forced into retirement by his son, who puts the best face onto his situation, boasting to an old friend that "I am a lucky man. I have a fine son, and he married a grand girl, and together they produced this incomparable child."

Though Petrakis's stories have their share of weaknesses—some passages of purple prose, occasional sentimentality, a tendency to stereotype the sexes into bearers-of-offspring and planters-of-seed—those weaknesses are overshadowed by the humanity and compassion evident in characters such as these. And by the fact that, if there is an underlying thread that ties the variety of these stories together, it is that they all bear the stamp of a knowledge gained through hard-won experience and immense sympathy. A knowledge, finally, of the infinite varieties of love that make life both worth living and nearly impossible to bear.

About the Author

Bernard F. Rodgers, Jr. is Vice President and Dean of Simon's Rock College of Bard in Great Barrington, MA. He is the author of *Philip Roth: A Bibliography* and the Twayne United States Authors series volume *Philip Roth*. His essays and reviews on modern and contemporary literature and culture have been published in *The Berkshire Eagle, Chicago Review,* the *Chicago Tribune, Critique: Studies in Modern Fiction, The Fitzgerald/Hemingway Annual, Illinois Issues, Magill's Literary Annual, Masterplots II,* and *The World & I,* and broadcast on WBBM-AM and WNIB-FM in Chicago.